CROSSING CULTURES

An Anglo-Australian working in Aboriginal Communities

Papunya 1982
Coonamble 1989
Yarralin 1995

Barbara Jackson

Barbara Jackson acknowledges the Traditional Custodians of the land upon which we live and work, and pays her respects to Elders past, present and emerging.

First published in 2023
by Barbara Jackson, www.crossingcultures.au

Revised reprint July 2023

Text and photographs copyright © Barbara Jackson 2023
Maps and illustrations copyright © Alex Hotchin 2023

ISBN 978-0-6457136-0-2

The moral right of the author has been asserted.

Disclaimer

This is a work of non-fiction. However, I have changed the names of some individuals for privacy reasons, but the events described are factual.

Readers of this book are advised that it contains the names and images of Aboriginal people who may be deceased.

 A catalogue record for this book is available from the National Library of Australia

Cover design: Sarah Allen
Maps and illustrations: Alex Hotchin
Interior: Nan McNab

Contents

Introduction	**5**
Map of Papunya	14
Part 1 One year in Papunya	**15**
1 Setting the wheels in motion	16
2 Working across cultures	27
3 Papunya Tula	48
4 A new doctor and cats	55
5 Heartbreaking challenges	65
6 The demise of Lyappa Health Service	69
Map of Coonamble	76
Part 2 Two Years in Coonamble	**77**
7 Coonamble and the CDEP	78
8 CDEP turns unemployment on its head	95
9 Racism and goodwill	111
10 Woodwork, the Warrumbungles and art	127
11 Dark and light sides of Coonamble	139
12 Leaving Coonamble	148
Map of Yarralin and surrounds	154
Part 3 Two years in Yarralin	**155**
13 4,000 kilometres to Yarralin	156
14 An old man is dead	175
15 A fraught history	183
16 Mistakes, achievements and failure	192
17 Upskilling Yarralin's young workers	208
18 A council clerk is never bored	221
19 The Health Infrastructure Priority Project commences	234
20 Reflections	242
Appendix 1: Massacres in the Victoria River Region 1884–1925	247
Appendix 2: Victoria River Downs Station	251
References	255
Acknowledgements	265

Introduction

When I arrived at Alice Springs Airport, a surprise was waiting for me. Instead of my skinny, balding father, Bill, waiting to greet me, there was a tall, gorgeous, bearded man holding a sign with my name on it. Bill's time-management skills had been overtaken by too many tasks so he roped in his friend Homer Coderre, to do the 'meet and greet' for him. It became a pleasure for both Homer and me as we clicked.

To my delighted surprise, Homer took the afternoon off and gave me a tour of Alice. After a stroll up the main street, we walked along the wide, sandy Todd River bed. Homer told me when the river flooded from time to time, it was very dangerous. Not that day though; it was peaceful and shady. Walking in the Todd gave me my first unexpected sight of Aboriginal people. They were sitting on the sandy riverbed chatting in groups and looked very much at home. It was my first recognition of difference, as I couldn't imagine White people sitting comfortably on a sandy riverbed with not even a picnic blanket.

A short drive took us to the lookout at Anzac Hill for the splendid, panoramic view of the layout of the town. I was captivated by the flat desert plain, rocks in all shades of ochre, white-trunked gums, a sky bluer than blue and crystal-clear air. The early frisson of romance heightened when Homer promised me a sightseeing trip next time I was in Alice Springs.

Alice Springs was the starting point for my week's holiday at Ali Curung Aboriginal community where my father, Bill, was the housing manager. After a pub dinner with Homer, Bill and I were heading 400 kilometres north to Ali Curung. Homer and I met Bill at the front bar. He was with his Aboriginal mate Benny Robinson who had volunteered to drive so Bill could enjoy a few beers with us. The four of us headed to the pub restaurant. This became my first encounter with Alice Springs racism. Benny was wearing thongs and a round necked t-shirt. At the door of the restaurant he was forbidden to enter because he was not dressed appropriately. I was witnessing the Alice Springs version of the colour bar. Because most Aboriginal people wore thongs on their feet and round-necked t-shirts, these items of clothing were banned in what became the White areas of the pub. I was shocked and wanted to go somewhere else to eat, but Benny had already vanished. Bill told me we'd meet him later at the service station. It was great catching up with Bill as we had plenty to talk about. Although Bill, Homer and I ate and laughed and joked together, the shock of racism left its mark on me. I pondered the effect the racist exclusion had on Benny.

We had little time to linger after our meal with a four-hour drive ahead of us up the Stuart Highway. Benny drove while Bill snored and I gazed out at the blackness of the night. It was after midnight when we finally turned off the Stuart Highway onto the corrugated dirt road that led to Ali Curung.

As we drove into the sleeping community it seemed to be a normal town of dirt roads with street lights, a school and houses. Knowing what a 'bushy' Bill was, when we pulled up at his house, I was relieved to find it had all the amenities of normal living. A kitchen with a fridge, a dining table, vinyl lounge, shower, indoor toilet, and best of all, a bed for me to crash onto. I was exhausted.

Next morning the appearance of normality evaporated when I awoke to discover a town like no other I had ever been to. Ali Curung was not a town of flower gardens, neat fences, concrete driveways and letterboxes. To my city eyes, it looked to be a neglected, run-down town. The housing was metal cladding and cement block, stained with the red dust from the roads. Instead of a gate and letterbox at the front of each house, there was an old forty-four-gallon drum used to burn household rubbish. If there was a fence at all, it was decrepit, tumble-down wire fencing. Old cars were parked here and there. Kids in scrappy clothing played in the sandy streets. Women carrying their babies walked along the roads.

In a typical Australian country town with a population of 700, one would expect to find a small shopping centre with a supermarket, maybe a café doubling as a gift shop, a pharmacy, a small boutique, service station and probably an op-shop. In Aboriginal Ali Curung there were no shops. Instead there was a general store, garage and post office located in the council office. Government services consisted of a primary school and health clinic. This was not the outback country town I had expected. It was a ramshackle Aboriginal community town provided by the government.

Ali Curung, Northern Territory, was the first Aboriginal community I visited. It was like no place I'd ever seen.
Tamara Wastl Munnich

My sightseeing tour of Ali Curung did not take long. The first port of call was the council office where Bill introduced me to the council staff and some of the councillors. Next was the health clinic where I met one of the nurses, a terrific woman. Bill's job kept him very busy, so when I could, I accompanied him to his work. At other times I sat on Bill's veranda and watched the Ali Curung world go by or wandered around the community by myself. Men and women with their children sat chatting in the little park, or under shady trees near their houses. When I smiled and said 'hello' to people walking, they smiled back but seemed to be shy of me, a foreigner in their town.

Late one afternoon, I was preparing food for our dinner when I heard the sound of wailing coming across the desert air. I quickly looked out the kitchen window to see what was happening. Not far from the house I could see bare-breasted women heading away from the community to the empty desert. The women were covered in what looked like white paint or powder. I had never heard wailing before. The sound was haunting and deeply disturbing and the hair on my arms stood up. When Bill arrived home I learned there had been a death in the community and the women were expressing their grief culturally, being 'Sorry'. The haunting wailing and painted bodies were part of their grieving process.

No alcohol was permitted on Ali Curung as it was a 'dry' community. Bill had some time off work so we decided to drive 40 kilometres to the Wycliffe Well roadhouse to have a beer together. We were sitting on the roadhouse veranda sipping our beer, enjoying some father–daughter time, when two small bubble-nosed Heli-Muster choppers flew in and parked at the edge of the car park. The young cowboy pilots jumped out of their helicopters and headed for the bar. I was astonished, to say the least. Even by Territory standards this must be an unusual sight. Bill agreed it was.

'Are they allowed to drink and fly? Or are they just getting a cup of tea?' we wondered. We both hoped the latter, but guessed the former.

The desert fascinated me: the feeling of emptiness and endless space of land and sky, the red-coloured earth and tough vegetation of Mitchell grass and acacia trees. This was, as Bill said, the real Australia, our vast and timeless land. My life in the city seemed alien and artificial. In a strange way, I had the feeling of coming home.

My three-week holiday passed far too quickly, but it was long enough to convince me to ditch my job in Melbourne and move to the Northern Territory. My comfortable, predictable life was over. I was seduced by the isolation, the desert, the desert people, the strangeness, the dislocated feeling of being White in a Black world. I was hooked by this unknown Australia. I wanted to work and live amongst the original inhabitants of our vast timeless red-earth country.

Bill and I left Ali Curung just on dawn for the drive back to Alice Springs. The desert air was soft and the landscape appeared more gentle and inviting in the early-morning light. Bill had a full day of appointments and purchasing ahead of him. My flight didn't leave until the next morning so I had the day to myself. My mission was to register with the Commonwealth Employment Service, or the CES as we called it, to find a job in the Northern Territory. Bill and I would catch up for dinner and Homer would join us. I was tickled pink that I would see Homer on my last night. It would be a great way to end my holiday. Deep inside I nursed the hope that we might be at the beginning of a special friendship if I could find a job that would return me to the Territory.

The CES was a friendly and efficient service which advertised jobs all over Australia. Such a difference to the privatised money-driven job providers of today. I was interviewed by a pleasant young man who seemed to think I would be able to find a job without much trouble. I completed the paperwork and started scanning the jobs. My luck was in. There was a job advertised at Papunya for a health-service administrator at the Lyappa Health Service. I carefully wrote all the details in my notebook so I could write my application and update my resume as soon as I got back to Melbourne.

At dinner that night, I excitedly related all the details of the Papunya job to Bill and Homer. Bill sat back and thought for a minute. 'Hmmm. Papunya. It's got a bit of a reputation but I think you'll be able to manage it.'

'What do you mean, "it's got a reputation"?' I asked. 'What happens there?'

'Oh, it used to get a bit wild from time to time but I think it's settled down now. You'll be fine, Blossom.'

I knew I would, so I didn't worry about what might or might not happen. My only concern was to win that job.

In the old days before the internet, it wasn't easy to find out what the tasks of a health-service administrator on an Aboriginal community might be. I scanned advertised health administration jobs in the newspapers and they seemed to be mostly work schedules, budgets, maintaining records, rosters. I figured I could do all of that. After all, I had been a salaries team leader in the Department of Immigration, accounts payable in Jones Lang Wootton in London, travelled all over Europe in a Kombi without a map and was currently a branch manager in a building society. I wrote up my application, amended my resume to suit the role and posted it off.

I was on tenterhooks for nearly a month before I heard from the CES. Finally I got the phone call I had been waiting for, inviting me to attend an interview at Papunya. I was thrilled to bits, but felt a bit stunned to hear that I would have to fly to Alice Springs at my own expense. However, I quickly agreed to that condition as I wasn't going to let the price of an airfare stand in my way. An interview date was set in two weeks' time. The CES told me that a council vehicle would collect me from Alice Springs and drive me to Papunya. I was ecstatic.

Bill hooked me up to stay in Alice Springs with Wendy, another friend of his. Bill was a very friendly guy and had many contacts willing to do him a favour. As well as letting me stay at her place, Wendy picked me up from the airport.

I had thought long and hard about what to wear for my interview. My previous experience in Ali Curung told me that it should be a darkish colour so any stains from the red dust didn't show. It needed to be businesslike as I wanted to look efficient and capable. I scoured my wardrobe and chose my neat, navy-blue dress with a sunray-pleated skirt, suitable for admin work and looking like I meant business.

The next morning I saw a Toyota troop carrier pull into the driveway. It was the Papunya vehicle. The driver nodded me to the front passenger seat and I dutifully climbed in. His family filled up the rest of the vehicle. There was plenty of chatter along the way but not in English, so I remained silent for the entire three-hour journey. That was fine by me as I had plenty to look at on the 250-kilometre journey west to Papunya, hoping that I'd soon be driving over this road myself. The road was badly corrugated and stretched through a vast and empty red-dirt land of spinifex, saltbush and desert oaks. From time to time I could see abandoned cars. The signs of irregular grading could be seen by the piled dirt rows on the sides of the road.

When we finally pulled up at what looked to be the council office, no one came out to greet me. I straightened my shoulders and I walked through the door that led directly into the office, and came face-to-face with my interview panel. There were two Whitefellas and about eight or nine Aboriginal people, all staring at me. One of the Aboriginal people was a young, unsmiling woman whom I later discovered to be Alison Anderson. At that time Alison was employed in administration and interpreting. She later became the council clerk, an ATSIC commissioner and a Northern Territory member of parliament. I stood waiting uncomfortably until a middle-aged, slightly overweight White man in a check shirt and casual pants introduced himself as Ron Moroney from the Department of Aboriginal Affairs. He introduced me to the Aboriginal councillors, the Lyappa Health Service staff and finally to Adrian, the other White guy wearing scruffy jeans and a blue shirt who was one of the doctors for the health service.

Mr DAA, as I silently named him, invited me to sit on the grubby three-seater couch in the middle of the open office for what I expected would be a general chitchat before the interview. *After all*, I thought, *interviews are held in private small rooms*. I chose the middle seat of the grotty couch, feeling relieved that my dress was navy blue. I folded my hands in my lap, with my neatly sandal-clad feet together in front of me. I had hardly caught my breath when I realised my interview was here and now, in the open office.

In fact it was already underway. I looked around the room. Some eyes were on me, other people seemed to be ignoring me.

As the interview proceeded, my neat navy dress and sandals felt more ridiculous by the minute. So did my prim posture of hands in lap and feet together. I put my hands beside me and crossed my ankles. I turned in my seat. It was too late to shift to the end of the couch. I was stuck in the middle and I looked a right prat.

As Ron from DAA asked me questions, all eyes turned on me. I tried a couple of half smiles and tried to looked pleasant. No one smiled back. I wasn't sure who I was supposed to look at. Some of my future male health-service colleagues were in one corner of the room, while my female colleagues were in another. I later discovered this was due to cultural avoidance practices.

So there I was, in my neat blue dress and neat Melbourne sandals looking completely citified and ridiculous in this strange office. Never before, or since, have I felt more spectacularly awkward.

While I had done my best to discover the duties of a health-service administrator and work out a few answers, in reality I was flying blind. I had no idea what my job would entail. Although most of the questions came from DAA Ron and Dr Adrian, I tried to direct my answers around the room. I was starting to get a swivel neck. At long last, DAA Ron asked the question which decided my fate, 'What is your current job?'

This was my moment! I launched into my easy-to-understand answer of helping people manage their money at my Hotham Building Society branch in Melbourne. I talked about my good reputation, how satisfied my customers were and that money deposits with my branch had grown consistently over the past twelve months. I told the interview panel that I helped people to save and take out loans.

Managing the financial side of the health service weighed heavily on the Aboriginal staff and council and my answer decided my fate. It seemed that my future Aboriginal bosses were delighted by my supposed financial genius at Hotham.

Despite the neat blue dress and looking like a total prat in the middle of the couch, I got the job.

Four weeks later, my work in finance was over and my tiny Port Melbourne home was rented. I booked a ticket to Alice Springs on the Ghan for me and my car. I packed my Subaru wagon with a portable cassette player, books, summer clothes, towels, bed linen, a pair of spare glasses and my camera. After driving for two days through Victoria and South Australia, I finally reached Port Augusta rail yards to have my car loaded onto the train. I felt a flush of pride at my momentous achievement when I gazed at my loaded Subaru tied down on a flat car for the train trip to Alice and took a photo.

My Subaru is locked and loaded as I prepare for the twenty-four-hour journey on The Ghan to Alice Springs
Jackson collection, 1982

The Ghan was originally known as the Afghan Express, taking its name from the nineteenth-century Afghan camel drivers who arrived in Australia and helped explore the country's remote interior. In 1982, when I caught The Ghan, the train departed from Port Augusta and terminated in Alice Springs, a trip of 1200 kilometres that took nearly twenty-four hours. I could have driven faster than the train, and I would have, but for my fear of driving more than a thousand kilometres in isolated and unfamiliar territory. The perennial fear that women have rose up in me at the thought of being stranded on that long empty highway if my car broke down. Much better to travel on the Ghan and arrive safely in one piece in Alice Springs.

As I sat on the train watching the desert slowly pass by, I tried to imagine what my life would be in Papunya. What I knew about Papunya could have been written on a postage stamp. When qualms arose, I beat them down with my personal mantra of *it'll be all right, just keep going*. I had gleaned a little information from Bill who had worked in the housing team at Papunya a few years back. He told me of the tough time he had working there and the poor conditions endured by the community people, however, Bill knew little about Papunya's history. Australia's colonial and racist past was pretty much a blank page for me.

Before leaving, I had phoned Wendy with the good news of my Papunya job. Bill had suggested that I ask Wendy to rent me a room for the occasions I would be in Alice Springs. I was pleased she agreed. When my car and I disembarked from the train, I drove straight to her house. After a welcome cup of tea, I quickly stowed my possessions in my new bedroom and packed a bag of essentials for my first weeks at Papunya.

My instructions were to wait at Wendy's house for the health-service vehicle to collect me. I spent the Sunday morning chatting with Wendy when finally, around lunchtime, the health-service troop carrier arrived. Both Papunya doctors, Adrian and Jenny, were on board. I climbed in the back, stowed my bag in the midst of the supplies and took a seat near the rear door. Adrian was dressed much the same as he had for my interview, scruffy jeans and a blue shirt. He was a slimly built, intense, intellectual-looking kind of bloke. I guessed he was in his early thirties. Jenny on the other hand, looked about sixteen years old, fair-haired, blue-eyed and attractive in a hippy way. Although I was only thirty-three years old, I felt very middle-class, middle-aged and uncomfortable with both of them, as if I was from another era.

As we drove up the Stuart Highway and turned west on the long dirt road to Papunya, Adrian and Jenny made desultory conversation with each other. Jenny directed a couple of polite remarks to me, but neither of the doctors seemed friendly. As we drove along, I made a couple of chatty remarks but they weren't reciprocated.

'This is going to be fun, I don't think,' I muttered to myself.

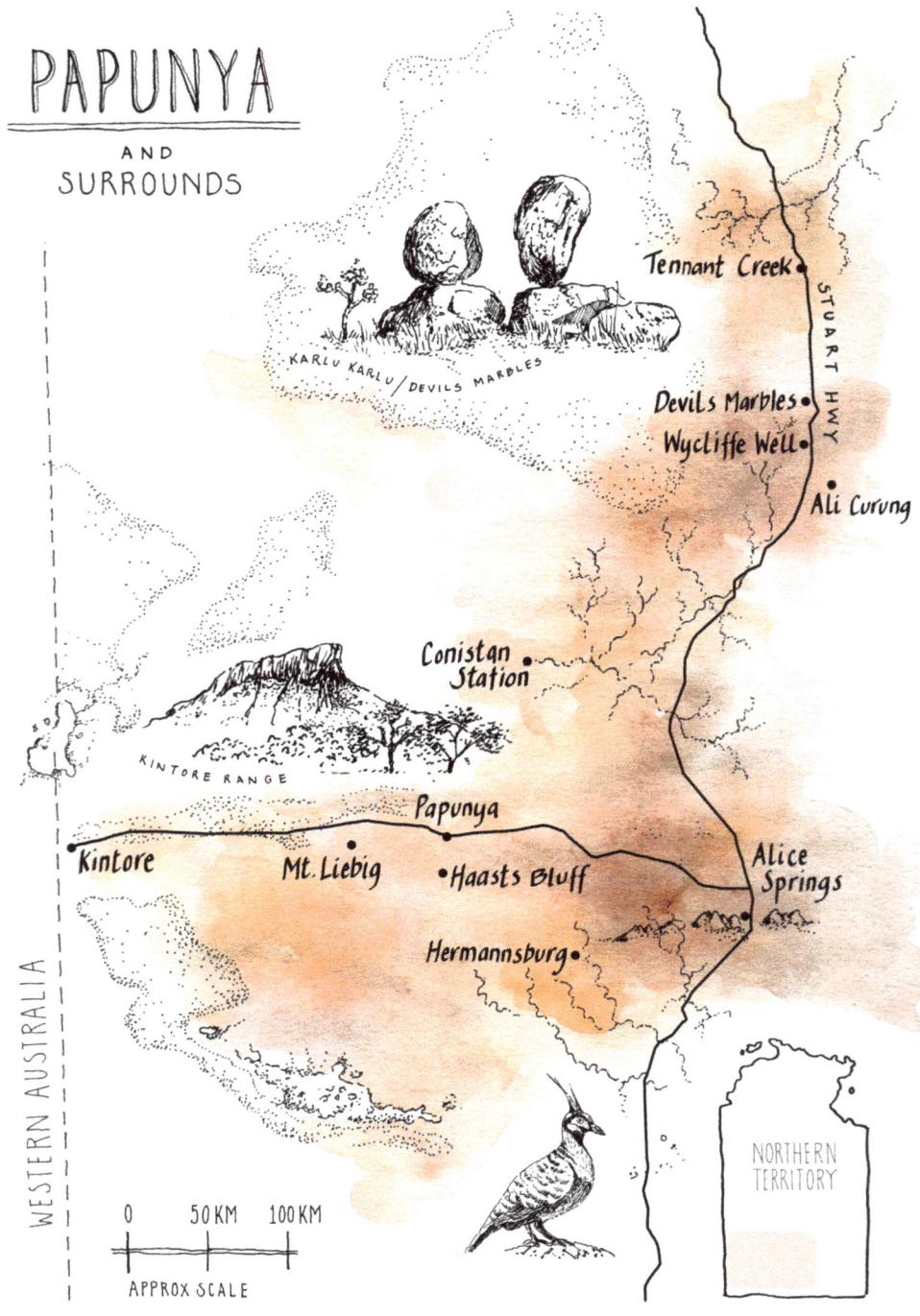

Part 1

One year in Papunya

1 Setting the wheels in motion

My accommodation was a shared house with Dr Jenny and Liz the Aboriginal midwife. Liz was much friendlier than the doctors. She had three young children and didn't seem to rest or sit down for a minute. As I was to find out, Liz was a dedicated nurse, seeing her patients at the clinic or visiting them at their camps at all hours. Mostly her children went with her. Her blessing was a wonderful Papunya woman called Topsy who was on hand day or night to help with the kids. I'm sure Liz couldn't have managed without her. Liz and her children often stayed with Topsy so she was rarely in our share house.

Settling into my new abode with my meagre possessions took about two minutes. I decided to check out the hospital clinic and the general store before starting work the next day. Dr Jenny gave me a set of hospital keys and directions but didn't offer to come with me.

'Bloody hell. You'd think she could at least be a little bit friendly and come with me,' I grumbled to myself, as I walked up the sandy road to visit my new place of work.

Papunya hospital was a forlorn, rectangular building of besser brick stained with red dust. No signage, no trees or flowers, no welcome mat. I unlocked the door and stepped into a large room which was a combined clinic and waiting room. I looked around at the motley assortment of chairs, the reception counter, filing cabinets, desks and baby scales, thinking it looked a dismal place.

I saw a passageway and took an exploratory walk. It was a bit eerie. It felt as though there were two realities. On one hand, the building looked like a small regional hospital. On the other, it looked nothing like a hospital. No polished floors or clean painted walls here. Instead, the surfaces were impregnated with red dust. I figured the two large rooms down the corridor were wards as they had lonely metal-framed beds positioned next to non-functioning oxygen and suction connectors. Unlocking one of the doors, I found a room that looked like the labour and delivery room, a sluicing area and a small operating theatre that was currently acting as a storeroom. This was a hospital that *wasn't* a hospital!

I remembered Bill speaking about the Papunya hospital as one of Whitlam's grand plans that had come a cropper. Bill had seen it as a complete waste of money. It was to have been a small regional hospital that enabled outback Aboriginal people to have access to modern medicine and health services like all other Australians. Instead of sick people being transported by plane or road ambulance to Alice Springs, they would be treated at Papunya.[1] If the hospital and health-care system had been constructed within an Aboriginal world view and staffed with Aboriginal and non-Aboriginal staff, it would have been a marvel. Instead, a combination of changing policies and budget priorities in Aboriginal Affairs had seen the concept come to nothing.[2] I wondered if the hospital had ever been commissioned. Had the air conditioning ever worked? Had the oxygen flowed in the wards? Had the small surgery ever been used? Had the incinerators for 'feminine waste' in the toilets ever worked? Somehow I doubted it. The only room that I definitely knew had been used was the birthing room and that's because I saw afterbirth in the sink. I must admit I gasped when I saw it. The tour of my new work space left me feeling thoroughly confused.

The next stop was the Papunya general store. Although I had followed Dr Jenny's directions, when I got to the location, I couldn't find the store. What I saw was a large, rough-looking tin shed with steel mesh. I stood still, staring at the structure, wondering what it was. If it was the store, it didn't seem to have a door. It looked forbidding. I must have looked like a lost galah staring at that shed. Eventually, a young Aboriginal man emerged carrying a bag.

It is the store, I decided. *I'll take a look.*

I plucked up my courage and cautiously walked into the building. As I looked around the gloomy interior I noticed most of the shelves had lots of empty space. Walking around, I saw drums of flour, bags of rice, sugar, tea, powdered milk, golden syrup, canned meat, soft drinks and a few stale vegetables. Everything was expensive. As my eyes got used to the dim light, I saw an Aboriginal woman sitting behind a counter.

Ahaa, it definitely is the store, I determined. *And she must be the checkout staff.*

To make sure, I nervously asked. 'Is this the store?'

The woman didn't answer but a White man appeared from behind a door and brusquely replied, 'Yes.'

'Can I get a coke please?'

'Yeah, just take one from the fridge and she'll take the money,' he said, nodding towards the woman.

I silently handed the woman some money and she put the change on the counter. I picked up my change and walked out of the store.

My God. This is a weird place, I thought.

When I commenced work at the Lyappa Health Service at Papunya, it was staffed by two doctors, one male and one female, an Aboriginal midwife, six Aboriginal health workers and the newly appointed health-service administrator … me! Although I didn't realise it at the time, working for an Aboriginal-controlled health service was an amazing opportunity. Nearly all the other health services on Aboriginal communities were run by the Northern Territory Department of Health with no doctor and two nurses.

Aboriginal community-controlled health services are initiated and operated by the Aboriginal community. They provide holistic primary health-care services, not only for the physical wellbeing of an individual, but also for the social, emotional and cultural wellbeing of the whole community. It is a whole-of-life view and includes the cyclical concept of life-death-life. The first Aboriginal-controlled health service started in 1971 in Redfern Sydney. The Lyappa Health Service was formed in 1978.

My first week was an orientation of sorts. I was introduced to the director of the health service, Andrew Bullen, and the health workers. Everyone seemed to be shy, including me. In truth, I was quite bamboozled as I could scarcely tell one Aboriginal health worker from another. I feel highly embarrassed to confess to this, but that's how it was. Fortunately, after a week or so, my eyes and mind had adjusted to my Aboriginal circumstances and I realised how easy it was to recognise my colleagues. In fact I was amazed that I hadn't been able to differentiate between them previously.

The admin office consisted of a couple of desks and typewriters with an odd assortment of stationery. Setting up the office became my first task which gave me my inaugural office-run to Alice Springs from where all the office and medical supplies were purchased. I learned the town of Alice Springs, one stop at a time: stationery, second-hand furniture, car parts, supermarkets, the bank, the accountant's office, Alice Springs hospital and the Central Australian Aboriginal Congress, which provided primary health care, support and advocacy for Alice Springs Aboriginal people. By good fortune, Ali Curung used the same accountant as Papunya. On one of my early runs into Alice, my father was down from Ali Curung. He took me to meet the accountant, Peter, and gave him the word to look after me as I settled in. Peter was helpful and he patiently answered my numerous questions. He also ensured that my lack of experience and know-how did no harm to the health service.

Understandably, my supposed financial genius as a branch manager did not equip me in the slightest for health-service administration. In fact, in my first couple of months at Papunya I was awash with feelings of shock, horror, amazement and bewilderment. I reeled from thinking, *How hysterically funny this is!* to *What on earth am I doing here?*

But not once did I seriously think of leaving. I was going to succeed at this job or bust with the effort of it.

Dr Adrian gave me a couple of weeks to settle into the job and set up the wages and account systems. Then he thrust on me the real reason for my employment. It was to repair and maintain the vehicles which were constantly in use, driving thousands of kilometres each week on rough roads from Papunya to Kintore and other outstations as well as to Alice Springs.

Just two weeks previously my knowledge of vehicles had consisted of putting in petrol and checking the tyre pressure. Now I had to become a 4WD expert. Of course I did just that, because when there is no choice, you just do it.

The vehicles were one of the biggest headaches of the Lyappa Health Service. There was one fully functioning eleven-seater Toyota troop carrier with side seats, commonly called a 'troopie'. Most times, the second troopie needed to be push-started and was in desperate need of quality repairs and maintenance. A third Toyota was pretty much stuffed and needed to be hauled out of Papunya and sold for parts and scrap. There was also a small Subaru sedan which limped along and needed to be sold off as it was totally unsuitable for the conditions. My task was to get the two Toyotas in good working condition and put in grant applications for two more vehicles that would be fitted out for the bush. Considering my previous car knowledge, this was a highly challenging task. I had much to learn before I could solve the vehicle dilemma.

I realised the distinct lack of enthusiasm with which the Whitefella health team greeted me was because their preferred candidate for the job was a mate who knew all about vehicles. It was a real blow to them that I got the job.

Well, too bad, I thought. *I'll get the vehicles sorted out and they can eat their words*.

Because my father, Bill, had worked in Central Australia, he'd gotten to know many Alice Springs businesses and he was able to point me to the best places for bush supplies, stationery, spare parts and vehicle repairs. His contacts in Alice Springs were a godsend to me in sorting the vehicle issues. Bill put me in touch with a bloke called Les Harkin who owned a garage. Les would arrange for a semitrailer to drive out to Papunya to pick up the dead and wounded vehicles and bring them back to him for repairs or scrapping. It would have been so much more difficult without him. Thank goodness for Bill.

In the 1980s when I worked in Papunya, there were no telephones in the outback. All communication was through the Royal Flying Doctor Service which provided a twenty-four-hour radio service. The RFDS radio schedule, known as the 'skeds', was the communication lifeline for Aboriginal communities and cattle stations alike. Talking on the radio was a very outback thing. A call sign was allocated to each radio. When someone finished a question or comment, the caller was required to say 'over' to let the receiver know it was their turn to speak. Each call was limited to a couple of minutes so there was no time to muck around. Everyone wanting to make a call was queued and had to wait until the operator called their call sign. Everyone waiting heard the current conversation. Privacy didn't exist.

As I prepared to make my very first call on the radio to Les Harkin, my stomach churned and my hands shook. I knew that everyone queued would be listening to me. I didn't want to sound like a complete 'newbie' so I wrote down our call sign and exactly what I wanted to say. Our call sign to VJD was Victor Mike Eight Papa. VJD was the RFDS call sign. Because I didn't want the doctors overhearing my quaking voice, I used the radio in one of the vehicles. My call to Les was simple and straightforward. He was to book the semi for the next week. I would come to Alice and travel back to Papunya with the driver and semitrailer.

A week later I was beside myself with excitement sitting in a semitrailer driving on the sandy red road to Papunya. I had to pinch myself. Was this really me? A city girl from Hotham Building Society in Melbourne. When we arrived in Papunya, I directed the driver to the waiting vehicles near the ramp. I hiked over to the hospital and picked up the working troopie. The idea was to set up the working Toyota with the dead vehicle, nose to nose, bull bar to bull bar. Then, using the bull bar of the working Toyota, push the 'dead' vehicle backwards up the ramp onto the tray of the semi with me steering it. With that accomplished, I then had to steer the 'just working' Toyota up the ramp onto the tray of the semi, also backwards. I was pretty nervous backing the Toyotas but the truck driver guided me and I managed it okay. I was totally elated. Me, Barbara Jackson, had organised a semitrailer and transported a couple of vehicles out of Papunya into Alice Springs.

With the vehicle repairs underway, my next priority was to order two new 4WDs fitted out for the bush. The specifications included bull bars, long-range fuel tanks, snorkels and air filters, roof racks, two spare tyres, built-in water containers, car radios and antennas. The list went on and on. I knew I needed good advice. Hundreds of trucks passed through Alice Springs every week, all with diesel motors, all fitted out for the bush. Who better to ask? And I knew where to find them. The pub. As Ted Egan said, 'They've got some bloody good drinkers in the Northern Territory'. It didn't take much to persuade Homer to come to the pub with me. After we'd settled in with a drink, I took stock of the pub and spotted a few burly blokes in the bar. I refreshed my lipstick, checked my hair, asked Homer to wish me luck, and set off to introduce myself.

'Ah, hello, I'm wondering if you are a truck driver?' I asked smilingly to the friendliest-looking bloke. He looked me up and down, and grunted 'Yep.'

'I work at a health service and one of my jobs is to buy two new vehicles and have them fitted out for the bush. I really need some advice about the specifications. Can you help me?'

He gave me a big smile and said, 'Is that right? Whaddaya want to know?'

I pulled my notebook out of my handbag and started my checklist of questions. He was happy to help and told me a few very funny tales along the way. Poor Homer was a bit cheesed off by the time I got back to him, but when I told him all the great information I had collected he laughed and gave me a hug.

I put together the information I had gathered and presented it to the health service. Dr Adrian had done his homework too. In the end we decided to buy two Nissan Patrols. Nissan was trying to break the Toyota stranglehold in the outback and their prices were very competitive. In addition, their service seemed better than Toyota. I was determined to get everything right for this major health-service purchase. For a small fee, the Automobile Association of the Northern Territory acted on our behalf to ensure the vehicles would be delivered according to the specifications. The AANT added a few more requirements to my list of bush-fit extras and I placed the orders.

It took about a month for the vehicles to be delivered to the AANT for inspection. When I received a radio call from the boss of AANT in Darwin I was horrified to hear there were thirty-two faults requiring rectification. I received the documentation a couple of days later and called Nissan in Darwin. By this time, I was an old hand at the two-way radio. I joined the skeds queue and waited my turn. Finally I was on. I asked for the Nissan manager and then proceeded to tell him about the vehicles not meeting the ordered specification.

'I'll tell you some of the problems if you want?'

Foolishly he agreed. I proceeded to read out the entire list of faults. What was hilarious was that a normal RFDS sked call runs for only a couple of minutes, but this time, there were no interruptions. The sked queue of people wanting to make calls had decided to stay silent so they could hear the gory details of Nissan's mistakes with the vehicles. After all, a good vehicle can be the difference between life and death in the outback. Even as I slowly read out the interminable list, I felt a bit sorry for the Nissan bloke who knew that this horror list of faults would be gossiped about all over the Territory.

As it turned out, buying the Nissan Patrols proved to be a great mistake. Although the initial faults were rectified, these were not the only problems. Nissan vehicle research had obviously been inadequate because a design fault showed itself within a few months. The corner windscreen pillars were simply not strong enough for the conditions and they began to crack. When my phone calls to Darwin were ignored, I started phoning Nissan in Japan. This was confusing, funny and also expensive as I had to invariably wait until an English speaker could come to the phone to hear my complaints. When this tactic had no acceptable outcome, my next foray was to the media. I was interviewed on Alice Springs radio and I gave Nissan a huge serve and recommended to all the listeners to buy Toyota in future. Eventually our campaign succeeded. For no cost we had the cracks welded and bush bars fitted to stop the problem from getting worse.

With four working health-service vehicles, we regularly had three in the field and one being serviced. As well as the pillar cracking, the wretched

Nissan Patrols were sensitive to dust and would suddenly conk out. It was a matter of waiting and then repeatedly trying to start up the motor until finally the vehicle would chug back into life. It was such a pain. Once again, it was the truckies in the bars who helped me when they advised me to learn how to bleed the lines on a diesel. I asked the mechanic Les Harkin to show me how, and my new skill got me out of trouble a few times. I was inordinately proud of my ability and I boasted about it continually. Eventually the filter problems were fixed and the Nissan Patrols were able to chug along the sandy roads without breaking down. Hurrah!

Health-service staff depended on the fleet of vehicles.

Bill and I had always exchanged letters and phone calls, but apart from my trip to Ali Curung, we had not seen much of each other for many years. It was an enriching experience for both of us to reconnect in the Northern Territory as we were friends as well as father and daughter. He used to sign his letters Bill/Dad and I addressed his letters the same. We had fun together. I inherited Bill's sense of humour and his droll sense of the ridiculous so there was always something we could have a laugh at. Now we had our shared experiences of working on Aboriginal communities. Bill was very proud of me for having a go at doing something worthwhile in Papunya. We met in Alice Springs when we could.

Although our communities were different and more than 500 kilometres apart, Papunya and Ali Curung were remarkably similar, with issues such as poverty, overcrowding and a lack of services and infrastructure. There was also an abiding sense of frustration as the one-way street of top-down government policies and their implementation inevitably stifled or thwarted community aspirations. Bill was a practical man who aimed for practical solutions. At times he was wildly frustrated, but at others, he laughed his head off at the ridiculousness of it all. He enjoyed being able to share his stories with me.

The Honey Ant Dreaming design of Papunya Community
Max Stollznow, 1976

When the design of the Papunya community was first conceived, a long-term supporter of Aboriginal people, Reverend Jim Downing, worked with the people of Papunya to design the town plan. The people drew their Honey Ant Dreaming and the concept was accepted.[3] The administrative buildings were in the central hub with housing for the different language groups in the outer rings. It's a wonderfully creative idea, but for me, a woman suffering from no sense of direction, it was perpetually confusing.

When I visited Bill in Ali Curung, I had found the layout of the community easy to navigate, and I could wander around on my own without getting lost. It was quite the opposite in Papunya. Of course I could find my way to the main places, such as the council office, the school and the garage, but I was blowed if I could work out where people lived. The various language groups lived clustered in geographically separate areas which looked great in the Honey Ant Dreaming design of the community but it made a problem for me. I could never remember in which area people lived. When I drove someone home from the hospital, I had to rely on my passengers to give me directions. This was when I discovered an interesting cultural behaviour habit. Aboriginal directions consisted of a small flick of the hand or pursed lips pointing to the dirt road I was to turn down. Although I tried valiantly to catch sight of the lip or hand movement, my peripheral vision was completely inadequate for this sign language. It wasn't long before I gave up trying to see the small movements and just drove until people shouted at me to stop. I'd reverse back to the turn I had missed, then drive till they shouted again as I passed their abode. I'm sure they thought I was extremely stupid but it was the best I could do.

At times I felt overwhelmed by Papunya, but mostly I embraced the new experiences in my life. One of my greatest pleasures was driving back to Papunya after my admin run. I always timed it to drive through the dawning light. It would still be dark as I drove out of Alice Springs on the Stuart Highway to the turn-off to Papunya. The Toyota troop carrier would be loaded with supplies for the health service: medicines, bandages, dressings, office stationery, a second-hand filing cabinet, a new battery for one of the vehicles and a wheelchair. I never tied anything down. I just put the seats up and shoved everything in the back willy-nilly. I guess the gods were smiling on me as I never had to do an emergency brake, which could have been a disaster.

It was only a twenty-minute drive on the bitumen before I turned west on the corrugated road leading to Papunya community. My headlights picked out the dark road, its red colour hidden by the night. A faint early-morning glow behind me heralded the approaching dawn. The foothills of the West MacDonnell Ranges were on my left. Dark and secretive. As the day started to break, the red soil emerged from the dark shadows cast across the road. On my right, I could discern the desert trees and bushes as the lightening sky dispersed the shadows.

The next half-hour was pure joy as the colours of the road, sky and bush broke through the dawn dark. The vibrant red ochre of the land. The pale, pearly sky turning to clear, vivid blue. The deep dark green of the bush transforming into the olive, grey-green that is so familiar to us. It was at this time the bush turkeys showed themselves. I loved to see these birds strutting along with their heads held high. Their correct name is the Australian Bustard. I kept a sharp eye out for kangaroos foraging near the road. Although the troopie had a protective bull bar for my safety, I adored the kangaroos and drove at a speed that enabled me to stop if one decided to hop over the road in front of my vehicle.

All too soon, the sun rose into the sky and the mystery of dawn was dispelled into the brilliant light of the Central Desert. The corrugations on the road revealed their full horror as the troopie shuddered along. I drove steadily on, but in this clear light, my mind turned to all that I had learned about Papunya and what more I would come to know through my work in this complex, uncomfortable, sad and troubled community.

Driving through the red dirt landscape gave me time to breathe, reflect and re-set.
Rhiannon Stevens, 2019, ABC RN

2 Working across cultures

In 1982 I don't think I was much different to most Australians at that time. Our schooling taught us British history, with the original inhabitants of the British penal colony being relegated to a footnote as a primitive people, unable to assimilate and dying out. As I write these words, I feel appalled at the unthinking, uncaring attitude and character of White Australia. Is this an unconscious British legacy or did we develop this way consciously? To this day, I don't know the answer to this question.

Papunya Native Settlement was established in 1959, only twenty-three years prior to my arrival. However, I had been in complete ignorance of its beginnings. As I wrote this book, I realised I needed to search into the past. My search revealed that the history behind this move began in 1862, when John McDouall Stuart became the first explorer to successfully cross from the south to the north of Australia and return. A decade later, the Overland Telegraph Line followed virtually the same route. The telegraph line linked Adelaide and Darwin through an overseas cable to Java and on to Europe, reducing Australia's communication time with Europe from months to hours.

These events led to the opening up of the Aboriginal lands of the central Australian desert regions of the Northern Territory, South Australia and Western Australia. Initially there was little contact between the Aboriginal people and the explorers, but this changed as the telegraph stations and pastoral properties were established and mining fields opened.

With the influx of men with their guns and cattle spreading across the lands and contaminating the waterholes, the Aboriginal people were facing an existential crisis. Their food supply and watering holes were severely threatened. They fought back, spearing cattle and threatening the White intruders. Drought exacerbated their desperation and guerrilla warfare broke out. Official and unofficial reprisals from the Whites in shooting parties resulted in killings and massacres of Aboriginal people. The White men, unaccompanied by women, bribed and stole Aboriginal women. The children resulting from the sexual encounters, referred to as 'half-castes', were removed from their families by federal and state government agencies and church missions. The venereal disease that came with the White men became endemic, further decreasing the Aboriginal population.

Overland Telegraph Line
https://collections.slsa.sa.gov.au/resource/B+78437

In a brief summary of the punitive expeditions of 1874–91, Reverend Schwarz from Hermannsburg Mission believed that many of the actions against the 'Blacks', and especially the men, were taken with the object of exterminating them. From the squatters' point of view either the 'Blacks or the cattle had to go'. It is thought that some 500 Aboriginal people and quite possibly upwards of 1,000 were shot in Central Australia.[4]

The guerrilla warfare continued on the most remote stations into the 1890s, and indeed into the 1920s. The Coniston Massacre of 1928 was to be the last major recorded massacre in this bloody frontier history. Coniston was, and still is, a cattle station about 250 kilometres north-west of Alice

Springs. Historians estimate that at least sixty and as many as 110 Aboriginal men, women and children were killed in the Coniston Massacre.[5]

The Hermannsburg Lutheran Mission offered a refuge for the Arrernte people from the frontier violence. It was established in 1877 on the banks of the Finke River, 125 kilometres west of Alice Springs. The missionaries played a key role in mediating the conflicts between pastoralists, the police and the Aboriginal people. The missionaries spoke out publicly about the violence between the groups, which led to an intense national debate on the treatment of Indigenous people.[6]

In an address given by Territorian Ted Egan AO in 2019, Ted noted that Warren Williams, a local musician who was born and raised on Hermannsburg, believed that the survival of Aboriginal people was in large part due to the missionaries at Hermannsburg. Williams said, 'If the missionaries had not come to Hermannsburg, there wouldn't be any Blackfellas in Central Australia'.[7]

The need for Aboriginal labour on the cattle stations shifted the control strategies of the pastoralists from wielding guns, whips and dogs against Aboriginal people, to the role of employer and welfare provider. In the Northern Territory, the Aboriginals Ordinance 1918 gave pastoralists the power to maintain the workers, their relatives and dependants. This shift from violence to controlling the labour of Aboriginal people was consolidated in the 1930s when Aboriginal people were being born on stations and had become accustomed to their labour relationship with pastoralists. Indeed the pastoralists realised by the 1930s that White labour was not going to fill the labour needs of the industry. The Territory's Chief Protector of Aborigines, Baldwin Spencer, noted that pastoralists had become dependent on Aboriginal workers. Aboriginal labour was not only abundant, but also highly skilled.[8] Aboriginal people had to work for their food and keep, but were not paid.

Lutheran missionaries and anthropologists strongly advocated the need for inviolable Aboriginal reserves. These reserves were to keep Aboriginal people in and keep pastoralists, doggers and explorers out.[9] In 1929 the Haasts Bluff Land Trust, not far from present-day Papunya, was gazetted.[10] A cattle station had been established in the Haasts Bluff area (east of the Kintore Range) for a few years around 1911.[11] In 1940 the government bought back the lease and grazing licence and created a Haasts Bluff reserve. The eastward drift of Eastern Pintupi and Warlpiri Aboriginal people towards Alice Springs and cattle stations created government concern and provided the rationale for establishing Haasts Bluff as a ration station in 1941. It became an offshoot of the Hermannsburg Lutheran Mission.[12]

Haasts Bluff to Papunya
Elize Strydom, 2015, ABC

The Lutherans established Haasts Bluff with government subsidies to cover building a store, employing a storekeeper and providing rations for aged and infirm people, women and children. In the early times, many people used the depot as a convenience to trade dingo scalps for food and return to the bush.[13] The storekeeper held cash to pay men for dingo scalps, kangaroo skins and curios as well as rations. By 1948 vegetable gardens had been established and several buildings erected including a church and a house for the missionary and his wife who was a nursing sister.[14]

Following the 1928 massacre of Anmatyerre families at Coniston Station, Anmatyerre people moved to Haasts Bluff joining the Eastern Pintupi and Ngaliya Warlpiri. Jeremy Long, anthropologist and patrol officer with the Welfare Branch in Central Australia, estimated that of the 263 people in Haasts Bluff in 1941, about one-third were Pintupi, one third were Ngaliya Warlpiri and the remaining were Kukatja, Pitjantjatjara, Ngaatjatjarra and Anmatyerre. Long stated that because of the considerable intermarriage that occurred between these groups, the inter-tribal lines of division, never clear-cut, became thoroughly blurred. The disparate Aboriginal groups, brought together and forced to communicate, created a shared history and a modern identity was forged. These groups became amalgamated into the Luritja.[15]

Initially, Luritja or Loritja was the name applied by the Arrernte people to all Western Desert speech groups. The Pintupi-Luritja language developed as a lingua franca for the various family groups who first moved to Haasts Bluff in the 1940s. Over time, during the settlement of people in Haasts Bluff and Papunya, the meaning of the term Luritja shifted dramatically and the Luritja-speaking people became self-identified as a group.[16]

In 1954 the Northern Territory administration assumed direct responsibility for Haasts Bluff and began to invest more development money and provide work for able-bodied males and some women. More yards and fencing were built for the cattle station which enabled the cattle-raising project to expand and become a valuable asset. The total meat requirements of the settlement were drawn from this source.[17]

Pintupi at Papunya

The settlement of Papunya came about as a result of the drinking water at Haasts Bluff. When the government realised the water supply at Haasts Bluff was unfit for human consumption, it decided to develop a new settlement further north at the Papunya bore where there was abundant water of good quality. Papunya was constructed during the period 1957 to 1959.

The Pintupi people entered Papunya from the 1960s. Rather than integrating into the broader community as the government hoped, they lived in a kind of isolation from the rest of the Papunya settlement. Their settlement in Papunya is a tragic and confronting story of cultures colliding, racism and a one-size-fits-all bureaucratic approach. One of the worst things was that, once the Pintupi were in Papunya, they couldn't go back to the way they were.[18]

Native Welfare Branch files show that of the seventy-four Pintupi people who arrived in Papunya in the eighteen months to August 1964, thirty-five died. The deaths were from malnutrition, pneumonia, chest and gastro infections, heart failure, tumours and injuries. Four people died from 'unknown causes'. It was generally believed these people died from severe depression worrying about being away from Country. In those early days at Papunya, a teacher reported that the children were herded into the kitchen and given food they had never seen before. Children of four years of age weighed less than 9 kilograms.[19]

Being Pintupi means coming from the Western Desert which includes the Gibson, Great Victoria, Great Sandy and Little Sandy deserts. These 'people from west' spoke a common language with dialectical differences. The Gibson Desert is a harsh environment mostly of sandhills with spinifex grass and areas of desert oaks. Pintupi survival depended on their detailed and expert knowledge of their environment for their food and particularly the location and usability of water. The availability of water determined their group size and the movement of the people.

Pintupi stories of early contact emphasised the quantity of food that White people carried with them. It seems clear that a strong motivation for Pintupi contact with White people was an assured food supply.[20] Another was the increased accessibility of roads into White settlement areas. The roads were built as a by-product of mining exploration and the nuclear bomb experiments at Maralinga testing site in South Australia. Blue Streak rockets built to carry nuclear bombs were test-fired from Woomera in the South Australian desert, right across the middle of Australia to the Indian Ocean, just south of Broome. This was known as the Line of Fire, and by coincidence, it was the same distance as London to Moscow. Not all the Blue Streak rockets reached the sea. Some crashed into the West Australian desert.[21] This missile testing was in part responsible for the relocation of Pintupi people to Papunya in the 1960s; not because authorities were concerned about falling projectiles, but because the grading of tracks through the desert increased accessibility to the region. Wherever there are roads, contact and engagement open up. The new desert roads exposed the Pintupi to White men, new ways of life, motor cars, camels, machinery and food.[22]

There are various versions of why and how the Pintupi came to Papunya and other communities such as Balgo, Warburton, Docker River, Wiluna and Jigalong. These versions include the government encouraging, moving, rounding up or coercing Aboriginal people to leave their Country and settle at a ration point or government settlement. However, understanding the relocation of the Pintupi as 'active participants, as people making choices and decisions about their lives, rather than as helpless victims'[23] is to me a more plausible version.

By the early 1970s, in the words of Geoffrey Bardon, Papunya was a 'hellish, dysfunctional community near Alice Springs, forcibly created by the government's racist policies during the 1960s'.[24] The settlement was plagued by poor housing and sanitation, health problems and tensions between various tribal and linguistic groups, including the local Luritja people, Arrernte from the south-east, Anmatyerre and Warlpiri from the north and Pintupi from the west. More than 1,000 Aboriginal residents were living in Papunya, twice the number originally intended. The hardship of this overcrowding is quite shocking when it is remembered that in the past, Aboriginal people lived in groups of around twenty to fifty people.

An insight into the assimilation policies of the early decades of Papunya can be found in *The Papunya School Book of Country and History* (2001) which was written collaboratively by students and staff with the support of a children's writer. It was originally produced as a resource to be used for the Papunya School Curriculum. An example of the school assimilation policies noted that:

> In those days children had to have a shower and change into school uniforms when they came to school. They lined up and went into their classrooms. At the end of the day, children put their camp clothes on again. At this time children were not allowed to speak their own language at school. They were meant to learn only the whitefella way of doing things. Teachers were very strict.[25]

In 1978, just four years before I arrived in Papunya, the governing of the community was handed to Aboriginal people and the Papunya Council and Lyappa Health Service were formed. This was the first step for the Aboriginal people to take control of their own lives and community, and to become independent. If Papunya had been an African country, it would have been gloriously referred to as 'independence' and 'removing the colonial shackles'. But this was Australia and for the most part this small step to independence went unnoticed by the Australian population. It wasn't until 1999 that some of the land was handed back to its traditional owners after a successful land claim. [26]

Lyappa Health Service

My admin office at the Lyappa Health Service was in a room just to the side of the clinic. I could see the mothers nursing their sick babies. I watched as the medical staff listened to tiny lungs with their stethoscopes, peered into little ears and took the babies' temperature under their arms. I saw the pregnant mums come in for their antenatal examinations. One evening, there were only two health workers and me at the clinic when some people came with a woman who was about to give birth. The health workers told me to get Rose, a trained midwife and the wife of the adult educator. I leapt into the troopie and drove madly to her house. She was a good woman. She didn't muck around, just put a couple of things in a bag and jumped in the troopie with me. We rushed to the birthing room and I was actually there helping out, when this new life came into the world. I haven't had children myself, but at least I have been at a birth. Awesome!

It was a busy clinic with the patients ebbing and flowing throughout the day. The patients suffered from a whole gamut of chronic conditions such as kidney disease, respiratory and cardiovascular disease, diabetes and mental health problems. I saw old people sick with pneumonia. People with cataracts and trachoma. I was in the clinic the day Dr Adrian was thrilled to agree to a man's request for the traditional healer to come to the clinic. I watched as the healer sucked small stones from the abdomen of the sick man. I felt very privileged to see this healing and I hoped it helped the man get better.

The medical work was intense for the staff as there were call-outs at night as well their clinic work all day. The call-outs were often from fighting related to alcohol. Papunya was a dry community and many people were teetotallers. But there were those who liked a drink and grog-runners were happy to supply them. The three police in Papunya tried hard to prevent grog runs, but the grog still got through. On more than one occasion, I can remember waking in the night to the chilling sound of shouting and screaming drifting across the still desert air. Patients would struggle to our house for treatment. Sometimes the police brought them.

There was a red, hard-covered book in the clinic office that was kept in a locked cupboard. It was an historic document that recorded all the births in Papunya. This book also recorded the deaths and the causes of death of the babies and children. The book recorded waves of childhood diseases such as measles and diphtheria sweeping through Papunya killing the little ones. It was a grim read, a legacy to the lives and misery of the people brought into Papunya over the past decades. Because this book named children who had died, out of cultural respect it was kept away from the health workers.

Liz told me that, prior to 1978, when the Lyappa Health Service started, health care for Papunya was provided by two nurses and a visiting doctor. She said that health care was forced on the people without them understanding what the immunisation programs and screenings were about. While people seemed to know about the power of 'needles', the trachoma program was massively resented. Nurses used to visit the camps and flip back the peoples' eye lids looking for turned-in eyelashes, a telltale sign of trachoma. It is an uncomfortable procedure and the people did not understand why the nurse was hurting them.

All humans beings want to be able to drink clean water, wash themselves and use a sanitary place for waste. The importance of basic public health measures, of a clean water supply and good sanitation, has been known for decades, forever actually. I could not understand why the water and sanitation was in such a run-down state through the community camps. It seemed to me that neither the Territory government nor the Department of Aboriginal Affairs had the capability, or the will, to supply the necessities of taps, showers, toilet blocks and rubbish collection to the Papunya community. I thought it was quite bizarre that modern-day knowledge and technology could put a man on the moon, but it couldn't supply a regularly cleaned ablution block on an Aboriginal community.

The National Immunisation Program greatly reduced the incidence of childhood diseases, although from time to time, cases of measles and whooping cough appeared in Papunya. While vaccinations and antibiotics ensured children did not die, in general, the health of children left a lot to be desired. A sizeable number of young children suffered from issues related to low birth weight. There were many chronic gastrointestinal, chest, ear and skin infections which were swiftly treated with antibiotics. If recovery was not as expected, the child was evacuated to Alice Springs hospital. The Royal Flying Doctor Service was a godsend to Aboriginal families and communities.

The policy of the two doctors at Lyappa Health Service was to use the same criteria in Papunya to admit people to hospital as they would if the sick person had presented to the emergency department in Alice Springs. The level of sickness was such that Flying Doctor planes were a regular feature of the health-service routine. I will never forget one day when I drove a particularly ill patient and his family to the Papunya airstrip for evacuation to Alice Springs. As the patient was helped on to the plane, the family members, suspecting a sad outcome, started wailing. Oh my gosh! My hair stood on end. I felt very shaken and had to wait a couple of minutes until my nerves settled before I could drive again.

Kintore

The work of the medical service was unrelenting for the medical staff. At that time, there were around 600 people living in Papunya, 160 people at Kintore and about thirty at nearby Mt Liebig. In 1981, the year before I arrived, the Pintupi people had decided to return to their traditional homelands at Kintore, locally known as Walungurru. This outstation was 250 kilometres west of Papunya. The Lyappa Health Service was determined to provide a health service that would assist this nascent homelands movement. There were medical teams going back and forth from Papunya to Kintore as the Kintore health clinic was slowly set up.

I had been hearing about Kintore for months when finally I got an opportunity to drive there myself with a troopie full of supplies for the health service. When the Pintupi people moved to Kintore, the only essential service they had was a single hand pump for water. A top priority for this new community was the construction of an airstrip for the Flying Doctor to land when sick people needed medical treatment. This was closely followed by the need for a primary school for the children and a health clinic. In the meantime, the Lyappa Health Service provided their medical care. A small caravan was set up on-site at Kintore with basic medical supplies under the supervision of health worker and ngangkari Benny Tjapaltjarri. Ngangkaris are traditional healers who look after people's physical and emotional health.[27]

I loved the long drive to Kintore. As well as supplies, I had a bunch of Pintupi passengers so I was never in any danger of getting lost. They knew every tree, rock and geographical contour on the road home to their Country. The love and passion I had been hearing about in relation to the move to Kintore had built the place up in my expectations and imagination. I thought it would be a desert paradise.

When we finally arrived after five hours of driving, we pulled up near the health clinic caravan. I climbed wearily out of the troopie and took in the environment and the landscape. It was truly horrible! Flies immediately found my eyes and stuck there. My practised Aussie hand wave was nothing to these untrained annoying flies. I had to wipe my hands over my eyes and literally push them away. Then there was the wind. Incessant. Blowing sand in my face. And of course the heat. The only relief in the landscape was a bluff standing stark in the desert, the Kintore Range. *Bloody hell! The Pintupi must truly love their home country*, I thought. *I wouldn't live here for quids.*

For the Pintupi, Kintore was a major step towards becoming autonomous and not under the control of the Papunya Council. They were reasserting their cultural control over their circumstances by leaving destructive outside influences. Their plan was to create further outstations in the Gibson Desert and there were already Pintupi living at Kiwirrkura 100 kilometres west and at other small centres. Their persistence and determination paid off as the Department of Aboriginal Affairs acknowledged the Pintupi Homelands movement to Kintore with an enquiry at the end of 1981. This resulted in a grant to Kintore of $76,800 for the year 1982–3.

During my experience of working in Papunya and Kintore in 1982, I was able to gain a rare insight into the unhappy collision of cultures in a post-colonial world. It was indescribably awful that the Pintupi, Luritja, Arrernte, Anmatyerre and Warlpiri people, who had once called more than a million square kilometres home, were cooped up in the less than 5-square-kilometre settlement of Papunya and locked out of their traditional lands. Where once they had walked, made love, had children, played and hunted, there were cattle grazing on land now owned by pastoralists. White people owned and controlled most of the country on which Aboriginal people had lived freely for more than 60,000 years.

In the first couple of months, while I worked with Aboriginal people every day in the office and the clinic and said 'hello' to people at the store, I didn't know them. In fact, I struggled to understand their English. With yes, no and good, being the only Aboriginal language words I knew, conversations were next to impossible. I was also single with no children which made me strange to them. I was an outsider, a foreigner in their land, and they were foreign to me. I was friendly and polite but I couldn't find anything in common to talk about – except of course the weather.

My communication with the health workers improved over time as they became more used to me, and I, them. In fact, I discovered that they knew quite a lot of English but they were not a chatty lot outside their own language. It was my wages-training program, Admin for Health Workers, that helped our worlds come together, albeit in a small way. As can be imagined, pay day was the most popular day of every fortnight. In those days, the wages were paid in cash which had to be ordered from the bank in Alice Springs. As I carefully counted the money and put it neatly into the pay envelopes with a payslip, some of the younger women health workers would come to watch. When I asked them if they would like to learn how to do the wages, there was a most enthusiastic response.

The Adult Education Officer helped me to work out a training program. Although the younger health workers had attended primary school, their arithmetic skills were not strong. Adding and subtracting were manageable but multiplication and division were challenging. Although from an educational point of view, it was deemed necessary for students to be able to perform calculations manually, I was very thankful for calculators.

Punata Nungurrayi was one of my favourite health workers. After leaving school, Punata trained for six months as a nurse's aide in Darwin, then worked as a health worker in Papunya. Punata was the daughter of Billy Stockman Tjapaltjarri who was one of the first chairmen of the Papunya Tula Artists cooperative. Billy Stockman Tjapaltjarri was an infant survivor of the Coniston Massacre of 1928 and was raised by the family of his 'brother' Clifford Possum Tjapaltjarri who became one of Papunya's most famous artists. Punata grew up being told by her father to watch and learn as he taught her painting. She eventually became an accomplished artist herself.[28]

Although Punata was younger than me, we could always share a laugh together. She had an open and friendly face and loved working at the hospital. Punata had three children. I rarely saw her older children but her toddler was gorgeous. I loved having him in the office with us. As part of her health-worker duties, Punata was responsible for Central Australian Aboriginal Congress radio skeds and restocking in the clinic. Punata's reading ability was low and she wanted to improve it. She was not used to hearing the alphabet, so when I spelt out words for her, she found it difficult to understand me. Punata, however, did know the phonetic call codes Alpha, Bravo, Charlie and so on. We decided to help each other. Punata taught me the call codes and I spelled out words to her in the code. It was great fun. Punata became a good speller and I still remember the phonetic alphabet codes all these years later.

It was Punata and her friend Joy who were most interested in learning how to pay the wages. It was an exciting time for those two women as they deciphered the intricacies of the manual Kalamazoo payroll system. It looked ferociously difficult but it was deceptively simple. The women learned how to use a calculator and to count the correct cash money for each wage packet. It was thrilling for the young women to hand out the pay envelopes they had prepared for their colleagues on payday. For me, it was one of the highlights of my time in Papunya.

The success of the wages-training program inspired me to educate my trainee health workers in how the budget for the health service worked. This required a much higher level of financial understanding. I was only into the program for a couple of weeks when I realised that I had bitten off more than I could chew. I didn't have to stop the program. Because I had confused the health workers so much, they voted with their feet and stopped attending my training sessions. They stuck with the payroll though. They loved putting the money in the envelopes and handing it out to their colleagues.

I was thrilled when Dr Adrian announced that we would have some cross-cultural training and an introduction to the Pintupi language with Ken Hansen. Ken and Lesley Hansen were linguists from the Summer Institute of Linguistics who spent many years living and working with Pintupi people in Papunya and various outstations. During that time the Hansens compiled the Pintupi dictionary. Indeed, the Hansens were among the very few people who could speak to Pintupi people in their own language and had witnessed the morbidity and misery of the Pintupi in Papunya. Although we learned only a few words, we gained a small insight into the importance of relationships within the Pintupi culture. In the construction of the Pintupi language, a specialised vocabulary is used for different close relationships. I found it bamboozling but fascinating.

From my narrow cultural perspective, Aboriginal and Anglo-Australian understandings of kinship, spiritual life and cosmology, rights and obligations, a sense of time and social behaviour, seemed to be incompatible. For the life of me, I couldn't work out how to cross the cultural bridge. I had no clue how to develop relationships with people who were so different to me. All I could do was to keep smiling and be polite.

In Papunya, the clash of cultures between a people with a 60,000-year-old culture and the results of the colonial invasion 200 years earlier was continuing to play out. Try as I would, I couldn't make much sense out of Papunya. I suspected that, for many Aboriginal people, their lived reality made little sense to them too. In 1982 when I left my city job in Melbourne and entered the fraught environment of Papunya, I managed to become a health-service administrator because I was utterly determined not to fail. I listened, I made mistakes, I learned.

My lack of experience, and my lack of cross-cultural understanding, should have been offset by an Indigenous orientation training program to help explain the cultural setting in which we non-Aboriginal staff were working. I found it interesting to learn later that as a colonial power, Australia had developed the Australian School of Pacific Administration (ASOPA) to train patrol officers in Papua New Guinea. They received education in subjects such as law, government and anthropology. Later, ASOPA was used to train administrators and schoolteachers. I could not help but wonder why the Indigenous people in Papua New Guinea warranted the training of White administrators and teachers but the Indigenous people of Australia did not. I still don't understand.

For me, a basic confusion came from the fact that, although I came with my best intentions and friendship, and did the very best I could in my job, it was not nearly enough. My deep ignorance of Aboriginal culture, and my inability to grasp the framework of their previous existence, made me question why I was there and what I could achieve. I suspect this type of ignorance was similar to that of many do-gooder missionaries, as well as the mercenaries who come for the money, and the misfits from mainstream life who could be more or less accepted in remote communities. Most White people fitted somewhere in this trio of meanings. I labelled myself as a do-gooder and a bit of a mainstream misfit. Although do-gooder was a derogatory label, I was proud to do-good. I wouldn't want to be any other way.

Pintupi and Warlpiri skin names

The skin-name system was another huge mystery to me. I was bemused, and rather pleased, when the health-service mob gave me the skin name Nampitjinpa. Skin names are inherited at birth and form part of the kinship system. Most of the health workers were Nampitjinpas so I guessed that I was to be a 'guest-sister' Nampitjinpa.

When I next saw my father, Bill, I told him with great excitement about being a Nampitjinpa. He looked at me, shaking his head slightly, and said, 'I'm sorry, Blossom, but you can't be a Nampitjinpa because I am a Tjapanangka and they don't have Nampitjinpa daughters. When you get back to Papunya, you tell the health workers that your father is a Tjapanangka.'

TABLE 1 Pintupi and Warlpiri kinship system[29]

Gender	Subsection name	First marriage preference	Children will be
Male	Tjapaltjarri	Nakamarra	Tjungurrayi, Nungurrayi
Female	Napaltjarri	Tjakamarra	Tjupurrula, Napurrula
Male	Tjapangati	Nampitjinpa	Tjapanangka, Napanangka
Female	Napangati	Tjampitjinpa	Tjangala, Nangala
Male	Tjakamarra	Napaltjarri	Tjupurrula, Napurrula
Female	Nakamarra	Tjapaltjarri	Tjungurrayi, Nungurrayi
Male	Tjampitjinpa	Napangati	Tjangala, Nangala
Female	Nampitjinpa	Tjapangati	Tjapanangka, Napanangka
Male	Tjapanangka	Napurrula	Tjapangati, Napangati
Female	Napanangka	Tjupurrula	Tjakamarra, Nakamarra
Male	Tjungurrayi	Nangala	Tjapaltjarri, Napaltjarri
Female	Nungurrayi	Tjangala	Tjampitjinpa, Nampitjinpa
Male	Tjupurrula	Napanangka	Tjakamarra, Nakamarra
Female	Napurrula	Tjapanangka	Tjapangati, Napangati
Male	Tjangala	Nungurrayi	Tjampitjinpa, Nampitjinpa
Female	Nangala	Tjungurrayi	Tjapaltjarri, Napaltjarri

I found this confusing but I did as Bill told me. It wasn't long before I heard myself being called Napangati, which is the skin name of the daughter of a Tjapanangka. I quite liked the sound of that name, but I felt a bit sorry that I wasn't a sister to the health workers any more. I felt like a bit of an orphan in that Nampitjinpa, Tjampitjinpa health service.

It would be many years before I gained an inkling of how the gift of my Napangati skin name provided me a guest-position in the complex kinship systems across Central Australia. Their system determines how people relate to each other and their roles, responsibilities and obligations to one another, ceremonial business and land. The kinship system determines who marries whom, ceremonial relationships, funeral roles and behaviour patterns with other kin. Hence my entry into this complex system as a worker in relationships with Nampitjinpas, Tjampitjinpas and their relatives, required that I be given my place. Or as it turned out, the place of being the daughter of my father who was in relationship with Warlpiri people in another community. All in all, it was fascinating.

The Pintupi and Warlpiri kinship systems were almost the same. The male names begin with *Tj* and the female names with *N*. With my father being gifted the name Tjapanangka, I became a Napangati. My marriage preference was a Tjampitjinpa and we would have Tjangala and Nangala children.

Housing, food and song

Papunya was more neglected and run-down than Ali Curung and had less of a sense of being a coherent town. There was a serious housing shortage and overcrowding. In general there seemed to be three types of housing: European-style houses, transitional housing and bush camps. All the White people who worked in Papunya lived in normal besser-brick houses as did some of the Aboriginal people who, in some way, had a position of influence. The transitional houses were small, two-room iron shacks with louvre windows and roofed verandas at each end. They were part of a staged approach to teach Aboriginal people how to live in houses. But the transitional houses did not have electricity or running water, making this a difficult task for them. Those awful iron shacks were built in rows with no consideration of the social patterns of the people. I had driven past them from time to time and wasn't sure if anyone actually lived in them.

Many Aboriginal people lived in bush camps made with sheets of iron and local bush materials. The Director of the Lyappa Health Service lived like this with his large family. I recall feeling shocked when I first drove him home, but I accepted this appalling housing situation as another fact beyond my understanding. It did, however, answer my question-to-self, as to why so many people used the showers at the hospital. It was because they had no shower at their camp.

I was told that Aboriginal people referred to Papunya as a sad place where everybody was mixed up. There was too much grog, too many fights and they were too far from their Country. It certainly seemed like a sad place to me. For the Pintupi, Arrernte, Warlpiri, Luritja and Anmatyerre there was little economic life and a pervasive air of just existing.

Everyone without a job existed on welfare cheques and spent their money at the store. Fresh fruit and vegetables were expensive and poor quality. In fact, because everything was expensive, every two or three weeks I bought all my groceries from Alice Springs supermarkets. I had little idea of what Aboriginal people ate each day. I had seen large 20-kilo tins of flour and shelves of golden syrup at the store so I knew they liked their damper with golden syrup. I saw camp-pie tins lying around people's camps so I presumed that was a popular meal. From time to time, I saw a Toyota with a dead kangaroo slung over the roof rack, and every now and again, I knew that the women and children would go out to collect bush tucker. I had also heard that they liked to eat 'pussy cat'. A good thing too, as feral cats are a scourge on Australian native wildlife.

Almost every week, there would be a knock at my door, usually a man, asking me for meat or milk powder. I would have liked to have been helpful, but I never bought meat out to Papunya and my loathing of milk powder taught me to drink my tea black. I did, however, have plenty of cans of beans for protein – baked beans, kidney beans, Heinz 4 bean mix. I offered these beans to the hopeful meat eaters but they always shook their head and walked away.

What was vibrant and dynamic in Papunya was the Warumpi Band. It was Neil Murray, a singer and songwriter, who helped to start up the Warumpi Band in 1980. He came to Papunya as a schoolteacher but his greatest achievement was joining with the other founding members of the Warumpi Band, Sammy and Gordon Butcher and George Rrurrambu.

A musical backdrop to many Papunya evenings emanated from a large Nissan hut where the Warumpi Band practised. The name Warumpi comes from a honey-ant dreaming site in Papunya. The young musicians were loud and played with great enthusiasm and I enjoyed hearing their songs improve over time. The Warumpi Band sound was a blend of Indigenous country rock and American R&B, with songs sung in Luritja, Gumatj and English. Indigenous Australia loved them. Their fame grew, and after being voted the best band at the 1983 Aboriginal Country Music Festival, they played as a support act to Midnight Oil. The Warumpi Band was the first Australian rock group to have a hit song in an Indigenous language; the Luritja single Jailanguru Pakarnu, or 'Out from Jail'. In 1986, Midnight Oil and the Warumpi Band embarked on the iconic Blackfella/Whitefella Tour which reached some of the country's remotest locations.[30]

The Warumpi Band seemed to give hope to the community. For most people there was nothing much to do in Papunya except visit relatives and sit around. For a town of 600 people, there were scarcely any employment opportunities. A few people were employed at the council office, a couple of young men worked at the garage, a couple of assistants at the Primary School, the check-out staff at the store and a few men with the Housing Group. The Lyappa Health Service was the largest employer of Aboriginal people in Papunya and Kintore with eighteen full- and part-time health workers, cleaners and drivers.

Warumpi Band *Big Name No Blankets* album photo shoot, 1984
Neil Murray website

Alice Springs interludes

I connected with Homer at each trip I made to Alice. It wasn't long before our romance was in full bloom. I adored Homer. He was as close to 'bohemian' as I was ever likely to find. Material possessions didn't interest him. He worked only to live and enjoy each day.

I always tried to fit as much as I could into my Alice Springs trips so Homer's quiet, easygoing life was turned upside down when I showed up. Our time together was filled with intense conversation interspersed with romantic picnics and swimming at one of the gaps or waterholes. Homer lived in a caravan and shed that were sheltered by a stand of magnificent desert oaks on a 5-hectare block a few kilometres outside the town. The land was owned by his artist friend Peter, and Homer was very careful to comply with all Peter's rules as he loved living there. Although I kept my room at Wendy's house, I more or less moved into Homer's caravan when I was in town.

Homer was a draftsman with a firm of architects and occasionally turned his considerable talent as an artist into an actual drawing or painting and made some money on the side. Homer was a good-humoured, easygoing man. He was interested in science and the cosmos and loved the vast emptiness of Central Australia. I was surprised to discover he was an ardent bridge player. He played bridge religiously with his pals from Pine Gap, the local name for the US satellite surveillance base 18 kilometres out of Alice Springs. Although I poked and prodded, it seemed Homer had never questioned his American pals about the secret goings-on at the base. Perhaps he was just interested in playing bridge. Homer was a libertarian, which I found puzzling. I could understand valuing individual freedom and equal rights but I thought he was incredibly misguided in objecting to wealth redistribution through welfare programs.

Homer was the highlight of my Alice Springs interludes.
Jackson collection, 1982

The architect firm where Homer worked designed the new Anglican Church in Alice Springs. Homer invited me to join him at a joint celebration of the architects and church. I met quite a few of the congregation and they seemed like nice church-going people. Things changed when they learned I was working in Papunya. Suddenly the pleasant conversations became tinged with hostility. Never one to back away from a good enquiry, I encouraged further chat. The complaints issuing forth were interlaced with words such as dirty, thieving, up to no good, lazy. The crimes they spoke about were young Aboriginal 'troublemakers' stealing money, or food, breaking a window, or at worst taking their car for a joy ride.

I was fascinated by the different tone. While I felt a certain sympathy for their fear of robberies, I was bemused by the intolerance. They didn't seem to grasp the irony of complaining about Aboriginal petty thieving and troublemaking against the massive theft by White people of the entire Aboriginal continent, and the subsequent and ongoing trashing of their culture and the natural environment. These good church folk lived comfortably, obeyed the law and were kind to their neighbours. Yet they viewed many Aboriginal people living in the town camps and in the dry, sandy Todd riverbed as outcasts beyond redemption.

Many townies had a mindset about White people who worked on Aboriginal communities. For a start, we were either *mercenaries, missionaries* or *misfits*. Next were the derogatory labels of *do-gooder* and coming from *down south*. Looking like a young, middle-class White woman from Melbourne, I was immediately eyed off and given three of the labels – missionary, do-gooder and from down south. It was a big hurdle to overcome when I wanted some help and cooperation, particularly for my vehicle headaches. Women don't have the mateship angle to draw on so we have to use other tools in the making-good-relationships box. It was my good fortune that I inherited my father's great sense of humour and his ability to tell a funny story. This, accompanied by my genuine smiling face, seemed to get me most things I needed.

On one memorable day in Alice Springs, I had a long list of items to either purchase or collect. It took me to businesses all over town as well as the hospital. I remember collecting some previously ordered parts from a surly, overweight bloke behind a counter. 'Oh yeah,' he said. 'I heard about you from my car-detailing mates. You're the do-gooder from down south who didn't tell them the Subaru was a "coon" car.'

This was true. I had rung up for a quote on detailing the Papunya Subaru to make it ready for sale. I got an acceptable price and had the car taken there. The company was furious that I didn't tell them the car was from an Aboriginal community. It would have been a very different price if I had told them. While I had some sympathy, given the grotty state of the car, their attitude was horrible so I thought, *Stuff them. I'm not going to pay any extra. I won't be getting any more cars detailed so who needs them.* Not a good attitude on my part and I had obviously become infamous as a result of it. I silently picked up the goods thinking that I'd better find another supplier ... soon.

This uncomfortable encounter was offset a couple of hours later by Dr Andy at the hospital. He had gone to endless trouble to order in some supplies for Lyappa. I was very grateful and suggested we have a cuppa if he had time. He did. We chatted away and shared a few stories. It was good. When I headed off, he said, 'You are a breath of fresh air around this place.' It was such a comforting thing for me to hear. I held those words close whenever I felt the judgement and disapproval that abounded in Territory life.

3 Papunya Tula

It was Dr Adrian who told me about Papunya Tula painting and its history. If it had not been for his education I may never have realised its importance. I was surprised that Homer hadn't told me about this amazing Aboriginal art. Although Homer mixed with other Alice Springs artists and indeed Peter, his landlord, had an art-supply shop, neither of them mentioned Papunya Tula art to me. Adrian had told me the story of Geoff Bardon, a schoolteacher who had come to Papunya in 1971. Bardon noticed that his pupils drew in the sand with their hands. He encouraged them to use school paints to draw the Honey Ant Dreaming in the traditional style of body and sand ceremonial art. This was the tiny spark that set off the Western Desert art movement. Bardon noticed some of the older men were intrigued by the children's painting. He encouraged the men to start painting and showed them how to use brushes and acrylic paint. The idea grew and resulted in the creation of a mural depicting Honey Ant Dreaming on an external school wall. Traditionally, Papunya is the epicentre of Honey Ant Dreaming where songlines converge. It was momentous for the Aboriginal community to see their mural on the school wall and it forever changed Papunya, and later, Kintore.[31]

In the eighteen months following the painting of the mural, 600 paintings and 300 smaller artworks were created by Luritja, Pintupi, Warlpiri and Anmatyerre men using acrylic paint on boards, depicting stories from the ancient past.[32] This was the beginning of the Papunya Tula movement, of which Bardon said, 'the paintings reflected precisely the circumstances in which they were produced'. Despite the hellish situation of Papunya, men from different Country were bound by their association with songlines and shared ceremony. In large part, it was this collision of remarkable individuals from disparate Country that sparked the creative energy from which Papunya Tula art has grown.[33]

Honey Ant mural at Papunya School
Geoffrey Bardon collection, 1971, Miegunyah Press, Melbourne University

Honey Ant mural with school grounds, June–August 1971. The mural was destroyed in an act of cultural vandalism.

Geoffrey Bardon collection, 1971, Miegunyah Press, Melbourne University

Papunya Tula artists and Geoffrey Bardon engrossed in their work
Geoffrey Bardon collection, 1971, Miegunyah Press, Melbourne University

By 1982, when I arrived in Papunya, the school mural was long gone, callously, or carelessly, painted over by Northern Territory Education Department contractors. It was 'an act of cultural vandalism', according to Judith Ryan, Senior Curator of Indigenous Art at the National Gallery of Victoria.[34] The significance of this art had yet to penetrate my heavy veil of ignorance. When artists knocked at my Papunya door to sell me their work, it didn't occur to me that I was being offered the opportunity to purchase Aboriginal history and culture in the form of a boomerang, goanna or emu artefact. Instead, I viewed these carved and painted artworks as interesting mementos, in much the same way I had purchased lacquerware in Burma and carvings in Java and Bali. I nearly always bought the offering. As well as helping the local economy, it also gave me a wonderful chance to have a small conversation with the locals.

At that time, most of the artists were men as it was not until 1994 that women generally began to participate in the art movement. However, some of the women I worked with at the health service were artists who painted artefacts. Word must have gone around that I was an art buyer, so they brought beautifully painted coolamons to the clinic for me to buy. I had noticed women using coolamons to carry their babies or sometimes for bush tucker so there was real meaning for me. I was glad to buy them and I have them on display in my home today.

Over the next months, I learned more about the art and the artists organisation Papunya Tula. I asked Homer about it and he told me there was a shop in Todd Street where many artworks were sold. As soon as my timetable allowed, I strolled down the street until I found the shop. The paintings were beautiful and colourful but I found them confusing. Why were the paintings made in dots? What did the pictures mean? What were the stories in them? They looked like abstract art, but they weren't.

I was at Kintore when Adrian introduced me to Nosepeg Tjupurrula, telling me with a grin that he was a very important and famous man. I wondered if he had got his name from being a cameleer. I said hello to Nosepeg as I would to anyone, having no idea that he was a fair dinkum VIP. I later discovered that Nosepeg was certainly famous and he had travelled far and wide. In 1954 he was chosen to meet the Queen of England in Toowoomba. He had been a guide and interpreter on Welfare Branch patrols and with the Australian Institute of Aboriginal Studies (now AIATSIS) filming trips over decades. He was also a movie star with appearances in films including *Jedda* and *Journey Out of Darkness* as well as the television series *Whiplash* and *Boney*. Nosepeg was a cross-cultural negotiator who was a friend of politicians as diverse as Gough Whitlam and Malcolm Fraser, and a force behind the outstation movement of the 1960s, 70s and 80s.[35] Nosepeg began painting at the beginning of the art movement in Papunya in 1971.

My work life in Papunya and Kintore was being intersected by Papunya Tula artists although I did not know it. Unbeknownst to me, Andrew Bullen, the director of the health service, had begun painting for Papunya Tula in 1979. Andrew's paintings usually depicted Kangaroo and Native Tobacco Dreamings from the Docker River area and a Man's Dreaming story which he received from his mother and uncle. One of Andrew's paintings and a photograph of him are featured in the magnificent book *Lives of the Papunya Tula Artists* by Vivien Johnson. Andrew is just one of the many artists I actually met, but did not realise they were artists.[36]

Johnny Scobie Tjapanangka painting, *Women's Dreaming*, 1972
Geoffrey Bardon collection, Miegunyah Press, Melbourne University

For the Pintupi people, the discord and disempowerment experienced at Papunya brought forth an increasingly urgent need for them to return to their homelands west of Papunya. When the 1976 Aboriginal Land Rights (Northern Territory) Act came into being, it showed them a way forward. This Act was the first attempt by an Australian government to legally recognise the Aboriginal system of land ownership and put into law the concept of inalienable freehold title. The Land Rights Act was a fundamental piece of social reform.[37]

Many of the visionary and dedicated Pintupi men who were actively engaged in the homelands movement were Papunya Tula artists. As they painted their dreaming and ancestral lands, their art practice became a means to advocate to their fellow countrymen and the broader community for their return to Country.[38] Their creative artistic energy, combined with their yearning to return to their cultural homelands, helped the Pintupi Homelands movement to forge ahead.

The Pintupi were strong supporters of a Kintore Aboriginal-controlled health service modelled on Lyappa Health Service. Some of the important health-service founders were also Papunya Tula artists, such as famed artist Johnny Scobie Tjapanangka, a charismatic man with a keen political sense. He was a strong supporter of the health service and a long-serving chairman of the Kintore Council. He was also one of the original shareholders of Papunya Tula Artists, although he had to stop painting for a few years when his council duties took over his time.[39]

Other activist artists were Ronnie and Smithy Tjampitjinpa, who were prime participants in the move to Kintore. Artist and health worker Benny Tjapaltjarri, who tried his hand at painting in the early 1970s, had put his artwork aside to work for the Pintupi return to their homelands.[40] Benny was our main contact at the Kintore clinic. He was a ngangkari or traditional doctor and he worked closely with the medical staff. In 1982, after Kintore was established, Benny began to paint regularly. Benny was an energetic and fiery man. I don't think I registered on his radar at all, although he certainly registered on mine as he demanded his health supplies – now! I was more attuned to his wife, Kawayi, who was always up for a laugh.

Dr George Tjapaltjarri, whose 'doctor man' powers were regarded with awe, was one of several ngangkari attached to the Kintore health clinic. George painted for Papunya Tula in the 1970s and then again in the late 1980s at Kintore and Kiwirrkura. In the late 1990s, he took his family to live in Alice Springs and began to fulfil his earlier ambition to see more of the world. He was eagerly promoted by private dealers as one of the new stars of desert art and travelled to capital cities in Australia.[41]

The convergence of art, homelands and health was happening under my nose. But as is often the case, these significant and historic happenings were obscured by the momentum of going forward. Only in hindsight did it become clear to me.

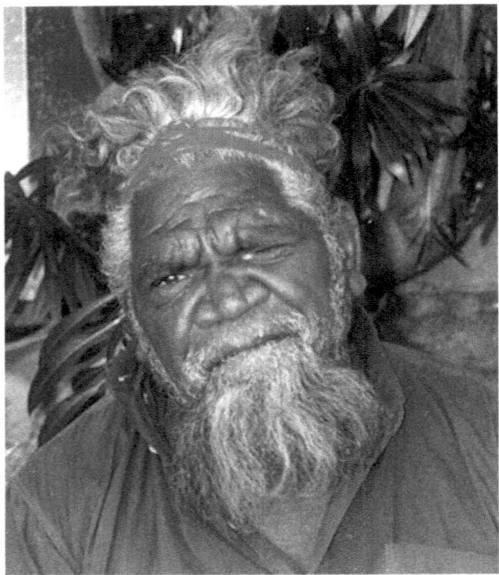

Dr George Tjapaltjarri, whose 'doctor man' powers were regarded with awe, was one of several ngangkari attached to the Kintore health clinic.
Gallery Gondwana

4 A New doctor and cats

Doctor Jenny and I had muddled along relatively well in our shared house. Our basic incompatibility was made easy by our frequent house guests and my regular absences in Alice Springs. Our shared lives came to a close after six or seven months when Jenny put in her resignation. I must admit to feeling a tiny bit relieved as I always felt that I didn't quite measure up. Jenny seemed to be a naturally confident and self-possessed young woman, as well as being a very good doctor. I, on the other hand, was always overcoming buckets of self-doubt and redoubling my efforts to do the best I could. I wondered if I would ever gain enough self-confidence to not worry about what other people might think of me.

Dr Jenny and me in our backyard
Jackson collection, 1982

In replacing Jenny, Adrian was determined to reach out to doctors who were 'fresh' to the Northern Territory and keen to work in the environment of an Aboriginal-controlled health service. The Lyappa Health Service followed the guidelines of the Central Australian Aboriginal Congress Health Service in Alice Springs, providing both a preventative and curative approach. In fact, it was Congress that assisted in the establishment of Lyappa Health Service in 1978. In this service model, health factors were not considered to be separate from housing, education, employment, land rights, food, recreation and community development.[42] The approach included a long-term training program for health workers and traditional healers or ngangkari who would treat people either before, after, or alongside medical staff. Ngangkari were held in high regard. Traditionally, Aboriginal people believed that all illness and death was caused by magical or supernatural influences. Serious sickness was caused by bad spirits and was cured by a ngangkari who knew the law and could see into people. They were also trained to restore the wellbeing of the soul or spirit. Traditional healers provided strong spiritual and social support within the community.[43]

Adrian wanted the replacement doctor to enthusiastically support those values and help build a trusted Aboriginal community-controlled health service. My job was to place advertisements in the *British Medical Journal* and the *Medical Journal of Australia* as well as the Sydney and Melbourne newspapers. The advertisement emphasised training Aboriginal health workers, noting there was an excellent opportunity to learn as well as teach. Although the work was demanding, it was a rare opportunity to experience life in a remote Aboriginal community in the unique environment of Central Australia.

I truly expected that we would be flooded with enquiries and applications. After all, who wouldn't be excited about living in an Aboriginal community, having amazing experiences working with Aboriginal people and revelling in magnificent Central Australia. Medically it would be challenging and far removed from the mundane coughs and colds of cooler climes. What could be better?

With each mail plane, I eagerly collected the mailbag from the council office and searched for applications. One letter arrived from England and another from Sydney. That was it. Only two applications. I was flabbergasted. I had thought Aussies were adventurous, willing to have a go. Apparently not. It seems our love of the great outdoors and having adventures is limited, and it certainly does not include living in Aboriginal communities.

'What a bunch of conformist wimps we Aussies are,' I thought disgustedly. *'No sense of adventure!'*

Both applications were impressive. The English doctor was highly qualified and very keen. Adrian approached the Department of Aboriginal Affairs for assistance to facilitate a migration application. Unsurprisingly this was not forthcoming. It was Doctor Phil from Sydney who got the job and I was glad. He was an easygoing fellow, much more approachable than Adrian, as well as being a very competent doctor. He settled in well and took to the challenges like a duck to water.

With Phil settled, Adrian moved into his next phase of introducing doctors from Alice Springs hospital to doctoring at the front line in Papunya. It was a brilliant idea and says a lot about Adrian's powers of persuasion and his professionalism. Every few weeks a doctor from Alice would do a few days' shift at Papunya. From what I could observe, I think the doctors thought it was a most worthwhile venture.

Meanwhile, Phil was 'eyeing-off' the small but non-functioning hospital surgery. Most of the basics of a surgery were there – the operating table, a stainless steel trolley and a steriliser – but there were no globes for the operating lights and various other bits and pieces were missing. After discussing it with Adrian, Phil enthusiastically took on the job of getting the surgery up and running. The missing items needed to be ordered in or cadged from Central Australian Aboriginal Congress or the kindly folk at Alice Springs hospital. This venture gave me much more practice on the radio. I was forever phoning Adelaide, Melbourne and Sydney ordering parts for the surgery. Most of the suppliers were surprised to be talking to a woman on the RFDS radio from Papunya in the desert of Central Australia.

Finally the day came when Phil declared the surgery was ready for business. It was my little adopted wild cat Tjapa that was to be the first customer, with a castration. Tjapa was a kitten, just a few months old, and had been given to me by neighbour Johnno the mechanic.

'It will be for the good of the community because there are already too many cats in Papunya,' both doctors declared.

I acknowledged the justice of this as I knew that wild cats are devastating to the wildlife. I found the cat basket and loaded poor Tjapa into it and drove us to the surgery. Phil was waiting, grinning from ear to ear and holding a deadly-looking scalpel.

'Come to me, pussy cat,' he crooned.

'Now don't you be making any terrible mistakes, Phil,' I warned darkly. 'Or I'll tell the locals you're up to no good.'

Then I skedaddled out of there. There was no way I was going to watch my kitten lose his cat-hood. I only had to wait a few minutes before Phil gave a shout to me, saying it was all over and I could come in. Poor little Tjapa was lying on the operating table with shaved bits and only the tiniest mark on him. I had to admit, it looked like a proper surgeon had given him the 'snip job'. Phil was as pleased as punch. Everything had worked just as he had planned. The operation was declared a smooth success.

Thanks Tjapa.

Taking Tjapa for the snip
Jackson collection, 1982

A shortage of accommodation for the White employees was an issue in Papunya, as it nearly always was in Aboriginal communities. When Dr Jenny left the health service, Liz the midwife moved out of our share house with her three children to live with Topsy. That left just me in a three bedroom house. I needed to find other accommodation to free up the house for Phil and his wife. Fortunately one of the four single-men flats became vacant. These flats had been built some years earlier to accommodate the workmen who had constructed the hospital and built housing in the community. They were one-bedroom flats which had recently been renovated. There was a small lounge and dining area, a bedroom and a bathroom cum laundry. I was delighted to learn that all the mod cons worked, the fridge, air con, stove and hoover twin-tub washing machine. I gave the unit a good spring clean and moved in.

Spunky Johnno, the mechanic

My neighbour Johnno was a young mechanic originally from Sydney who had been in Papunya for about six months. He was a good bloke and from time to time we'd share a cup of tea. One day I was complaining to him about finding dead cockroaches in my cupboards and having to wash all the plates. Johnno gave me a great housekeeping tip.

'You don't have to wash the plates,' he said. 'Just leave the dead cockies on the top plate. It's like a deterrent. You'll find no other cockroach mates join them. Just lift up the cockroach plate and take the next one from under it. Easy!'

It was great advice. Johnno was right. The plates didn't build up a collection of cockroaches and it saved me mountains of washing up.

During our cuppa time, Johnno would tell me tales about the cars and how the Aboriginal bush mechanics held them together. One afternoon, I spent a couple of enjoyably entertaining hours watching the cars going in and out of the garage with their bonnets, doors or bootlids missing and some with their tail pipes dragging on the ground. I used to wonder what Mr GMH or Mr Ford would think if they saw their vehicles. I found it hugely funny.

By now I was used to seeing cars being push-started by being shunted in the rear end by a vehicle with bull bars which pushed it along until the dead motor car roared into life. I remember how horrified I was in my early days at the health service, when Neville the driver came to my office and asked me to push-start the dodgy troop carrier. I had thought he wanted me to come and personally push the troopie until it got up enough speed to start. This had been the norm in my youth with all the dodgy cars my friends owned, but I was long past doing that. I looked at him with astonishment and said, 'Neville, go and ask one of the men to help you. I'm not going to push a vehicle for you.'

Neville remained silent, he turned around and walked away. He came back the next day and asked me again, 'You come, push the vehicle.' He made a small motion with his hand.

'No, Neville, sorry, I won't.'

On the third day, poor Neville returned to my office for another try. By now he had worked out the White woman from down south didn't have a clue about push-starting vehicles. This time, as Neville said, 'Push, push,' he smacked the knuckles of his fist into the palm of his other hand. Then he made a key-turning action with his hand. I stared at him and he repeated the action.

Hmmm, he wants my Toyota keys, I thought to myself.

I took them out of my drawer and handed him the keys. Neville shook his head and beckoned me to follow him. He got into my vehicle and gave me a demo. I was to drive slowly and connect my bull bars to the dead troopie and then push.

'Aah, right! Okay, Neville I've got it.'

A big beam lit up his face as he realised, 'Finally she's got it.'

I jumped into my troopie and started it up. Neville jumped into his. Driving slowly, I edged up until the bull bar was up against the back of his dead vehicle. I put my foot on the accelerator and gathered some speed to push his vehicle. Suddenly his troopie started and he drove off. Bonza!

That afternoon, I had just got home from work when there was a knock at the door. It was Johnno holding a kitten in his hand.

'I've got to go to Alice and this kitten is going to get ripped up by the dogs if you don't take her.'

I stared at him. 'And what am I supposed to do with the kitten when I go to Alice Springs myself every two weeks?'

'I know, I know. But I don't want her to die. She's such a nice little thing.'

He was right. She was a very cute little kitten.

'Well, you'll have to feed her when I'm not here,' I demanded.

'Done,' he replied handing me the little animal.

I wondered what to call her. I thought of my skin name Napangati.

'That's it. I'll call her Napa and she's going to be my cat sister.'

Only I would know and it appealed to my sense of humour to pass on my skin name to my house cat. Napa and I bonded well. She was an easy kitten to get along with. Very obliging and quite docile. I enjoyed her company and it was much nicer to return to Papunya with a little animal living in my flat.

It was only a few weeks later when Johnno turned up again at my door with yet another kitten.

'Two is no more trouble than one,' said Johnno. 'You have to take this one as well, otherwise he's a gonner! Don't worry, I'll pop in and feed them both when you're not here. No worries.'

I glared at him and said, 'This is the last one, Johnno. I'm sorry but the next kitten will just have to be eaten by the dogs. I'm not taking any more!'

This kitten was wilder than Napa. A little spitfire. It only took a few seconds for me to name him Tjapa. He was now officially my cat brother. My flat was filling with relatives! Tjapa put an end to my calm life with Napa. He loved to fight and tease her. He jumped on her, jumped on me, leapt all over the furniture and generally ran amok day and night.

Night time was the worst. Tjapa would attack Napa and the fight would be on, round and round my tiny unit, which had no bedroom door to shut them out. I worked very hard at my job and went to bed exhausted with my mind awhirl with all the tasks I had waiting for me the next day. I needed my sleep. It was not to be with Tjapa. The cats would leap on top of my sleeping body, growl and hiss at each other, and then leap on to the chest of drawers and back to the tiny lounge room. By the time I got back to sleep, the next chase would be on. I had to make a choice. Either I would have to learn to sleep through cat mayhem or Tjapa would have to go and face his fate. Having made this decision, much to my complete surprise, I learnt how to stay asleep with cats fighting and jumping on top of me. It is truly amazing what we humans can do when we set our minds to it.

I was glad my cat problems were solved. They were very entertaining to watch and good company. On nice sunny mornings, I would take my cup of tea to the seat at my front door and let the cats out for some fresh air and exercise. My flat must have been near Old Mick Tjakamarra's camp because he often came round the corner of the block of units and saw me with the cats. He used to grin widely and laugh saying, 'Good *kuka* those ones.' I knew that Aboriginal people like to eat pussy cat so I didn't know if he was teasing me or if he really meant it. I'd laugh too though and protest, 'Oh no Old Mick. These are my cats. They're not for eating.' Old Mick would laugh again and continue on his journey. Because of his high ceremonial status and his knowledge of songs, stories and designs, Old Mick became one of the most important artists painting for Papunya Tula in its first decade. I knew Old Mick as a lovely old man who liked to tease me and always gave me a laugh. I wish I had also known about Old Mick's capacity as an artist.

Men's business

My job was to weave vehicle repairs and purchasing trips with the routine fabric of admin – paying the fortnightly wages, paying the bills, and making sure we didn't run out of the essentials that kept things ticking. Paying the bills was a three-part process. Firstly, rounding up and matching invoices to orders, secondly, achieving two signatures on our health-service cheques and finally freighting the cheques and invoices for payment to Peter the accountant in Alice Springs. Peter was one of the cheque signatories which made the Alice Springs side of the process easy. The Papunya side was a different story. I had to track down Andrew Bullen, our health-service director, or front up to the council office and get one of the councillors to sign the cheques. I loathed going to the unfriendly, joyless council office where a smile would have cracked someone's face. My fortnightly mission became catching Andrew when he had business at the hospital.

Andrew was a busy community man and a mainstay of the health service. When I worked with Andrew in 1982, he was only around fifty-two years old but he seemed to me much older than that. I thought he was in his sixties. Andrew was a Pitjantjatjara man who had been born in the desert, north of Docker River near the Northern Territory and Western Australian border. He was about twelve years old when his family came into the mission at Haasts Bluff, hundreds of kilometres north-east of their traditional Country. As a young man, Andrew did stockwork, mustering cattle south of Haasts Bluff. Later he was employed by the Papunya Council as a health worker. He also served as a community councillor.

Andrew's duties as director were leadership and liaison with just about everyone. Catching Andrew and pinning him down required devoted observation and timing on my part. I would spy him from the corner of my eye and then keep him under observation as he interacted with Dr Adrian, the senior health workers, the driver Neville and perhaps one of the male patients. As soon as he drew breath, I would beamingly front up to him with my order book, invoices and cheques, and attempt to pin him down for the dreary and laborious process of cheque signing. Andrew was a very polite man and would never have groaned out loud in dismay, but I could sense the groan. I'd caught him.

The process of cheque signing was laborious because Andrew didn't read English. I guess we could have chosen the quick way of me saying, 'office supplies' and Andrew signing the cheque. But I took him down the long path of me reading out the invoice. For example, Territory Office Supplies, Kalamazoo payroll system for the wages and the amount.

I considered the full run-through of the accounts to be a vital part of my role as I had heard numerous stories of corruption and theft in Aboriginal communities, and I didn't ever want to be suspected of it.

I'll never forget the day I overstepped the boundaries between the Aboriginal and non-Aboriginal worlds. As usual, I hurried up to Andrew with my invoices and chequebook at the ready. With a quick greeting, I plonked my papers down in front of Andrew and started to explain the first payment to him. Unbeknownst to me, as most things Aboriginal were, it was a time of ceremony and men's business. Andrew was in a hurry to leave the clinic office to go on men's business.

'I gotta go,' he said.

This is where I should have stood up and headed off to get the cheques signed at the unfriendly office. However, I knew it would only take Andrew and me about thirty minutes to complete the cheques. Could we get through our business before he had to leave? I fervently hoped so.

'How long will it be before the vehicle taking you to business arrives?' I asked him.

Andrew's reply was vague. I started reading the next invoice and cheque.

'Will they come in and collect you? Can I drive you there?' I persisted.

Another vague reply so I read out the next invoice as Andrew carried on signing.

Andrew said, 'I gotta go.'

'There's not many more Andrew, can't we finish them?'

Andrew was a polite and kind man, but he had put up with my nonsense for as long as he could. Andrew stopped and sat in stillness for some long moments. Then he raised his head and looked directly at me.

'You're going to get me into big trouble.'

I was horrified. My drive to get my work done had given me a huge, selfish tin ear. I had sensed Andrew's anxiety but I had overridden it. This high-handedness combined with my lack of cultural understanding had taken me into the dangerous ground of interfering with men's business.

'Oh Andrew. I am so sorry.'

I quickly packed up the documentation and backed out of the room. I felt overwhelmed by my ignorance.

The only thing I knew about Aboriginal business was that it was serious. I had no idea of the responsibilities and obligations, the customs and the practices. I knew nothing of the strict regulations and penalties attached if the rules of traditional practices were broken. My inadvertent and very uncomfortable encounter with men's business was a wake-up call for me. In future, I would take more note of the mysteries of the parallel universe being lived at Papunya by the people who have ancestors who have lived in this country for 60,000 years or more.

5 Heartbreaking challenges

At one of the regular health-service staff meetings, Liz the midwife, raised the subject of petrol sniffing, putting forward the question 'What can the health service do?' I recoil from the smell of petrol when I fill up my car, so the thought of choosing to sniff petrol was quite bewildering. According to Liz, it was a growing social problem affecting Papunya primary-school-age children and teenagers, mostly male, who were sniffing their lives away on petrol.

When Liz made me aware of the issue, I realised I had already seen dazed petrol sniffers wandering around the community. They wore a tin hanging from a chain under their chin. I was horrified to realise it was petrol in that tin and the kids were sniffing it. Petrol sniffing gives a euphoric mood and the young sniffers shared their intoxication and hallucinations, enhancing the effects. There was a sniffers' subculture and they hung around together.

Parents, the council, health services and government bureaucracies all seemed helpless in the face of the petrol-sniffing scourge and were unable to control it. Customary Aboriginal child-rearing practices were highly permissive and parents seemed not to have the tools to help their children deal with the petrol-sniffing addiction. In addition, the sniffers were aggressive and thought to be abnormally strong. Young men had tantrums and threatened their parents and grandparents.[44] It was a lose-lose situation until 2005, a long twenty-three years later.

In 1992, an Arnhem Land community discovered that Avgas— aviation fuel—was not sniffable and could be used safely in vehicles that ran on regular petrol. Avgas was introduced into many Aboriginal communities, including Papunya, but sniffing continued more or less unabated until Opal petrol made by BP became available to communities and roadhouses from 2005. Opal is a high-performance fuel with low aromatic compounds that do not produce a high when sniffed. By 2011, petrol sniffing had dropped by more than 90 per cent.[45] In many communities, the introduction of Opal went hand-in-hand with youth-engagement programs.

When I saw petrol sniffing in 1982 in Papunya, it was not new. Sniffing had been around from the 1950s and 1960s. It seems incredible that it took until 2005 to find a major part of the solution to the petrol-sniffing addiction of young Aboriginal children and teens. A bloody disgrace really!

I found the trauma and addiction of Papunya most disturbing, and the only way I could process it was by simply accepting this as my new reality. Whenever the daily challenges started to feel overwhelming, I went for a walk. The desert entranced me. The clarity of the light. The deceptiveness of desert plants. How soft-looking leaves pricked me, while ruthless-looking plants were gentle to the touch. I loved the trilling sound of crested pigeons taking flight and the bobbing of their crests when they walked on the ground. I saw the awesomeness of nature in a long line of small caterpillars, positioned head to tail, making their way in unison across the red earth. I smelt the acrid scent of the early-morning dew rising from the ground and rejoiced in the peace and the quiet of the desert. The beauty of the desert stays with me always. It is the heart of Australia. It is there, sleeping and waking to each new day. Grounding us into this vast, beautiful country that offers us the freedom to be.

The challenges facing me were not only in Papunya. They were also in Alice Springs where I encountered hostile racism. It was not that racism was unknown to me. After all, I grew up in the time when Anglo-Australians happily called Italians and Greeks, *dagoes*, *wops* and *Ities*. Not in my family though. My parents were very open minded and welcomed my first boyfriend into the family. It didn't matter a jot to them that he was Greek.

When I was in Alice Springs on a regular trip, as luck would have it, I managed to catch up with my father, Bill. I don't know why Bill thought it was necessary, but on this particular Alice Springs get-together, he was on a mission to show me the ugly side of the town. He took me to a 'Whites-only' club. I think it was the Italian Club where no Aboriginal people were given membership. I perched myself at the bar to survey the clientele and said a friendly 'hello' to a drunk-looking chap sitting a couple of stools up from me. We introduced ourselves and I discovered he was one of the Northern Territory government ministers. As Bill and I ate our meal, I watched him continue drinking. What a disgraceful sight he was! So drunk that he was drooling.

How hypocritical, I thought, *that the Whites condemn Aboriginals for drinking when they set such a disgusting example themselves.*

After the club, Bill took me to the now-demolished Stuart Arms Hotel. He introduced me to Bruce Chalmers, supposedly a relative of one of the old Territory cattle-station families. Although it is said that one should not speak ill of the dead, it would be hard not to when talking about Bruce. He asked what I did and I told him I was working at Papunya. He told me that the only solution was to round up all the Blackfellas behind a fence and shoot them. I could hardly believe my ears. I became rigid with shock as he continued expanding his solution and opinions of Aboriginal people. I turned and strode out of the hotel into the night. I was completely engulfed in rage. Hot tears scalded my cheeks.

Bill had given me a hard lesson in the reality of White life in Alice Springs. That night stripped away my innocence and took away my trust in Australians. Over the next year I learned that racism was an endemic, structural, systemic part of Territory life. I heard it in the anger, the sneers, the intolerance and the well-worn constructed dialogue of the more educated. Even the names of many important Aboriginal 'men of knowledge' given to them by White men were disrespectful, such as Billy Boy, Jackie Jackie and Nosepeg. Racism is the dark underbelly of Australia.

Relaxing with Homer in his rural retreat gave me respite from the challenges and frenetic pace of my work. From time to time, people from Papunya would call in to Homer's caravan to ask me for help for one thing or another. When Homer's landlord, Peter, found out, he was furious. He didn't want 'those Aborigines' coming on to his property and he banned all Papunya vehicles from coming on to his land, including my troopie. Our idyllic life was ruptured forever by this. There was no choice for me and I moved back to Wendy's house. Homer decided to move with me.

I suppose it was a combination of the intensity of our relationship and the angst of the move that tipped Homer into the suppressed pain of his past. Our life together became filled with disagreements and tension. He became convinced that I was in love with Adrian. This was so silly it was laughable. Adrian drove me nuts. He was so demanding. But I guess it would have been feasible to Homer because I spoke about Adrian constantly. I denied any romance or feelings, over and over. But when jealously is fixed in someone's mind, there's usually no changing it.

I became very unhappy, so when I could, I reduced my time in Alice

Springs. Homer and I were drifting apart. Then I got a call from Bill. Homer was in the psychiatric ward of the hospital. I felt horrified, devastated and shocked. As soon as I got to Alice, I went to the hospital. More shock was in store for me. Homer didn't recognise me. In fact, he looked at me and said, 'You look like a nice lady. Who are you? Do I know you?'

All I could say was, 'Yes, we know each other.'

I felt the pull from the vortex of mental illness and stepped away. I knew the love I felt for Homer did not have the strength or endurance to stand with him through this crisis. Our relationship was too undeveloped. In a state of shock, I found my way out of the hospital and back to my vehicle. I knew I had to absorb the shock by myself surrounded by country, so I drove to my favourite spot at Wigley's Waterhole. As I sat there surrounded by rocks and silence, the peace flowed over me. I realised my dream was over. I was back in my reality of making my way in the world alone. I was, once again, a single woman.

On my return to Papunya, I had not regained my equilibrium and was feeling rather depleted, so it was a stroke of good luck that I ran into Daphne Williams. She always lifted my spirits. She was an amazing woman, unstoppable in her drive to support the Papunya artists. Our paths rarely crossed as she was an endlessly busy woman, driving back and forth from Alice Springs to Papunya and Kintore delivering supplies of canvas, boards, brushes and paint and collecting art for sale.

Daphne Williams had become the manager of Papunya Tula Artists around the same time as the Pintupi started moving to Kintore. She had run the gallery for Aboriginal arts and crafts in Alice Springs for many years and knew the painters and their families personally. It was her close personal relationships that enabled Daphne to stay in the job for longer than all of her predecessors put together.

The last time I had seen Daphne, I had expressed my interest in seeing some of the artist's work and she invited me round anytime when we were both in Papunya. So here we were, both in Papunya, with time to chat. It was calming and normal to have a cuppa and chat about art. I was definitely going to buy some paintings from Daphne before I left Papunya. I regretted not having had time to get to know Daphne better as she was a terrific woman. Strong, determined and utterly committed to the artists.

6 The demise of Lyappa Health Service

During the past year, the Kintore population had doubled, keeping Lyappa Health Service busier than ever servicing both Kintore and Papunya communities. The Papunya Council was not overtly supportive of the Pintupi homelands movement away from Papunya. Nor were they generally supportive of Aboriginal-controlled Lyappa Health Service working in both communities. Indeed, some Papunya residents resented the dual servicing role even though the second doctor had been appointed to help reduce the workload. An underlying tension between the council office and the health service rumbled on.[46]

I did not understand the political or financial implications of Aboriginal-controlled Lyappa Health Service versus the Department of Health model. However, I completely sympathised with Aboriginal people wanting to avoid the cultural bias of the White medical world. I had heard many stories of racist treatment of Aboriginal people at Alice Springs hospital. I had even witnessed it myself when, on a freezing Alice Springs winter night, I brought an Aboriginal woman to the hospital after seeing her lying in the middle of the road on a median strip. After the on-duty staff had decided she was just a drunk, the woman was ignored. I was terrified they would throw her out of the hospital and I couldn't find anyone willing to tell me what they intended to do with her. I refused to leave her until, finally, a doctor promised they would keep the woman in emergency until the morning.

The Central Australian Aboriginal Congress started in 1973 to meet the health needs of Aboriginal people. Until that time there had been nowhere for Aboriginal people to go for medical care as they certainly would not have sought out a White GP. In remote communities, the Northern Territory Department of Health controlled health services for Aboriginal people. It was obvious to me that Aboriginal people needed their own system of health care that understood their physical, social and spiritual needs.

Papunya was one of the few communities chosen to have an Aboriginal-controlled health service, the Lyappa Health Service. This was due to the intervention of Charlie Perkins in 1978 who committed the Department of Aboriginal Affairs to fund Lyappa Health Service.[47] Now it seemed that this was in jeopardy.

During the past few months, Dr Adrian had held discussions with high-level officers in the Alice Springs office of the Department of Aboriginal Affairs. Northern Territory Health officials had flown to Papunya to talk with the director and doctors. From my memory, the topics of conversations were mainly the costs involved in running two health services and the expensive Royal Flying Doctor Service evacuations. During one very well attended community meeting, many people addressed the meeting supporting the Lyappa Health Service and the RFDS evacuations. Call me naive, but I was astonished when the health official openly responded to the community, saying we needed to sit down and talk about this. I had thought that was exactly what was happening. Everyone at the meeting was sitting down talking about the issues. Of course what he meant was, that he was not inclined to the community point of view. He wanted a cost-saving solution to the financial issue. That is, evacuations should occur at the same restricted rate as the communities serviced by the Department of Health. Trouble was brewing. It seemed to be matched by the threat of storms with rolls of thunder and flashes of lightning in the distance. The storms didn't eventuate but trouble did.

The day the sky fell in at the Aboriginal-controlled Lyappa Health Service was like any other. A hot day with a clear blue sky. Patients were being seen by health workers. Liz was dashing here and there. Adrian and Phil were in discussion about something or other. Then seemingly without any warning, our sky fell in. I heard our driver Neville bringing the troopie to a fast stop in front of the clinic. Andrew Bullen walked into the clinic slowly. He was shaken and looked bewildered. He went to Adrian and they spoke for some time. Then Adrian addressed us all.

'The council have ordered us to the office. We are sacked and the Lyappa Health Service is finished.'

Ron Moroney from the Department of Aboriginal Affairs and Alison Anderson of Papunya Council delivered the message to us. The Aboriginal Papunya Council had disbanded their own Aboriginal-controlled health service. Rubbing salt in the wound and showing who was boss, Alison gave the White staff twenty-four hours to leave the community. I was completely bewildered.

'Why would they do that? Why would they hand back their control over health to the Northern Territory government?'

It was incomprehensible to me.

There was never a clear reason given for the demise of the Lyappa heath service. Like all tragedies, there was a combination of reasons. In a Central Australian Aboriginal Congress (CAAC) report written two years later, the finger was clearly pointed at the Department of Aboriginal Affairs for their lack of assistance to Lyappa. It was DAA that had prevented the CAAC from providing on-the-ground support and advice. The report also noted that the collapse of Lyappa Health Service highlighted the different understanding of community control, often embraced by health professionals, with how Aboriginal people perceived it. The report noted anthropologist Fred Myers' comment that for many Aboriginal people the delivery of health services was seen as a non-Aboriginal domain. That is, it was Whitefella business. Thus, the expectation that Aboriginal people would take over control of the day-to-day aspects of health services was unrealistic at that time.[48]

The Congress report hinted at 'private manoeuvrings by Territory and Federal authorities with support of some Aboriginal people' behind the forced closure in December 1982. In my uneducated opinion, a reason for the demise of the health service could be found by following the money. It was expensive running two remote health services with four vehicles, two doctors, two sisters, admin worker, health workers, driver and cleaners. These costs were being met by the Department of Aboriginal Affairs, but the major cost of evacuating patients to Alice Springs Hospital by the Royal Flying Doctor Service was met by the Department of Health. Department of Health services in other communities did not have staff doctors, and nurses were discouraged from evacuating patients. At Lyappa, patients were evacuated according to the same criteria a doctor would use at a hospital emergency department. This was expensive. The Department of Health did not want to foot the bill and neither did the Department of Aboriginal Affairs. Ergo, get rid of Lyappa Health Service and put the Department of Health in control at Papunya. Whatever the reason, it was over. Lyappa Health Service no longer existed.

I had never been sacked before. As I completed my outstanding work, I had a vaguely bitter taste in my mouth. I didn't have any friends except my cat-gifting neighbour Johnno. He was blasé about the sacking.

'Happens all the time in Aboriginal communities,' he said, airily dismissing my sadness.

As I was packing my few possessions, I realised I had not bought any Papunya Tula paintings. Fortunately Daphne Williams was in Papunya. I drove over to her house and knocked on her door.

'Daphne, I've come to buy some paintings. The health service has been sacked and we are leaving soon,' I blurted out.

She invited me in, gave me a cup of tea and some soothing common sense.

'Aboriginal councils do what they think is right for their community and their leadership. We need to accept their decisions and not take it too much to heart.'

'Let me see what I can find for you,' she continued. 'I wish you had come last week when I had lots of paintings for you to choose.'

Although I wasn't able to buy any signed paintings, I was very happy when she found me two wonderful paintings to buy. To this day, this art of the Western Desert hangs on the walls of my home and I treasure it.

The paintings hang alongside my treasured coolamons. These shallow carrying-vessels were painted by the women health workers. I also treasure the boomerangs, emu feet and a carved goanna made by the artists who knocked at my door selling their wares.

Papunya paintings, coolamons and artefacts (opposite and above)
Jackson collection, 1982

I had few possessions at Papunya – some clothes and books, and of course my paintings and artifacts. My big worry was about my cats, Napa and Tjapa. There was no way I was leaving them to become feral or attacked by the dogs. I found my cat basket and loaded them both into the Toyota along with my other possessions.

It was a sad and silent convoy that drove those 250 kilometres to Alice Springs. We went straight to the house of an Aboriginal Congress health-service boss to debrief. Over the next few days, Aboriginal and non-Aboriginal Congress staff bunkered down with Adrian, Phil and Liz to discuss the complex situation and search for potential solutions. I couldn't find any place for me in these discussions so I quietly withdrew.

My job was gone and I felt quite shell shocked. Only fifteen months earlier, I had flown to the Northern Territory to visit my father, Bill, in Ali Curung where I encountered Aboriginal people for the first time. That momentous holiday had changed my life. When I was selected for the health-service administrator job in Papunya, without a moment's hesitation I resigned from my Melbourne job and moved to the Northern Territory.

As the strangeness and foreign-ness of living in Papunya receded, I became more at ease. Each day became an experience in the 'unknown' and I relished it. It was an extraordinary job that required me to learn at warp speed – health clinic administration, training health workers and outback radio skeds. I also had to learn my way around Alice Springs' businesses and purchase two new vehicles fitted for the bush.

I was proud of my achievement of completing the annual operating budget. It was the first time I had done such work and I found estimating the costs for the next twelve months a mammoth task. Especially as there were no computers or Excel programs in those days. I also felt satisfied at the success of my purchasing system, which meant we always had enough medical and office supplies. No mean achievement working in a remote locality.

I had become familiar with living in Papunya and forged goals for the next year. I would renew my involvement with health-worker admin training, learn more of the Pintupi language and make friends with some of the locals. I was filled with hope and excitement for my next twelve months.

But now it was over. My Papunya life had closed down. I considered staying in Alice Springs and trying to find another job, but that was much easier said than done. I wasn't a nurse, schoolteacher, mechanic or a builder and other suitable jobs on communities were few and far between. Reluctantly I made my decision to return to Melbourne with my cats.

I was deeply disappointed for the Lyappa Health Service staff. It felt to me that they were the pawns in a financial power struggle. The Department of Aboriginal Affairs and Papunya Council had turned their backs on them and the work they were doing for their community. With the Northern Territory Department of Health funding and health-care model, most of them would probably lose their jobs. With money politics, the people at the bottom had lost yet again.

Papunya had taught me that we urban Australians know virtually nothing about the history of our country and of the first inhabitants. But then how could we have known? All we were taught at school was that Aborigines were primitive people and not important to Australia. I had much to learn about the Aboriginal history in Australia and their present-day situation. I started to read … I had a lot of catching up to do.

It was also the beginning of a big love affair with the Australian outback. Working in Papunya and being a Central Australian Territorian for twelve months had given me a deep love and reverence of the vast timeless interior of our country. The pungent scent of the desert air at dawn. The landscape of straw-coloured spinifex, stark white trunks of the ghost gums against the endless clear blue sky and the dusty green of the long needle-like foliage of the desert oaks, once seen, were never forgotten. I was entranced by the clarity of light that enabled each leaf to be viewed with new appreciation.

I was captivated by the hardy vegetation of tiny bushes and grasses that literally grew out of rocky outcrops. Over the next few years, my love of the outback took me across the Nullarbor to the West, from Halls Creek to Alice Springs on the Tanami Road, from Adelaide to Darwin and from Katherine to Wyndham as well as up the coast to North Queensland. I never tired of it. The unending road and far horizons blended with the gratitude I felt for living in this vast and beautiful country.

Although I had put the idea of working in an Aboriginal community out of my mind, the consuming challenge and intensity of my job in Papunya never left me. The mainstream jobs I held didn't measure up with *meaning* or challenges. In 1989, when I was at a turning point in my life, the memory of my work in Papunya rose up. I remembered the immense feelings of satisfaction I had working alongside Aboriginal people and trying my best to contribute to a future that had meaning in their lives. The thought of leaving the city and once again living in the far reaches of our country drew me like a magnet.

Could I find another job working with Aboriginal people?

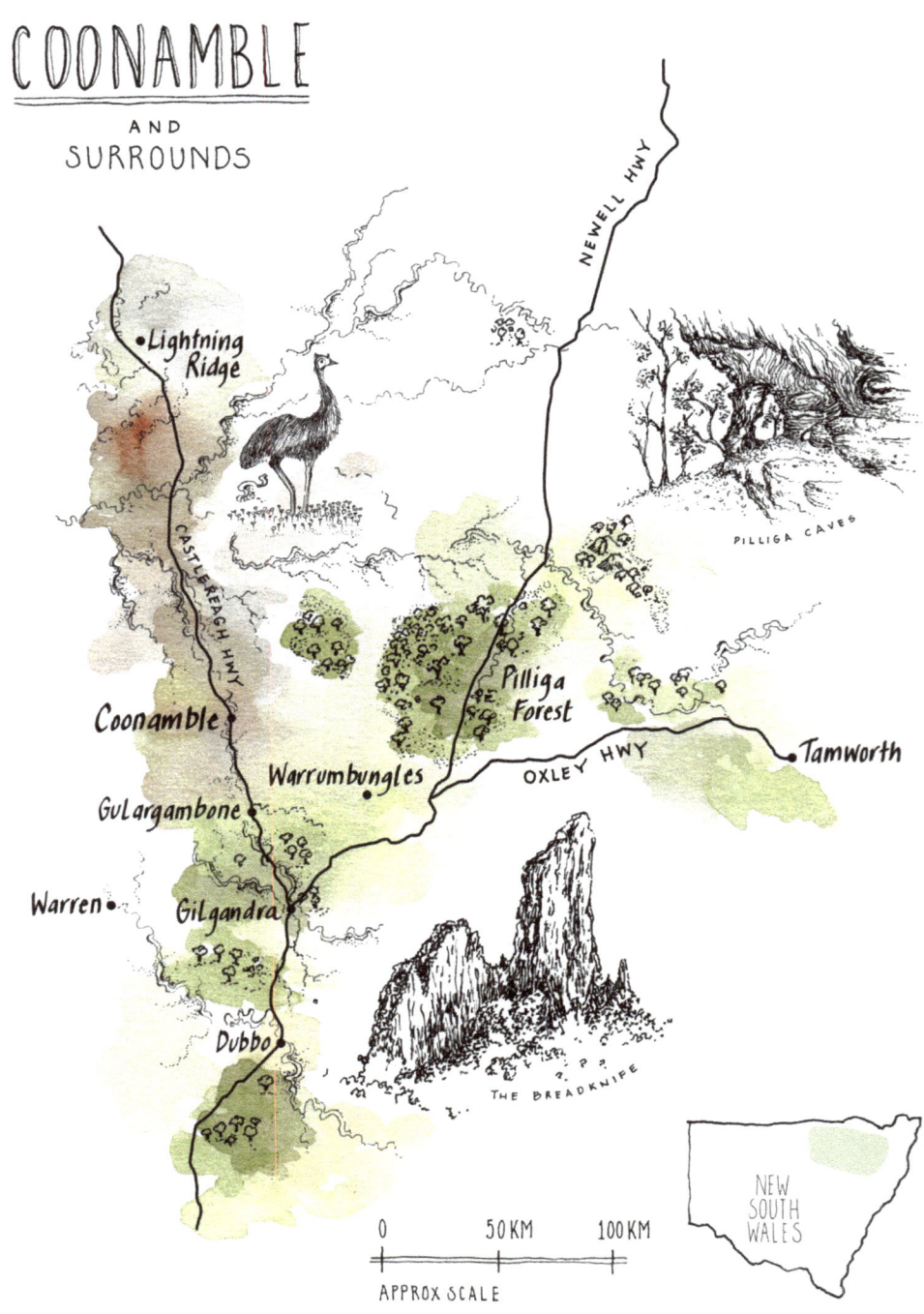

Part 2

Two years in Coonamble

7 Coonamble and the CDEP

I pulled up in front of the Coonamble Aboriginal Land Council and gave a sigh of relief. I had reached Coonamble. I climbed out of my car, straightened my shoulders and walked through the wide doorway. There was no one about. I ventured a tentative 'hello' and walked in a bit further.

Ahaa. I spied an office with a young Aboriginal woman sitting in it. I knocked and went in.

'Hi, I'm Barbara. I'm here to start work with the CDEP.'

The young woman looked up at me. 'Oh, hello, I'm Angela, I'll get Dad for you.'

Her father, Eric Fernando, was one of the leaders of the Aboriginal land council. He greeted me warmly and offered a welcome cup of tea. Eric told me how the town was looking forward to the start of the CDEP (Community Development Employment Project).

'Angela will help you settle in,' he said. 'We're pleased that we have found you a place to live,' he said, 'Ellen will be coming this afternoon to take you there. Ellen has a good job at the ANZ bank,' he announced.

The CDEP was a 'work for the dole' scheme that was both a community development program and an employment program. I was thrilled to be a coordinator of one of the first schemes in New South Wales. The Aboriginal land council was sponsoring the start-up of the CDEP with office space and support to get the scheme up and running.

CDEPs had been operating successfully for many years in Aboriginal communities in the Northern Territory and remote areas of South Australia, Western Australia and Queensland. From the late 1980s, the scheme was further expanded into regional, urban and even metropolitan Australia.[49] As well as Coonamble, a sister CDEP was starting up at Gulargambone, the small town I had passed halfway to Coonamble. There were also CDEPs at the opal-mining town of Lightning Ridge about 200 kilometres north and the cotton town of Warren about 100 kilometres south-east of Coonamble.

The CDEP scheme was introduced by the Fraser Government in 1977 for 'Aboriginals who live in remote or separate communities where normal job opportunities are inadequate' or 'who do not form part of the open labour market'.[50] Many thousands of Aboriginal people in remote areas were employed under CDEP. As well as receiving the 'dole' money to pay participants, CDEPs received a loading for on-costs and capital funds to support the program. CDEPs were the most extensive program in the Aboriginal policy arena.[51]

Before we could talk about my job, Eric was called away.

'Are you going to be working with me, Angela?' I asked hopefully.

'I can give you a bit of a hand here and there, but I'm busy with my job here. That is your desk over there,' she said pointing.

The land council had supplied me with a desk, stationery and an empty four-drawer filing cabinet. *What on earth am I going to write on that paper and file in those drawers?* I wondered.

My desk looked naked as there was no computer sitting on it.

'Is there a computer for the CDEP?' I asked Angela.

'You'll have to get one from the CDEP funding,' she replied.

That was positive, I thought. *At least there is money for a computer somewhere.*

It was soon lunchtime and I saw a couple of people heading out for lunch. Angela grabbed her bag and went out the door with a 'see you after lunch,' flung over her shoulder.

'Okay. Right. I guess I'll walk up the street and find some lunch.'

As I walked the couple of blocks to the main street, my impressions of a few weeks ago on my first trip were confirmed. Coonamble was not a charming town. It was flat and ordinary. Although the population was around 3,000, on my short walk it had the feel of a much smaller town. The people were casually dressed and the men wore battered narrow-brimmed hats. They seemed not to be in a hurry. I didn't see anyone who looked Aboriginal and I wondered where they were and what they did?

The main street had all the basics: supermarket, newsagent, pharmacy, hardware store and a couple of clothes shops. Halfway down the street, there was a country-style hotel with a balcony, amazingly called the Sons of the Soil Hotel.

'How very Aussie,' I chuckled to myself.

I was later to find out it was the 'cockies' pub, as the farmers were called. I was pleased to see Coonamble had three video shops.

At least I'll be able to watch videos in my spare time, I thought, picturing the empty evenings ahead of me. My experience living in the Aboriginal community of Papunya in the Northern Territory had taught me the importance of books and music to keep loneliness at bay. Here in Coonamble I would also have videos to keep me company until I got to know a few people. A bit further on, I found a small shop selling sandwiches and pies and bought my lunch.

Midway through the afternoon, Ellen, a young Aboriginal woman, turned up to take me to my new home and introduce me to the landlady. We both got into my car and Ellen directed me over the Castlereagh bridge before heading to the outskirts of town. My heart sank when I saw a demountable, my new home, sitting in a bare paddock next to a spindly tree with no shade.

Castlereagh, the 'upside-down river'
Aussie Towns website

'Rental accommodation is scarce in Coonamble and this furnished demountable was the only place available,' Ellen said apologetically.

My new home was grim. It was furnished with a beaten-up laminex table, four unmatched chairs and an uncomfortable-looking two seater green vinyl lounge. The bedroom had a metal-framed single bed with a disreputable-looking mattress, a small wardrobe and a cupboard. Mod cons were a small fridge and hoover twin-tub washing machine. I put a smile on my face and tried to look pleased as I was introduced to my landlady.

Castlereagh River and Castlereagh Highway leading into Coonamble
Coonamble Times

After taking Ellen back to the land council, I returned to the demountable to empty my possessions from my small Nissan Pulsar. I set up my 386 computer on the kitchen table and placed the TV and video player on top of the cupboard in the bedroom. There was no way I would be relaxing on that ghastly couch in the living area. I put away my clothes and placed my few books on the kitchen bench. The only place for the cassette player was on the floor. I was done. I could not have imagined much worse. Drearily curtained small windows looked onto flat paddocks with a few sparse trees stretching into the distance. The monotonous view was relieved only by barbed-wire fencing. As I sat at the table writing out my shopping list for essentials to fill my cupboard and fridge, I didn't know it was going to get worse.

For my first evening, I made a simple salad for dinner and boiled the jug for a cup of tea. That done, I thought I'd have a look at some television. I went to the bedroom, turned on the TV and connected the portable antenna. Snow!

No reception at all. My heart sank to the floor. No TV. I quickly plugged in my cassette player and put on some music to raise my spirits. Then I got to work and connected my TV to the video. Thank goodness I had brought a few videos with me that I could watch until I started hiring them. I put visiting the video shops in town at the top of my 'To Do' list.

At dawn the next morning, I found out just how awful my new home was. The early-morning dew had settled on the bare earth littered with sheep droppings. The damp odour entered my sleeping nostrils and brought me abruptly to wakefulness.

'Good grief! What is that horrible smell?'

As I took in my new surroundings and remembered where I was, I realised the smell was sheep manure. I buried my face in the pillow and pulled the sheet over my head, but it was too late. I was well and truly awake. I swore to myself that I would leave this dump as fast as I could. There was no way I could live in a sheep paddock.

As I ate my breakfast and sipped my cup of tea, I reflected on my 1,000-kilometre journey from Melbourne to Coonamble. The final 100 kilometres from Dubbo to Coonamble had been like driving in another country. Gone were the rolling hills of Victoria's gentle countryside. Instead I was driving through flat, grass plains scattered sparsely with trees. Dorothea Mackellar's poem 'My Country' came to mind. As well as sweeping plains, there would be pitiless blue skies, drought and flooding rains, and nearby, the ragged mountain range of the Warrumbungles.

In a similar way to Papunya, I was starting my new life in Coonamble pretty much as a blank slate. My entire body of knowledge consisted of knowing a handful of dot points.

- Coonamble is 575 kilometres north-west of Sydney.
- Geographically it lies almost midway between the Warrumbungle Range and the Macquarie Marshes.
- The town is one of the stepping-off points to the outback of New South Wales. Approximately 10 per cent of Coonamble's population of around 3,000 people were Aboriginal people.
- Coonamble's economy was based on agriculture and it was well known for cattle, sheep, wool and wheat.

I would need to be a sponge soaking up information to learn about the Aboriginal community and figure out how the town worked. My next few months were daunting.

As a Victorian, I knew next to nothing about the history of New South Wales. It wasn't until I started writing my stories that I started to rectify that. Thank goodness for Google. My searches informed me that the first Europeans arrived in the Coonamble area with John Oxley, the land surveyor-general in New South Wales. Oxley's survey exploration of 1818 discovered the Castlereagh River and Warrumbungle Range which led to the opening up and settlement of the district.

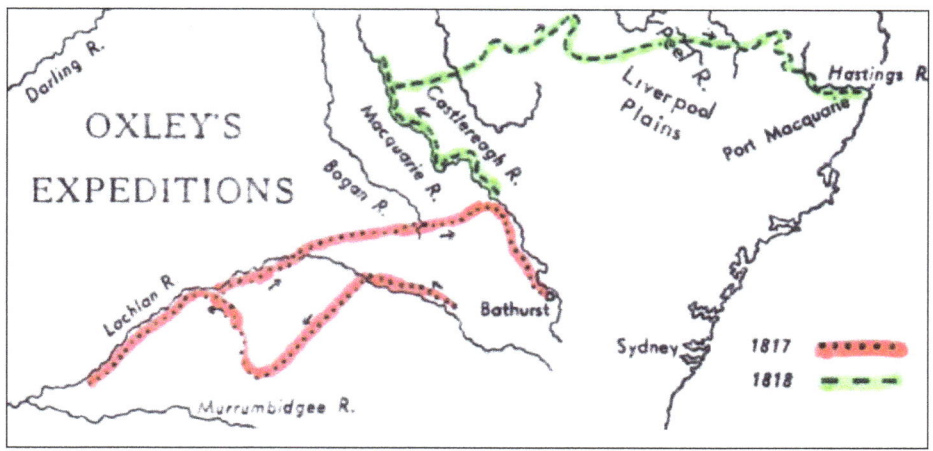

As a Victorian, I had no idea of the historical significance of Oxley's expeditions.

From the 1840s, squatters moved into the Coonamble area establishing large cattle and sheep runs. The Coonamble Post Office was opened in 1859 and the first selection of blocks of land was sold by auction in 1861.[52] Coonamble was proclaimed a town in 1861 and a municipality in 1880.[53]

Historically, Coonamble Shire sits at the convergence of the territories of three Aboriginal language groups, the Kamilaroi, Wiradjuri and Wailwan peoples. They all moved through the area, however, the Wailwan are the traditional custodians of the land.[54] Although the Wailwan population prior to the arrival of the Europeans is not known, it would have been significantly less than the Wiradjuri population of 3,000. The Wiradjuri were the largest Aboriginal group in central New South Wales during European settlement.[55] Little is known about the history of Aboriginal people in the Coonamble area prior to the Europeans. However, it is known that Aboriginal people were living on Wailwan land near Quambone in central western New South Wales in 1898.[56] Although

83

pastoralists dispossessed Aborigines of their land, the Aboriginal people continued to live on the fringes of settlements. This uneasy coexistence continued until 1935 when Aboriginal people were moved to Brewarrina.[57] It is not known how many Wailwan people there are today.

The name Coonamble is derived from an Aboriginal word meaning 'bullock dung' and 'amazing sight'. The name reflects the rich alluvial plain and the landscape of the Coonamble hinterland.[58] Tribal boundaries were geographical landmarks such as mountains and rivers, however, boundaries were crossed in times of drought and for the trading of tools, weapons and stories. Along the Castlereagh River, which flows through a series of towns including Coonamble, Coonabarabran and Gilgandra, there are culturally significant artefacts. In the Coonamble area, these include scarred trees, bora grounds, burial grounds, fish traps and paintings.[59]

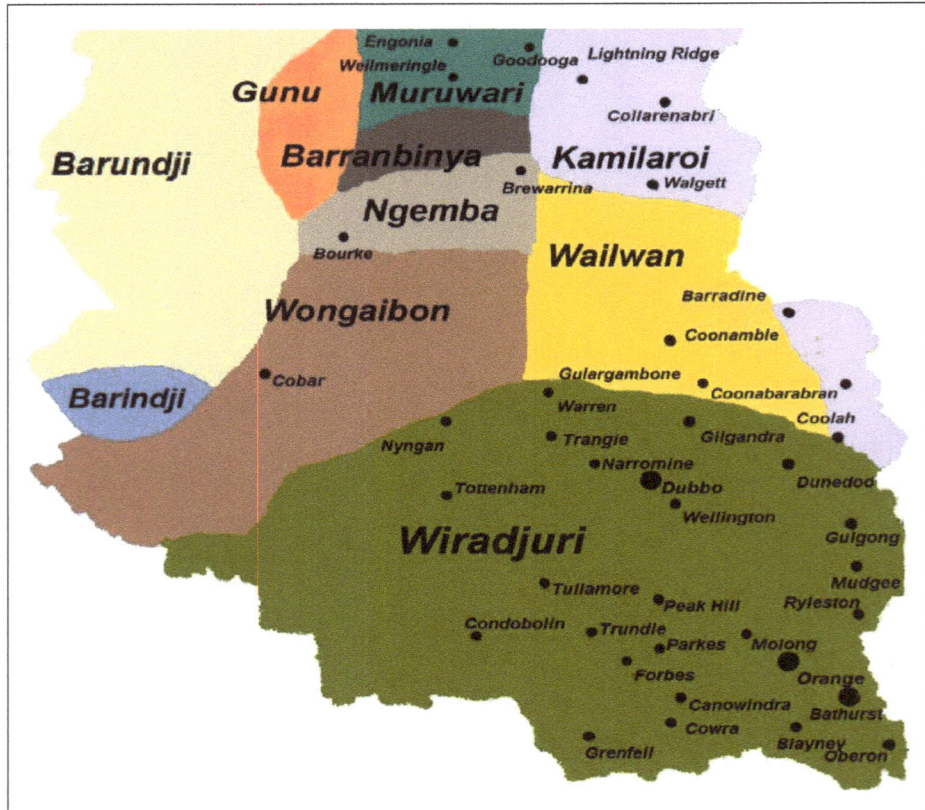

Map of languages in central New South Wales
Nola Turner Jensen, Aboriginal Language Research

Gail, my counterpart, starts work

Eric was in his office when I arrived at work. He gave me a small stack of papers that were related to the CDEP and told me that Andrew from the Department of Aboriginal Affairs (DAA) would be visiting in a few days. I was relieved that I would have something to do. I read the documents slowly to pass the time until I could think of something productive to do. I felt a sinking feeling in the pit of my stomach. How was I to do my job?

I didn't want to appear pushy so I waited a couple of days before tracking Eric down to discuss my need to have someone to work with. I knew I was getting on Angela's nerves with all my questions and I hoped she had spoken to her father about getting me off her back. I think she must have, because the next day Gail came to the office. She had been given the job of Aboriginal Trainee CDEP Coordinator. Gail was a young woman with dark auburn hair and a dash of freckles across her nose and cheeks. She gave me a warm and open smile as we were introduced and I took to her immediately. She was a good choice for the job with her background in administration work and her cheery personality.

'I'm so pleased we are going to be working together, Gail. We'll make a good team,' I said as I congratulated her on the job. I was very thankful that Gail would be by my side to start up the CDEP for the Coonamble Aboriginal people in this far-flung town.

Gail and I met with Eric Fernando the next morning to discuss how we would start. Eric reminded us that Andrew from the DAA was coming to Coonamble in two days. He would be giving us the guidelines and an initial work plan to set us on the path. I was heartily relieved to hear that. In the meantime I thought a Coonamble orientation tour would be most helpful.

'Let's drive around the town, Gail, so I can get an idea of the place.'

Gail agreed and we set off in my Pulsar for the grand tour.

Coonamble was a typical inland New South Wales country town with a mix of smart and shabby older-style weatherboard homes situated on large blocks of land. Most blocks had a couple of shade trees nearby the house to help cope with the hot summers. There was usually a patch of green grass and maybe a few flower gardens or bushes here and there. Invariably, there was a large shed in the backyard, sometimes two. Like so many towns in Australia, the original Coonamble town planner copied the old English ways making the street grid run east to west.

'My goodness, those houses must be hot in summer when the western sun burns down on them,' I commented to Gail.

She agreed. 'Sometimes it's better to sit under a tree than be inside.'

Gail's guided tour showed me that Coonamble was divided in two by the Castlereagh River. She told me the Castlereagh was known as the upside-down river. It is a most unusual river as water only seems to flow in the riverbed when there is a flood. On one side of the Castlereagh, there were four churches, a secondary college, four of the five hotels, the shopping street and supermarket. On the other side, there was a primary school, swimming pool, two clubs, one hotel and a smaller supermarket. I asked Gail where the Aboriginal people lived.

'We mostly live in Housing Commission places scattered over the town, although some of us rent from Whitefellas. It's not like Walgett where many Aboriginal families live out of the town where the old missions were.'

I found it interesting that every street seemed to be a mix of houses of various quality, some old, some new. It seemed there were no good or bad areas in Coonamble.

'What is there to do in Coonamble?' I asked. We were heading back to the shopping side of the Castlereagh, when Gail pointed to the bowling club.

'There's a good trivia night there on Friday nights,' she said pointing to the club. 'I don't usually go there but I'll show you the RSL where I sometimes go.'

She directed me down the main street to the RSL on the corner of Tooloon Street. As we drove down the street, Gail pointed out various shops including the newsagent.

'On Saturday morning, everyone goes down the street to catch up with friends or to pick up the newspaper. You should go down the street too.'

It sounded like a good idea although I felt a bit nervous that people would know I was a newcomer and give me the once over. Nevertheless, that's what I did on Saturday morning. I plucked up courage and drove into town. I parked round the corner from Castlereagh Street, squared my shoulders, and set off.

Gail was right. There were a lot of people walking up and down the main street. I saw a couple of the Aboriginal people I had previously met and was glad to smile and said 'G'day'. Being brand new to the town, I was highly aware of my surroundings. My antenna picked up a strange feeling as I noticed that the Aboriginal people and White people did not appear connected to each other. They each walked with their own kind. It was as though there was an invisible line separating them. I came to learn that this initial feeling of a divided town was true. While there was little overt hostility, a gulf did exist between the Aboriginal and non-Aboriginal communities. I was yet to learn that Aboriginal people were derogatorily referred to as 'darkies'. When I did know that, it brought the gulf between Aboriginal and non-Aboriginal people into starker relief.

A few days later, Gail and I were sitting in the sun having a cuppa out the front of the land council when Andrew, the field officer from the Department of Aboriginal Affairs, pulled up in his vehicle.

'I'll have one of those too. Put the kettle back on,' he said, smiling as he jumped out of the Toyota.

Andrew was a terrific bloke, easy to get along with and immensely helpful in guiding us with the CDEP work program for the next couple of months.

'The most important aspect of starting a CDEP,' Andrew instructed, 'is to have the active involvement of the participants. Right from the start, when you set up the CDEP operating rules and requirements, you need to avoid top-down decision-making and have the active involvement of the participants.'

This was right up my alley. Community development is working alongside people, shoulder to shoulder. It's their community and their daily reality, and they need to be involved in making and implementing the decisions that affect their lives. It was exactly the way I worked.

Most of the Northern Territory CDEPs asked their participants to work fifteen or twenty hours a week, however, Andrew told us that we could introduce the Coonamble CDEP with a twelve-hour working week to earn a wage equivalent to the unemployment benefit. A twelve-hour week made the hourly pay rate a more reasonable 'award' wage. If the participants wanted, they could increase the work hours at a later date. Andrew explained to us that the number of participants determined the operating grants the CDEP would receive. The larger the CDEP, the more financially viable it would become. I took careful note of this advice as I realised the success of the new CDEP would be determined by winning hearts and minds early in its life.

Finding employment for the participants was at the top of my mind. I knew that unemployment in regional Australia was generally higher than in the cities. Smaller rural towns had even higher numbers of unemployed. In Coonamble, the estimated unemployment rate was over 10 per cent,[60] but it was much higher for Aboriginal people. Andrew told us that he had held fruitful discussions with Coonamble Shire Council and St Vincent de Paul about opportunities for employment.

'I am confident both the shire and Vinnies will find work for the CDEP,' he said. 'As soon as you are up and going, make sure to get in contact with Jon, the Shire Engineer at Council, and Bede Waterford, who is very active with St Vincent de Paul.'

We promised Andrew that we would.

Gail and I set to work publicising the start of the CDEP program. We made colourful posters inviting people to a meeting to learn about the CDEP and placed them around the town. Gail made sure the posters were in the food shops where Aboriginal people shopped, the Coonamble Hotel, where many Aboriginal people drank, and on the lampposts most likely to be seen. The meeting was to be held at the land council office in one week's time. We waited excitedly for people to come and ask about this fantastic new program.

Over the next days, only a couple of people turned up to ask about the upcoming CDEP meeting. In fact, very few people seemed to visit the land council office at all. There did not seem to be enough interest and I was getting worried. I broached the subject with Gail, 'Why aren't people coming to ask about the CDEP?'

She looked a bit awkward and said hesitantly, 'It might be because people are afraid, or too shy, to come to the land council office.'

This didn't make sense to me. After all, it was an Aboriginal land council, and therefore, it was an Aboriginal place.

Gail saw I was confused and explained, 'The land council mob aren't their mob, so they hang back.'

I still didn't understand but I left it. Maybe it would become clearer to me a bit later. We realised that we needed to postpone the CDEP introduction meeting until we had promoted the CDEP concept and benefits to people.

Informal CDEP census

Reaching out to the community at a personal level was the only effective way to communicate the starting up of the CDEP in Coonamble. Gail and I decided to combine a home visit recruitment program with an informal census of the Aboriginal families in town. Amazingly, Gail knew practically everyone in town, White and Black. Street by street, we visited each Aboriginal family with our CDEP invitation and explained that people could have a job working twelve hours each week to earn their dole money. In a town where nearly all Aboriginal people were unemployed and held little hope of getting a job, this was very attractive. Young unmarried men were our prime candidates. Mostly they lived at home, and in nearly every case, if our household visit was in the morning, the young men of the house would still be in bed. It seemed they were up all night and in bed all day, living upside-down lives. Our list became an unofficial census of Coonamble's Aboriginal population.

The Aboriginal people of Coonamble were warm and hospitable and I always felt welcomed. The pattern of our visit was similar with each family.

'Come in, Gail, how are you, love?' A smiling mum would say as we were ushered into the kitchen or lounge room. Gail would start off introducing me and then explain the Community Development Employment Project we were starting up.

'I'm a bit busy with the housework and kids to have a job myself, but I'll let my husband and son know all about it,' the mum would explain to us.

As Gail's explanation came to a close, I would usually ask, 'What do you think about the idea? Do you think people will like it?'

The reply was usually, 'Oh, it sounds all right, it might work.'

I had been expecting a much more enthusiastic response but I became used to these low-key answers, and I was pleased that no one thought it was a doomed idea.

As we added each household to our spreadsheet, we made a note of everyone who seemed interested in being employed. Our census numbers grew until we recorded a total of 434 women, men and children on our spreadsheet. Gail was surprised at the number of Aboriginal people living in Coonamble, saying, 'I didn't know there were that many people here. I thought there were maybe 300 or 350.'

I found it disconcerting that a small number of people whom Gail knew to be Aboriginal did not identify as Aboriginal. When in doubt, she consulted Eric Fernando as to whether or not to include them in our census. Mostly Eric suggested we leave them out because it was probably better for their job or business if they 'passed' as White. We respected their privacy and choice and did not include them in our census. I had read about light-skinned coloured people passing in South Africa and condemned the South African system of apartheid. How shameful that my own country of Australia also had apartheid. How disheartening to realise White prejudice and discrimination resulted in people hiding their Aboriginality and cultural heritage. I hoped with all my heart the CDEP could help turn this around.

With our census and recruiting drive completed, we knew there was interest in the CDEP and Gail and I were keen to organise another community meeting. We put new CDEP posters around town and personally invited people to the meeting when we met them down the street. Our fingers were crossed that our second meeting would be successful.

The meeting day dawned. Andrew had driven up from Dubbo to answer questions and explain the program. Once again the meeting was held at the land council, but this time, even before the meeting time of 11 am, people were turning up. They were mostly men, from teenagers to older men in their forties, although a handful of women came too. This was to be the pattern of the CDEP. It was the men who wanted employment even if it was working for the dole. It was the men who had nothing to do, as they had no work and few hobbies.

Around thirty men signed up that day, more than enough to declare the CDEP a goer! Andrew moved immediately into our participation process.

'Before you all go,' he called to the assembled Aboriginal people, 'we're going to have a vote on the first rules of the CDEP.'

'The first thing to decide is – what time do you want to start work, 8 o'clock? 9 o'clock? 10 o'clock?'

There were a few moments' silence, then a chap from the back called out, 'Eight o'clock.'

'Any more ideas?' Andrew asked.

There was a bit of head turning and murmuring but no more suggestions.

'Okay, hands up if you agree to an 8 o'clock start.'

All the hands were raised. It was unanimous. Being paid weekly won the next vote. The final vote decided that an attendance book would be used to sign on and off. Andrew wrapped up the meeting explaining that the participants would need to elect their CDEP committee when it was up and running. Andrew gave the crowd a gentle warning, saying that it would take a few weeks for the CDEP to get going. He asked everyone to be patient.

Gail and I rented a double-fronted shop with two large workrooms at the back. Although the premises were shabby and run down, the shop suited our needs and the rent was reasonable. The location in Aberford Street, just a few hundred metres from the centre of town, was perfect.

We fitted out the sparse office with two desks, a single computer and our almost empty filing cabinet. We scrounged some tables, scruffy chairs and bench seats for the large rooms at the back. We found a small table for the sign-in attendance book and stuck a large poster on the walls with the rules clearly displayed. Someone donated an urn and we bought cheap mugs so we could all have a cup of tea together. Our start-up grant from the Department of Aboriginal Affairs was used to buy gardening equipment including a couple of lawnmowers and brush cutters. The CDEP had its premises and equipment. We were in business.

The CDEP employed Frank, an older local White bloke, as the works supervisor. He was an easygoing fellow who managed the rostering and organisation of crews. The CDEP was in its learning phase so a large portion of Frank's job was showing the new participants what to do and watchfully supervising the jobs. Fortunately for us, Frank owned an old ute which he generously used for transporting crews and equipment as long as we paid for petrol and servicing. We had no paid work at that stage but we kept the crews occupied helping Aboriginal families clean up their yards and doing odd jobs for them. It was a useful and heartwarming way to start the program.

The numbers of participants were increasing nearly every day and it was time to elect the CDEP Committee. In general, the committee would be expected to provide advice, support and guidance to help the CDEP deliver on the two goals of community development and employment outcomes. We promoted the election of the committee throughout the CDEP and asked everyone to spread the word and encourage community leaders to attend the meeting.

There was a good turnout and the result could not have been better. Well-known and respected Aboriginal elders were nominated and elected onto the CDEP Committee. Tracker Robinson was elected president. Tracker was known as a man of great integrity around Coonamble district and beyond. In his younger days, he had been the last official tracker assigned to the Dubbo police station. In his twenties and early thirties, Tracker had been a welterweight boxer, fighting all comers at Jimmy Sharman's boxing tent. For many years Tracker worked at the Pilliga sawmills and rural properties around Coonamble. We were lucky to have Tracker on our committee and his wise advice was always appreciated. In fact, the whole committee was terrific. They met regularly and kept in close contact with the participants. Because they had their ears to the ground, they knew the whole story when small issues raised their head. The committee contributed greatly to the success of the CDEP.

We had invited Andrew to attend the committee election. Sadly, he couldn't come because he had resigned from the Department of Aboriginal Affairs. A new body called ATSIC, the Aboriginal and Torres Strait Islander Commission, had been established under the Hawke Government earlier in the year.[61] The Dubbo DAA office had become the Dubbo ATSIC office. Unfortunately, it seemed there was no suitable place for Andrew. It was a real pity as Andrew's experience was huge and we would miss his advice and assistance. However, we looked forward to working with ATSIC. The commission was an exciting development for Aboriginal people. Many believed ATSIC would lead to self-determination as there were elected regional councils and an indirectly elected national board of commissioners. ATSIC's functions were to advise Governments at all levels, provide peak national and international advocacy for Australian Indigenous affairs, and deliver and monitor Indigenous programs and services.[62]

Coonamble Shire and Vinnies back the CDEP

From the beginning, the shire council and St Vincent de Paul were the mainstays of CDEP business. I had discovered the shire council featured large in Coonamble life as I was forever hearing people say 'the shire did this', or 'the shire said that'. This took me by surprise as I was accustomed to noticing my local council in Melbourne only when I received a rates notice or saw a garbage truck. The shire council was indeed a very important institution for Coonamble. As well as being the largest employer in the shire, the council was directly, or indirectly, involved in numerous aspects of the lives of shire residents. As well as the typical responsibilities of roads, rates and rubbish, Coonamble Shire owned the small local airport, managed the library, swimming pool, cemetery and the animal pound. The shire was also the point of contact or the initiator of many programs including drought relief, youth programs, aged care and cultural heritage.

During the CDEP learning phase, Gail and I had followed Andrew's advice and set up a meeting with Jon, the shire engineer. Jon was an experienced professional, and over time, he became a valuable friend to the

CDEP. I learned that I could always trust him to be straight and honest with his opinions and suggestions. However, this was our first meeting and we had yet to develop a working relationship.

Gail and I were directed to Jon's office. He was a tall, fair-haired man with an air of command about him. He was direct and to the point. There was no pussyfooting around with Jon. He opened the meeting by informing us that Andrew had addressed the council some weeks previously. Andrew had explained the background and purpose of the CDEP program and requested the assistance of Coonamble Shire Council in providing contracting opportunities for the CDEP.

Jon looked at us keenly as he asked pertinent questions.

'The council agreed to support the CDEP program. What I need to know is, to date, what is the progress of the CDEP? How many people have registered to work? Do you have transportation and equipment? Do you have a supervisor?'

I explained that CDEP has already grown with more than forty-five participants joining to date. We had gardening equipment and employed a supervisor who owned a trayback ute that we could use. I completed my small monologue with the important question: 'Will Coonamble Shire be providing the CDEP with work opportunities?'

Jon smiled his acknowledgement at my direct question.

'The council has discussed the CDEP starting up in Coonamble and welcomes the program,' he said. 'Andrew suggested the CDEP would start small then, over time, it would build its organisational capability and the participants would learn work skills.'

Gail and I nodded our agreement. Although the CDEP was very new, this was already happening.

Jon continued, 'The shire council would like to propose a program to support that approach. As a start, the council is offering the CDEP work such as mowing verges on the side of the road, cleaning out culverts and clearing up rubbish on council land. The work will be closely monitored by the council works supervisor and inspected before being signed off as satisfactory.'

This sounded like music to our ears. We had work to offer the men. A huge weight lifted from my shoulders. Jon asked if we had set our contracting rate. I had no hesitation in being up front and admitting we had no clue how much to charge for these works. I'm sure Jon was expecting this as he suggested the council would pay the CDEP the same rate it paid other contractors. He added that the council would expect the same value for money. He further added that if, at some later stage, we wanted to change the contracting payments, we could negotiate with the council.

As our meeting drew to a close, Jon suggested Gail and I make an appointment with Bede Waterford, a local solicitor who was heavily involved with St Vincent de Paul, or Vinnies as it was called. I phoned Bede Waterford as soon as I was back in our office and we arranged to meet with him the next day.

Bede's office was exactly as I pictured a country solicitor's office. Slightly old fashioned with leather chairs and law books lining the walls. Bede was a quiet, kind and unassuming man. He listened attentively to our CDEP story and committed Vinnies to supporting us. It was not a long meeting and Gail and I left feeling elated. Two promises of work in two days. What could be better!

8 CDEP turns unemployment on its head

We didn't have to wait long before we received notification of the CDEP's first council job. It was to clean out a culvert. A council works supervisor met with the CDEP supervisor Frank and the CDEP crew and explained what was required. The next morning the work crew loaded the ute and jumped on the trayback with Frank driving. I think all of us felt nervous about this first council job. Gail and I had to wait until Frank reported back to us that afternoon. It was great news! The men did a good job that easily passed inspection by the works supervisor. The CDEP had earned its first payment.

Bede's promised support materialised over the next weeks. Vinnies promoted the CDEP to its older clients who needed extra help, which wasn't available through Home Care. Many small jobs started coming to us from elderly people who needed help mowing their large yards and doing the heavy gardening. As well as gardening, our crews also helped people clear out their sheds, cart rubbish to the tip and generally keep their yards tidy and well maintained.

For many of the men, being employed on the CDEP was the first job they had ever held. It was also the first time they had to regularly get up early to be at work at 8 o'clock in the morning. The twelve-hour working week was spread over three days with most of the CDEP work being carried out in the mornings so the men had their afternoons free. Although Frank tried to organise the work roster, he became a work juggler instead. Frank didn't know from one day to the next how many workers would show up. If too few men turned up, he might have to reschedule a job. If too many men turned up for work, he had the shortage of equipment to contend with as there were not enough mowers, brushcutters or hand tools to go around. The morning starts were chaotic and fun.

Gail or I would get to the office early to open up and put the urn on for the early-morning cups of tea. The workers for the day would arrive, laughing and joking with each other as they grabbed a tea or coffee and checked out the jobs that Gail had written on the whiteboard the day before. Frank would turn up with his ute and the crews would select themselves for a particular job, with Frank overseeing the number of workers and equipment required. The first crew would load the equipment into the ute and Frank would drive them to the job. They would unload and Frank would come back to collect the next crew.

When participants turned up for work, we always did our best to send them to a job, even if there wasn't enough equipment. As it turned out, our shortage of equipment became a blessing in disguise. While the men were waiting for their turn to have a go on a mower or brush cutter, they chatted among themselves. By working together and chatting together, they got to know each other, enabling them to form strong bonds of friendship.

I had assumed that because the participants were all Aboriginal, had gone to school and socialised together, they were friends. But as I discovered, this wasn't the case at all. For many, it was the CDEP that brought the men together. In a participant survey I did at the end of the first year, the outstanding finding was, for nearly all participants, 'the best thing about the CDEP was the friends they made'. I had expected the participants would have noted the new skills they had learned, and that they felt more confident and in control of their lives. Well it did all that, but the best thing was making friendships. How wonderful was that!

Prior to the CDEP coming to Coonamble, only a handful of Aboriginal people were employed. Two Aboriginal people were employed in the private sector, Ellen with a job at the bank and a young man who was employed at the RSL club. A few men were employed by the shire council; the school employed Aboriginal teaching aides; the hospital employed some women as cleaners. From time to time, an Aboriginal person would be employed when government-funded training grants were available. Gail had been employed in administrative training positions at the secondary school and the courthouse. As often happened, at the end of the grant period, she was let go as her 'training' had finished, with no commitment to further work.

Men found casual work at the saw mill in the Pilliga Forest when it was operating, or picked up seasonal and casual work such as shearing, burr-cutting, stick-picking or 'mulesing'. Burr cutting and stick picking jobs were associated with the cotton farms in the region. Mulesing was a horrible task that I hoped would one day be banned. I felt sorry for the poor lambs.

As far as I knew, not one Aboriginal person was employed in retail or hospitality. Indeed, I was told that no Aboriginal had ever been employed in hospitality, as the White people in Coonamble would not eat food that was prepared or served by Aboriginal hands. I hoped this wasn't true.

While wheat, sheep and cattle have always been the economic mainstays of Coonamble, there were employment opportunities across the spectrum of jobs as the town was essentially a service centre for the shire. That being said, it was certainly not a vibrant economy with most young people leaving town to find a good job elsewhere. Nevertheless, the record of employing Aboriginal people was dismal.

The CDEP turned the past history of Aboriginal unemployment on its head. Within a few months, Coonamble CDEP had become the largest employer of Aboriginal people in the area. Slowly but surely the sign-ups increased, until almost without realising, eighty-four participants had joined the program. It was like a miracle. We were relieved, thankful and overjoyed.

The ATSIC operating grant that covered the CDEP wages and on-costs was apportioned according to the number of CDEP participants. Andrew had warned us that if the CDEP didn't attract sufficient participants, it could fail due to insufficient operating funds. With eighty-four people signing up to the program, it would certainly be financially viable. I no longer had to worry about failure. We had done it. The Aboriginal community of Coonamble had grabbed the opportunity to be employed, albeit working for the same small money they received on the dole. It was a breathtaking achievement.

Gail and I marvelled at how the low-key sign-ups had crept up, almost without us noticing. One man at a time had come to the office to join up. If needed, Gail would help him with the CDEP application form and then he'd leave, as quietly as he had arrived. The Aboriginal people of Coonamble were seizing the opportunity to work.

The CDEP was taking its first steps towards becoming a viable business with two streams of regular income. We had short-term contracts with the Coonamble Shire and a growing customer base of older residents who required CDEP muscle and equipment to keep their yards in order. This income allowed us to buy boots for the workers, pay for repairs and maintenance and buy small pieces of equipment. However, the CDEP could not have grown or prospered without capital grants from ATSIC. The latest grant had enabled us to purchase more mowers and slashers, bigger brush cutters and more hand tools. With this extra equipment, the CDEP was able to take on larger jobs with the shire and our Vinnies customers. This included slashing paddocks near houses and sheds to get rid of overgrowth and reduce fire risks. These jobs added welcome income.

A few weeks previously, I had attended the Welcome to Coonamble dinner which was a Coonamble tradition hosted by the towns' clubs, service organisations and churches. I was one of a large contingent of newcomers who had arrived during the past eighteen months including leaders from other local and regional Aboriginal organisations. During the dinner, each of the 'newbies' was asked to introduce themselves and talk about their role in their town. As well as learning about the other newbies, it was a great opportunity for me to tell people about the work of the CDEP and my role in it. During the mix and mingle time after dinner, I felt quite heartened as people approached me with good-luck wishes for the CDEP. The dinner provided a good opportunity for me to let people know I was looking for a place to rent in the town as I was desperate to leave the demountable.

My salubrious abode in Arthur Street, Coonamble
Jackson collection, 1990

My enquiries at the Welcome to Coonamble dinner paid off. A small unit had become vacant and I grabbed it. It was a one-bedroom unit with two single beds, an open-plan lounge with a dining table, tiny kitchen, and a small bathroom. There were five units in the block and we shared the laundry and clothesline. It was basic but I loved it. No more living in a crappy demountable sitting in a sheep paddock with the stench of manure waking me in the morning. Even better, the unit was in Arthur Street so I could walk to work and the shops. I would be a townie. My lonely life was over and I no longer needed to be polite to the owner of the demountable who referred to me as 'the woman who's come to put the darkies to work.' I was shocked when she said that to me. At that time, I didn't even know Aboriginal people in Coonamble were called darkies. It was even more woeful that she had no idea of the racism inherent in that name.

Now that I lived in town, I encouraged Gail and a couple of the CDEP women to introduce me to Coonamble nightlife. It was just as well I enjoyed a beer because Coonamble was a big drinking town. Although the total population was only around 3,000, there were five pubs, three clubs and numerous bottle shops to keep the town drinking. I heard from a person in the health sector that the Dubbo region was one of the biggest drinking areas in the state. If Coonamble was anything to go by, I believed them.

I learned that the pubs, all within walking distance of each other, catered for different groups in Coonamble. The farmers, or cockies as they were known locally, usually went to the famously named Sons of the Soil Hotel. By and large Aboriginal people went to the Coonamble Hotel and a mix of people went to the Commercial and Club House. Because the Terminus Hotel was on the other side of the Castlereagh River, which divided the town in two, I never went there and had no idea of their clientele.

The three clubs were the RSL, the bowling club and the golf club. The RSL was within walking distance of the four hotels and often had entertainment and dancing on a Saturday night. The bowling and golf clubs, which were over the bridge on the other side of the Castlereagh, mainly catered to their members but also held large functions. In every pub and club there were poker machines galore providing endless opportunity for people to run through their money on payday. Although I had little interest in gambling and found gaming poker machines boring, I was addicted to playing card poker with Gail on the RSL's only 'real' poker machine. We had uproarious fun drawing our cards, betting five cents on the side and doubling or nothing. The machine obviously didn't pay for itself and I mourned its loss when the management removed it about six months later.

Apart from drinking and playing the pokies, bingo would have been the most popular entertainment in town. I was amazed to learn bingo was played six nights of the week in Coonamble, at the bowling club, golf club and in church halls. I figured I should get into the community spirit and have a go at bingo myself. Gail's mother was a bingo fan and she invited me to go along with her to try it out. Bingo sounds like it should be fun and light hearted, but that's not the case. It is a very serious game. One needs to concentrate on the caller and the numbers in front of you. Money was at stake. You had to match all the numbers and call them out. Although bingo nights were portrayed as innocent fund-raising, it seemed like gambling to me. In any case, there was too much concentration required for my liking so I gave it away.

Between drinking, pokies and bingo, for Coonamble residents, including CDEP participants, the temptations were constant. It was Gail who opened my eyes to the problem long-term unemployed people face in managing their money. In the past, when I was unemployed and had overspent, I had savings that cushioned me. In Coonamble, most unemployed people had no savings. If they mismanaged their money on a Friday or Saturday night, it had a disastrous effect on their family budget until the next pay day. It was the lack of food for the children that worried Gail most. She had given the situation a lot of thought and had come up with a solution.

Advance pay scheme

'What about we give the participants an advance on their weekly wages? We give the advance on Monday morning and deduct it back from them on Thursday payday,' she suggested.

I thought it was a great idea so we called a meeting of the committee to share our concerns and discuss Gail's possible solution. We hadn't heard about any other CDEP giving advances and had no idea if ATSIC had a rule about this. Better to 'ask forgiveness rather than permission' we decided. In any case, we had yet to meet any of the Dubbo ATSIC staff. It seemed they were grappling with their new roles as they learned on the job and had no time to drive to Coonamble to give us support. We were left managing on our own. In many ways this suited us as we were able to develop our policies and programs without bureaucratic input. We flew the plane ourselves by trial and error.

The committee made the decision for the CDEP to pay advances on Monday so people could buy food for the week. Married couples with children could receive an advance of $100 with single people receiving $50. Advances had to be requested first thing on Monday morning and were paid at the end of the work day. The advanced amount was deducted from participants' pay on Thursday.

This simple decision of a payday advance changed the lives of the CDEP participants. Just about everyone took advantage of the scheme and incredibly beneficial outcomes followed. With less money in their wallets on Thursday, less drinking took place at the weekend. Kids were better fed and people began to have a bit of money in their pockets. As a bonus, less drinking meant less fighting and fewer working wounded on Monday mornings.

The success of the pay advance scheme led to requests from participants for help to pay off their rent arrears. For some people, with more than a thousand dollars owing, their rent arrears seemed insurmountable. We held discussions with the housing commission about the CDEP implementing a deduction system to pay off the outstanding rent. The commission agreed. With committee approval, we implemented rental arrears deductions. Bit by bit, people paid down their arrears until finally they were debt free. We had similar conversations with private landlords, and they too agreed to the arrears scheme. Before long, there was no more need for people to do a 'midnight flit' and they could remain in their homes.

Next came requests for help to pay off huge electricity bills. Some people had been living without electricity for months. We implemented a deduction system to pay the power bills and it wasn't long before people were able to turn their lights back on. Being able to stay in their houses and keep the power on was transformative.

Another cause of financial anxiety were the large book-downs at local food stores. I heard stories of some families, so ashamed of owing money, they couldn't look the shopkeeper in the eye. With the deduction scheme, families were able to get their book-down under control. Outstanding fines were another sought-after deduction. People hated having outstanding warrants as they were scared of being sent to jail for unpaid fines, even though the law had changed a couple of years earlier in 1987.[63]

As the financial lives of CDEP participants steadily improved, we began to receive requests for help to buy second-hand furniture on lay-by. We got in touch with Dubbo Disposals who were delighted to have a new stream of customers. They put fridges, washing machines and lounge suites to the side while the participants saved the payments through the lay-by scheme. The saving system caught on and one chap even saved up to buy a car. Amazing.

It is interesting to compare the flexibility and client-centred approach of the CDEP deduction scheme with the compulsory income management of the INDUE Cashless Debit Card. Because the CDEP deduction scheme was voluntary, people maintained their power to choose how they would spend their money. Participants could still buy a beer to drink with their friends or waste their money at the pokies. However, pay advances severely limited the amount of money available for alcohol, gambling or cigarettes. As families became accustomed to the scheme, they could choose to pay off rent arrears or excessive power bills through the CDEP deduction scheme. They could even choose to save for furniture and white goods. It was up to them.

Barb (above) and her Aboriginal counterpart Gail (opposite), hard at work in the CDEP office
Jackson collection, 1990

Gail had thrown herself into the huge task of paying the wages and managing all the deductions. She was in charge and I was the backup. It was, quite frankly, ridiculous that this highly competent young woman had previously only been offered Aboriginal traineeships. However, it was a very lucky break for the CDEP. Gail developed a manual system of Excel spreadsheets and lists. Although it worked, with the complexity of the deductions, it became clear that we needed to computerise and we needed help to do that.

We were in luck. Robyn, a dear friend of mine, was working in a hands-on role with a company that sold software. Although she was in South Australia, by using the telephone and fax Robyn was able to steer us through the complicated set-up of a program which met our needs. We were on the phone constantly with Robyn who figured out how best to set up the program, then patiently trained us and helped us get it up and running. The Coonamble CDEP was no ordinary payroll. We had to manage many facets of the participants' personal finances, tracking and deducting amounts for weekly advances, rent arrears, electricity bills, fines, lay-bys and debts to local stores. If we had the money, we would have employed someone locally to help us, however, there was no budget for this so we relied on Robyn's inexhaustible generosity.

The flexibility of the CDEP was changing people's lives. Another opportunity to help people improve their financial situation was brought to our attention. Phil was the designated spokesman for a small delegation of men who hesitantly came into the office.

'A few of us do casual work from time to time,' Phil began. 'You know, shearing, burr-cutting and stick-picking. But we don't want to leave the CDEP. If we go away for a job, we want to come back and be able to start work again.'

This was an issue for the CDEP because we had a waiting list. When a participant left we filled the position straight away. We knew we had to keep up our numbers or ATSIC might take a position away from us and give it to another CDEP. There was no way we would risk that.

'How long would you be away for?' asked Gail. 'We need to know that in order to work out what to do.'

Phil looked at the other men, and tentatively said, 'For a month or two, maybe three months, depending on the contract.' The other men nodded in agreement.

'Hmmm, we've got to worry about ATSIC taking away our positions you know. We'll have to think about this. We will need the committee's agreement before we do anything. Why don't you come back in a week and we'll try and have an answer for you.'

Workers hours bank

Gail and I set to work trying to figure out how the men's request might work. We knew that many of the men could easily build up hours as they worked far more than the required twelve hours each week. Gail made a spreadsheet using the attendance sign-in book to calculate the number of hours each participant worked. It took a couple of days for Gail to complete the figures.

'It's amazing,' she said. 'I've calculated that some of the men are working twenty or twenty-five hours a week. Considering they are paid to work for twelve hours, quite a few are working around ten hours for free each week.'

'What about we let the men build up time in advance so they can go away working,' I suggested. 'They are already working twelve hours a week. If they worked an extra ten hours a week for eight weeks, they could bank the extra hours. By adding their holidays, they could work away for ten weeks.'

Gail sent a message through one of the work teams to Tracker. He dropped into the office the next day. We explained the situation to him and he thought it was a good idea for the men to build up a bank of time. He told us to call a committee meeting so we could make a ruling on it.

The committee got together the next week for a lively meeting. In principle, they thought it was a good idea but they wanted the whole CDEP to be part of the decision. They also wanted to let the participants know that the committee was very pleased with the way the CDEP was going. I took note of some of the comments made.

'Letting the men build up hours gives them a great chance to get ahead by earning some short-term money.'

'It's a big decision so it's right that the participants get to have a say.'

'The CDEP is doing very well when so many of the participants are working extra for nothing. We need to let them know we think they are doing a great job.'

'It's about time we have a get-together so they can tell us what they like and don't like.'

'While we're at it, we can check with them that they are happy with their supervisors.'

It was the biggest CDEP meeting we had ever held. Gail and I got in early to set up the room. We placed a small desk for the speakers at the front. I was well prepared but felt nervous as we had a big agenda. The committee came early and took the seats on the side. The men streamed into the CDEP, laughing and chatting with their mates, their workboots clumping on the wooden floor. Gail and I took our place at the small desk. When I looked into the sea of faces of maybe forty or fifty men, my knees started to knock and my hands shook. It was the largest group I had ever spoken to and the most men I'd ever seen in a meeting.

I took a deep breath, 'Thanks for coming. It's great to see so many people here this morning. Okay, let's start. I'll say a few words then Gail is going to talk about an hours bank. After that we'll open up for other comments and suggestions from the workers.'

I went on to explain the idea of building up hours so when participants found casual work, they could remain on the CDEP and get their job back when their casual work finished. I handed over to Gail who I knew could explain the concept better than I could. When Gail finished, Tracker put the 'hours bank' idea to the vote. It was passed unanimously.

Tracker then asked the workers to put out their suggestions or complaints. At first it was a bit of a free-for-all with complaints about the workers not having proper workboots, broken equipment and a couple of participants not being picked up after a job. We wrote up the complaints on a whiteboard for everyone to see and promised to fix things as soon as possible. It quietened down, then one brave chap spoke up.

'I think we need to have regular elections of supervisors. That way, they know they have to listen to us.'

Gail wrote up the suggestion on the whiteboard. As it turned out, we didn't need to hold regular elections for supervisors, as invariably the supervisor would chuck the job when it became too difficult and the crews would elect someone else.

The CDEP work management team of Frank, the two supervisors, Gail and I were keen to respond quickly to the workers' demands. It was the CDEP's responsibility to supply workboots to the men, and we should have done it ages ago. There were a lot of feet that needed boots so it was a big project to organise. Ally Rutherford, one of our excellent supervisors, volunteered for the job. Ally collected the boot size of every worker and I made the Excel spreadsheet for the data. It was hard work for Ally collecting the boot sizes as many participants didn't know their shoe size. Finally, he gave me the completed spreadsheet and asked me to phone Bata, a recommended supplier in Sydney, with our order.

'No Ally,' I shook my head. 'This is your order to put through to Bata.'

'I don't know how to do that! I can't ring up Sydney!' he protested.

We sat down together and talked through the process and I made him a call script to follow. My goodness he was nervous, but he picked up the phone and organised the order. Then he followed it up with a confirmation fax. Ally was proud of himself, and so he should have been. It was a spectacular effort. The boots arrived on the train about a month later. Once again Ally rose to the occasion. He sorted out all the boots and handed them to each worker. There were a couple of stuff-ups that were easily fixed. All in all, it was a great job.

In the early CDEP days, when we only had Frank's ute, it was accepted that the men had to travel in the back of the ute with the equipment. Although the CDEP office was only a stone's throw across the road from the police station, we were lucky that no police eyes ever seemed to notice our illegal transportation to jobs. With a grant from ATSIC, it was time for the CDEP to lift its game and become work safe on the roads. Through Frank's connections, we bought an affordable twenty-two-seater bus in good condition. We were relieved that finally we were safe and legal with the men travelling in the bus while the mowers, brushcutters and other equipment went in Frank's ute.

Workers' complaints about broken equipment were only part of the story. Some of the breakages were due to carelessness while others to a lack of regular repairs and maintenance. Carelessness and faulty equipment are work-safe issues. We did our best to keep the workers safe, but in truth, it was a pretty rough and ready show we were running. Everybody was learning on the job to operate and manage our employment and community development program. There were no policy guidelines, no human resources section, no training section, no occupational health and safety section. The supervisor role was expanded to include monitoring the use and care of equipment, while Frank was charged with acting on maintenance and repairs more quickly. These measures helped a little, but our equipment problems stayed with us.

A new safety issue arose when the CDEP was offered tree-lopping work by the council. I learned that tree lopping was a pruning program carried out by the council every year or two. Quite a few participants were keen to be a part of the tree-lopping crew. The council had laid down a contract condition that crew members must have chainsaw proficiency certificates. The CDEP signed up with a good local program that offered training in the 'Operation and Maintenance of Chainsaws'. This was the first time that most of the men had been trained in anything. It was a hands-on training course and the crew members were very proud when they passed the training, gained a certificate, and took their place in the tree-lopping crews.

Finding work opportunities and managing a large employment and community development enterprise were new experiences for the CDEP towns of rural New South Wales. The Department of Employment, Education and Training (DEET) offered grants for the learner-CDEPs to visit more established CDEPs and other welfare employment programs in New South Wales to gain new ideas and approaches. Now that we had our twenty-two-seater bus to travel in, we successfully applied for a grant. It was a terrific learning opportunity for Coonamble CDEP and we made arrangements to visit the CDEP at Lightning Ridge and a welfare organisation in Tamworth.

Lightning Ridge excursion

Eight excited participants were selected for the excursion. We set off at 8 o'clock in the morning for the two-hour drive to the opal-mining town of Lightning Ridge, 200 kilometres north of Coonamble. It was great to get out of town and drive through the vast black soil plains dotted with wilga trees.

At Lightning Ridge we were meeting Sam Jeffries, the Barriekneal CDEP coordinator. The Lightning Ridge CDEP had been going for about twelve months and we were keen to hear what they were doing. Sam was a long-term Lightning Ridge resident. He explained to us that Lightning Ridge was not the same as other towns in north-central New South Wales.

'It's a unique town,' he explained. 'Different to towns like Bourke or Brewarrina. It's a multicultural mining town with more than sixty nationalities. And best of all, it's not racist like other towns. Ridge people respect the background of other people and there is a lot of intermarriage here.'

Sam told us there were around 2,000 people in the town and only six police. I was startled to hear how few police there were in Lightning Ridge.

Vastly different to other towns. I had heard that Bourke, with a population of 3,500, had thirty police, while Walgett had twenty police for a population of about 2,000. In Coonamble, we had twelve police for our 3,000 population. It seemed that the police ratio to population was an interesting gauge of the harmonious nature, or otherwise, of New South Wales towns.

'Everybody is the same at the Ridge,' Sam continued, 'they are all having a go. A lot of people who don't have the money to hire equipment to dig underground can find small pieces of opal by specking. Lots of people are on the dole, but they can pick up a bit extra to make ends meet, have a few beers at the pub and buy things they need.'

'What is specking?' we asked.

'That's when you go over a digging after the owner of the claim has given up and left it. Anyone is allowed to go over the mullock heaps and see what they can find. Normally you can only find a little bit here and there, but it all adds up. You know, black opal is worth more than gold or diamonds. It can sell for over $10,000 per carat!'

This seemed like an unimaginable amount of money to us.

'I thought mining was very expensive?' I queried.

'Opal is quite close to the surface. Maybe 15 or 20 metres underground. By comparison to other mining, ordinary people can try their luck. I mean, diamonds are very deep and hard to get so it's only big companies that mine. And you know how expensive it is to find gold … just look at Kalgoorlie. That's why there are so many people having a go at the Ridge.'

'Come on, I'll show you round the town,' he said. We piled into the van and headed off following Sam's direction. Lightning Ridge was a mix of houses, mostly suburban-looking houses, but there were also shacks that had no electricity. Our CDEP crew was amazed to learn that some White people lived in the shacks. It wasn't only Aboriginal people. We admired, and laughed at, some of the bush sculptures that people made out the front of the houses and shacks with pieces of tin, wood carvings and bits of old junk.

While we were driving around, Sam told us more about the spirit of the Ridge and how the community came together to make their own Olympic-sized swimming pool. The town raised money and provided equipment while the community provided their labour free of charge. We were most impressed. Lightning Ridge was certainly different to Coonamble.

Sam had his eye on the big picture for employment and business opportunities. The CDEP was the largest employer of Aboriginal people in the town. He told us about their plans to build housing for people in Lightning Ridge and their intention to buy the local Shell service station. There would be training programs too. As we drove back to Coonamble, we were hard put to think of ways our CDEP could have similar ventures to Lightning Ridge, but what we learned stayed in our minds.

Mullock heaps in Lightning Ridge
Aussie Towns website

Tamworth excursion

The next CDEP/DEET excursion was to Tamworth about 300 kilometres away. We were visiting a disability workshop that provided paid employment to its clients. The workshop was impressive, well organised, friendly and down to earth. But again, we couldn't see how our CDEP could follow the workshop model. Their success depended on contracts with local businesses to manually make things that required repetitive tasks. Unfortunately there were no similar businesses with requirements of that nature in Coonamble.

It was late afternoon in Tamworth when we decided to head to the local caravan park at which I had booked and paid a deposit for three on-site cabins for us to share. The park was next to the Peel River so we could have a walk before we prepared the food for our big barbecue dinner that night. We pulled up outside the campground office and I went in to register. I could see the owners were dismayed that we were a group of Aboriginal people. I was used to this racist stereotyping by now so I put on my best middle-class White-woman smile.

'Hi, we are really looking forward to staying here. It's a lovely caravan park,' I gushed.

The husband and wife looked at each other doubtfully.

'This is a very quiet park here, so it may not be what you are looking for. We're very happy to give you back your deposit if you want to go somewhere else,' the husband said hopefully.

'Oh no, it's perfect for us. We will be very quiet. We're going to have a barbecue and then go to bed because we'll be leaving early in the morning. And don't worry, we'll leave everything neat and tidy. Our crew know how to behave.'

The husband nodded and the wife smiled. What else could they do?

'Well so long as you're quiet and don't leave a mess, you are very welcome,' the wife said.

As we planned, Gail, Rhonda and I went for a walk on the riverside path where we met two young women who were also out walking. One of the women was obviously Aboriginal, while the other had fair hair and skin. After some general chitchat, Rhonda asked them what was the racism like in Tamworth.

The darker girl said, 'Oh it's not too bad.'

But it was the conversation Rhonda had with the fair girl that was most interesting to me. She said that she didn't worry about racism. As far as she was concerned, she was the same as everyone else and nobody treated her as an Aboriginal.

Rhonda stared at her, asking, 'Are you passing?'

'What do you mean?'

'I mean passing as White when you are Black.'

The girl look confused. 'Well, I suppose you might say that.'

'You can't do that,' said Rhonda. 'The Whites will never let you be White. If you are Aboriginal, you are Black. It doesn't matter what you look like and what your skin colour is. You'll never be anything but Aboriginal.'

There was an awkward pause, and the fair-haired girl looked away.

'We've gotta go. Nice meeting you,' she said abruptly.

As the young women walked away, Rhonda shook her head and said, 'She'll learn. Probably the hard way.'

I immediately recognised the truth of what Rhonda was saying. The CDEP had a couple of fair-haired, blue-eyed Aboriginal participants, but they could never pass as White people because of their Aboriginal family names. In a small town like Coonamble, people were labelled at birth.

9 Racism and goodwill

Coonamble looked and felt like any ordinary New South Wales country town. Although I had felt the gulf between Aboriginal and non-Aboriginal people on my first walk down the main street of Coonamble, the harsh racist attitudes I'd encountered in Alice Springs were not visibly present. During my employment in the early 1980s at Papunya in Central Australia, I had come to know Alice Springs quite well and discovered that racism in Alice was part and parcel of the town. I was thankful it was not the same in Coonamble. For example, there was no dress code serving as a colour bar in the pubs and locals did not make racist comments about Aboriginal people to me during casual conversations. Nevertheless, Coonamble's racism, like racism throughout Australia, was culturally ingrained.

The segregation of Aboriginal people at Tin Town is in Coonamble's memory. Tin Town was a makeshift shanty town on the outskirts of Coonamble at Warrena Creek. The dwellings were made mostly from materials discarded by the White townsfolk and landholders, 'scraps of timber, corrugated-iron sheets that structured the dwellings, with dirt floors and torn hessian bags for a door'.[64] It was a home for Aboriginal people from the early 1900s until the last family left Tin Town in 1978.[65]

Also in Coonamble's memory is the segregation of their movie theatre where Aboriginal people had to sit apart in the poorest seats. Not to be forgotten, until the 1970s, Aboriginal mothers were kept out of the wards and segregated to the hospital veranda to give birth.[66] Like many other rural towns, the medical neglect of Aboriginal mothers no doubt contributed to the high death rates of Aboriginal babies.[67] While the racism of segregation was in the past, other forms of racism and discrimination continued. The lack of employment of Aboriginal people made the gulf between White and Black communities highly visible. The derogatory term darkies, which was commonly used by White people to refer to the Aboriginal people, showed a continuing lack of respect for their Indigenous neighbours.

A typical house in a shanty town similar to Coonamble's Tin Town
© *West Australian Newspapers Limited*

My first personal experience of racism in Coonamble came from Mary, a senior Anglican church parishioner whom I had met at the Welcome to Coonamble dinner. We were chatting over a cup of tea, when Mary paused the flow of conversation, gave me a penetrating look and said, 'I need to let you know that Gail at the CDEP has changed her name.'

I knew from the way she spoke, she was implying that Gail was doing something wrong. I was caught off balance. Finally I said, 'I don't know about Gail's name. What's wrong with her changing her name?'

Mary looked slightly awkward. 'Well, um,' she started hesitantly, 'Aborigines change their names so they can get government money twice. She might not be doing this, but I thought I should warn you.'

It was a confronting moment for me. I had no idea about Gail's name change so I couldn't defend her. However, by not defending her, I felt as though I was betraying her. I felt angry with Mary for her racial stereotyping and prejudice, and for passing on this accusation. I was at a loss to know what to do. I said the only thing I could think of, 'Gail is on a wage, so it doesn't apply.'

I left Mary's house as soon as I could, thinking *If this is Mary's attitude, it doesn't bode well for Anglican support in this town.*

This thought proved true, for the CDEP received no active support from the Anglican minister or his parishioners during my time in Coonamble. My next encounter with racism was more disturbing. It occurred when I tried to rent a room for a CDEP women's sewing group above one of the shops in the main street. I had no luck with the first few shops so I was delighted when I received a positive answer at the newsagency.

'Yes we do have a suitable room for a sewing group,' the newsagent said. 'I'll take you upstairs and show you.'

He was right. It was a lovely room. It had good light, plenty of power points and the rent was reasonable. We agreed the CDEP would rent the room as soon as ATSIC had approved our grant application for sewing machines and overlockers.

As we came back down the stairs, the newsagent said he had heard that the CDEP was an employment program.

'Who are you employing and what is your role?' he asked.

I explained the program was for Aboriginal people and I was the CDEP coordinator. I told him that many people were interested in joining the program and it was very successful. In my naivety, I had anticipated my information would be greeted with smiles and congratulations. Not so! He turned to me and said abruptly, 'I'm sorry you can't have the room. I didn't know it was for Aboriginal women. I won't rent to them.' I was shocked but managed to stay polite as I asked him why.

'I'll show you.' He took me out the back of the shop where there was a small derelict house.

'Just look at this! They break into the backyard to drink, do drugs and other disgusting things. And I know they are Aborigines because they have graffitied their names all over the walls.'

'Do you know these people?' I asked, pointing to the names.

'They're kids,' he said. 'They are always getting into trouble.'

By this time his wife had joined us. When he told her what had happened, she remained quiet but looked sympathetic. I decided to point out the obvious.

'That little building is certainly an awful mess. But you know who did it.

I'm trying to rent a room for a sewing program. A room for women, for mothers. They are not the people who vandalised your building.'

The newsagent looked uncomfortable for a moment but responded with a hardening attitude. 'I'm not going to rent a room to them, and you're wasting your time with them!'

We stood there silently looking at each other. It was his wife who broke the silence of that awful moment.

'It's her life's work, Jim, you mustn't say that to her.'

There was nothing more that I could say. I turned away from him and went out into the street. Hot tears of anger scalded my eyes. I felt ashamed to be of the same Anglo ancestry as the newsagent. Because of my White colour, I was associated with the callous racism and prejudice handed out to Aboriginal people by this town and by much of Australia. I was so overcome by shame at the racism, that I didn't tell Gail or anyone at the CDEP what had happened. I hid it.

A few weeks later, during a conversation about retailers in the main street, I blurted out that the newsagent was a racist. Gail swung round and stared at me.

'What do you know about him. What have you heard?'

I'm not one to think quickly on my feet, so I had to confess that I hid the newsagent's racism because I was too ashamed to tell anyone. My goodness I got the rounds of the kitchen table for that. Gail reported me to the committee and I was heartily condemned for hiding what was properly Aboriginal business and told I must never do it again.

'How you feel doesn't matter. It's about us!' I was told. 'It's our right to know what is being said about us.'

You can be sure I learned my lesson and I reported back every racist incident that I came across.

My most profound learning occurred when the arrow of racism was shot straight at me. I was told an Aboriginal person at the land council had called me the 'White cunt' at the CDEP. The arrow hit deep inside and it hurt. Being called the c-word was bad enough, but the label White left me impotent. I couldn't become Black. This was my first experience of racism directed at me. Compared to what Aboriginal people suffer repeatedly, it was nothing. When I recovered from the shock, I realised the racist insult was actually a gift. It had given me a small insight into knowing and feeling a racist slur.

As a White woman and outsider to the town, I had no idea of the day-to-day racism that Aboriginal people were subjected to. When I did my shopping in Coonamble I found the retail staff friendly, helpful and happy to have a casual chat. Gail and I took turns buying the CDEP groceries, cleaning equipment and office supplies at a local supermarket, just a few minutes' walk away. The manager didn't speak very good English but she always said hello to me, and from time to time we exchanged pleasantries. I assumed it was the same for Gail. Not so!

We had shopped at that supermarket for many months when Gail burst into the CDEP office, announcing, 'You'll never guess what just happened! The supermarket manager said hello to me for the first time.'

I could hardly believe my ears. 'Are you serious? She has never greeted you before today?'

'Not once,' Gail said emphatically. 'I guess the changes the CDEP is making in town must have got through to her.'

The supermarket had been happy to take Aboriginal money, but that didn't translate into respect for their Aboriginal customers.

It was the same at the pharmacy which did very well financially from its Aboriginal customers. Yet, when Aboriginal people paid for their purchases and put their hand out for their change, the staff ignored their outstretched hand and put the money on the counter.

The supermarket's change of attitude towards Gail came at around the same time that two of our female participants noticed a change at the pharmacy. The chemist's staff had begun to put the change directly into their hands. The arrival of common courtesy in shops was like a signpost of change. It confirmed my feeling of hope that the CDEP was starting to make a difference in the lives of the Aboriginal community.

Although racism was commonplace, there was also goodwill, fairness and acceptance. From the beginning of the CDEP, it was the active support of the shire council that helped the program to become successful. Local government is the democratic sphere closest to the community and the shire councillors represented both townies and cockies. The votes by the councillors to support the CDEP gave a 'fair go' and employment to the Aboriginal community. I took it that their supportive stand must have been acceptable to their constituents.

Having the backing of Bede Waterford and St Vincent De Paul gave Gail and me, as coordinators of the CDEP, confidence and a sense of security. We knew we could always go to Bede for help and advice if we needed it. The support of Vinnies was a vote of confidence in the Aboriginal community and it set an example for the town to follow. The organisation provided us with work when it could, and so did the older folk associated with Vinnies. This work helped the CDEP to keep the participants meaningfully employed as well as being financially useful.

There was also acceptance from many other townsfolk. I had been struck by the companionable atmosphere at the bingo where skin colour and family background appeared to play no part at the bingo tables. Indeed, if bingo was the only thing I had known about Coonamble, I would have said it was *not* a racist town.

The goodwill also came into my office. One day as I was tapping away on the computer, a kindly-looking chap asked to come in. He introduced himself as Jim.

'I've come to thank you for a wonderful thing,' he said. 'The CDEP boys were in my street yesterday tree lopping and they were singing and laughing together while they worked. It was one of the nicest sounds I've ever heard in Coonamble and what they are doing is a credit to them.'

With that, he tipped his hat to me and headed back out the door. A smile stayed on my face for a long time as I thought over what he had said. For this man, the Aboriginal people were not 'just darkies'. Through their joy to be working together, the humanness of the work team had shone through and captivated the old chap. It was these precious moments that changed people's perceptions.

Jim wasn't the only friendly face to pop into the CDEP. Wal McKenzie was a lanky Aussie in his retirement years. His open friendly smile was matched by the twinkle in his blue eyes. Wal and I had several little chats, which somehow always turned to the card game bridge. I had been a fanatical 500 player in my younger days and boasted to Wal that I was known for my cutthroat bids.

'Bridge is similar to 500,' Wal said, 'but the bidding is much more interesting. I reckon you'd like it.'

On his next visit, Wal informed me, 'I'm putting a four together for bridge and I'm looking for new players. I reckon you'd be good so why don't you come along?'

The idea of learning to play bridge tickled my fancy, and I liked the idea of meeting more locals. My bridge partners were Stella, who worked at the hospital, and Geoff, who was a sheep farmer.

Wal and Joan McKenzie's home was the first non-Aboriginal home I had been invited to. Joan McKenzie was the local historian who wrote the biography *Just Lovely*. It was about the life of Aboriginal woman Aunty Jean Hamilton who received the Coonamble Citizen of the Year Award in 1984. Aunty Jean had grown up with her family in the Pilliga but moved to Coonamble during the war years. She told Joan McKenzie that there were very few Aboriginal people living in Coonamble at that time. Many families preferred to live together at Tin Town.

Getting to know Wal, Joan, Stella and Geoff gave me insight into the Coonamble life of White people that I hadn't previously experienced. From Geoff I learned what a tough time it was for sheep farmers. The wool price had crashed as markets in Russia and China evaporated. This was closely followed by a further wool-price crash when the government lifted the reserve price. Our bridge games gave Geoff respite from his frightful task of shooting and burying his sheep. We all felt his pain and sorrow and kept the game light and friendly.

From my perspective, goodwill, racism, townies and cockies were distinct features of the town that I could readily grasp. However, there were other layers and divisions in the town that I had little idea about. Fortunately, I had got to know Gloria when she opened a small and friendly café next to the CDEP. She was a motherly woman whose beaming personality was an automatic drawcard to passers-by. The café was a boon for Gail and me as we could pop in for a quick coffee and a sandwich whenever our stomachs, or stress from work, demanded.

One quiet afternoon, I ducked in for a cuppa and a sandwich and found Gloria with a bit of time on her hands. I was keen to collect information about the town and this was the opportunity I had been waiting for.

'How are you liking Coonamble?' Gloria enquired in her friendly manner. 'I saw you out for a walk the other day with a couple of ladies, so it looks like you've settled in okay.'

'Oh yes, I walk every week with Margaret and Brenda. It's good for the health, and it helps me to feel as though I live here, and I'm not just an outsider.'

'It's always difficult fitting into a country town,' Gloria said, nodding her head in agreement. 'The Johnny-come-latelies can find it hard to fit in when they only meet people from their workplace. If that happens, they might not get to know the town at all.'

'Johnny-come-latelies? Is that what I am?' I laughed.

'Newcomers to the town are often referred to as 'blow-ins' but I reckon that sounds like a piece of litter being blown around. I call them Johnny-come-latelies. It's got a better tone to it I reckon.'

'Who are all the Johnny-come-latelies? Where do they work?' I queried.

'For a start, most of the schoolteachers, some of the nurses, the bank managers, a couple of the business managers. Altogether there are quite a few. The teachers and nurses are good for the cockies' sons as they get a steady supply of nice young ladies and there have been a few weddings out of it.'

'How long have you lived here Gloria?'

'It'd be about twenty years I suppose, but that doesn't make me a local,' she grinned. 'You have to be born here to be a local. We outsiders all joke about it. You can raise your kids here and join in with the community. But at the end of the day, a born-and-bred local will see you as someone from outside.'

There were no customers in the café so I decided to dig a little deeper asking, 'How does this town work?'

'Aah, that's a good question. There is more to see here than meets the eye, lots of layers. You've got the cockies and townies and mostly they divide into Rugby versus League footy. You've got the business people and the workers, the Catholics and the Protestants. Then there's those that go to the bowling club and those who go to the golf club or RSL. There's the kids who went to the local high school and the boarding-school kids. And of course, there's the Aboriginal and non-Aboriginal folk.'

So many layers, I thought. *No wonder I'm having trouble working out who's who.* This brought me to my next question.

'Who do you think is the most influential person in the town?' I asked.

'Aah, that's a good question too.' Gloria thought for a few moments, then she replied, 'It would have to be Bede Waterford.'

I nodded my head slowly, thinking back to our conversations with Bede. He was a great support for us and I was very pleased to hear that he was so influential.

A couple of customers breezed into the café and Gloria dashed over to welcome them and sit them down at a good table. As I finished my cup of tea and sandwich I thought about how I fitted into the town. I realised I was similar to the business people who mainly associated with their work colleagues. The RSL was my main club where Gail and I uproariously enjoyed gambling away a few dollars playing card poker. I definitely belonged more to the Aboriginal group despite being a White person. My empty cup and plate said 'time to get back to work' so I got up to leave.

'Thanks so much for the chat, Gloria. You've helped me heaps.'

'Anytime,' she smiled. 'Pop in anytime. Bye for now.'

Gloria's description of the layers and divisions of the town gave me much to ponder. Apart from bingo, I had noticed very few situations where Aboriginal and non-Aboriginal people mixed as one group. At the footy there were groups of Aboriginal supporters and groups of non-Aboriginal supporters. At the clubs or pubs, the Aboriginal people laughed and joked together separate from the non-Aboriginal people. Individuals in the groups might cross the divide to say hello and pass some idle chitchat, but they would then drift back to their own group. Black and White lived in the town together, their cultures touched at the sides but they didn't stay connected. They disengaged and drifted apart.

My counterpart Gail made friendships at school with her non-Aboriginal classmates. On occasions when I was with her at the Chinese restaurant or at a club, Gail would stop and chat with her old White school chums and introduce me to the group. There was no invitation for us to join their group. We would keep moving.

It was the layers that Gloria spoke of. The Aboriginal people lived in one layer and the non-Aboriginal people lived in another layer. The layers might bump into each other at footy matches, the bowling club or RSL, or at major events such as the Coonamble Show or Rodeo, but for the most part, the layers co-existed without connection.

Gloria's description of Johnny-come-latelies brought home to me how much of an outsider I was in Coonamble. I wasn't a born-and-bred country girl and I didn't even come from New South Wales. I wasn't one of the usual Johnny-come-latelies with the backing of the major employers such as the council, schools, hospitals or bank. Although I worked for an Aboriginal organisation, I was an outsider to the Aboriginal community. Working for an Aboriginal organisation also set me apart from other White employees in the town. Quite simply, I didn't fit with either the White or Black communities.

Being an outsider is uncomfortable. Like most of the human race, I needed to feel like I belonged, that I fitted in. Even my clothing looked out of place in Coonamble. I couldn't change my circumstances, but I could change the way I looked. My clothing was more suited to the city of Melbourne than the hot, dry streets of Coonamble. As well as that, I worked with people who lived on unemployment benefits, and their clothing reflected their circumstances. I checked out the shops in the main street but the clothes were not cheap and they were a bit conservative and countrified for my taste. I found the perfect shop just down the road from the CDEP – the local op shop. It became my go-to clothing shop. If I couldn't find what I wanted, I would put an order in with the op-shop ladies. They'd keep a lookout for the garments I wanted and put them aside for me. One time I needed an outfit to go to the theatre on my next trip to Sydney. The op-shop ladies found me a selection of three outfits. Their service couldn't be beaten!

To fit in with my work colleagues and rural New South Wales, I also had to change the way I spoke. In the early days of the CDEP, I was interviewed by Bourke radio about my job and what was happening with the new CDEP in Coonamble. When I listened to the playback, I heard my citified Melbourne vowels sounding stuck-up and posh.

That Melbourne sound has got to go, I thought. *I need to sound more local.*

I attuned my ear to the way people spoke around me and gradually I learned to let go and relax into the Coonamble way of speaking – slower, broader, with flatter vowels. I even learned to say 'youse' and value its usefulness as a plural. I knew I had made the change when I heard myself asking at lunchtime, 'Are youse coming for a feed?' It was a victory for my new way of speaking.

New names to learn

One thing I was quite uncertain about was, what should I call Aboriginal people? When I worked at Papunya in the Northern Territory, it was common for both Aboriginal and non-Aboriginal people to use the terms 'Whitefellas' and 'Blackfellas' in a friendly way. I hadn't heard those terms at all in Coonamble, only the derogatory 'darkies'. Gail and I were alone in the office so I took the opportunity to ask her what I should call Aboriginal people here in town.

She said, 'We don't like being called Aborigines or Blackfellas. You can call us Aboriginal people.'

At that point, Gail's cousin from Sydney turned up. Gail brought her into the conversation asking, 'What do you think Barb should call us?'

Her cousin replied, 'She can call us Murris. Melbourne people are Kooris, but here in Coonamble we are Murris because we're pretty much in north-western New South Wales.'

I had never heard of Murris or Kooris before so I decided to stick to saying Aboriginal people.

There were new words to learn as well, like the term 'Gubba'. I had overheard Aboriginal people referring to me as a Gubba. I was puzzled about it and eventually asked Gail what it meant. She looked a little embarrassed as she explained that Aboriginal people call all White people Gubbas and that it came from the word government. She went on to say that in the past, Aboriginal people would call out 'Gubbamen' when officers were coming to take their children away or do something bad to the community. My face must have shown how uncomfortable I felt being classified as a Gubba, but Gail quickly assured me that it didn't mean anything bad now, it just meant White people.

Thank goodness for that, I thought.

The funniest new term I learned was 'Old Mate'. I heard Old Mate being referred to constantly in conversations around me. Someone saw Old Mate down the street. Another person heard Old Mate say this or that. Old Mate seemed to be everywhere. My curiosity mounted until I was forced to ask Gail.

'I keep hearing about Old Mate. Who is he, Gail ? Do I know him?'

Gail looked at me strangely and said, 'Are you asking me who Old Mate is?'

'Yes, that's right,' I answered.

Gail laughed and laughed until tears rolled down her cheeks. She called out to the other people in the office. 'Barb's heard us talking about Old Mate and she wants to know who Old Mate is!'

They all started laughing. It was the hugest joke for everyone except me. I stood there feeling like an absolute dill, not having the vaguest notion of what was causing the hilarity.

When the laughter died down, Gail explained. 'Calling someone 'Old Mate' is like saying 'what's-his-name' or 'thinga-me-bob' when you can't remember their name.'

I started to laugh too. It was very funny. From then on, I listened out for 'Old Mate' and sure enough, he really was everywhere, in Coonamble, in Coonabarabran, all over. He was a New South Wales icon.

Being an outsider had both advantages and disadvantages. One of the advantages was not knowing about past histories or events. I was able to take people at face value. As I got to know the town better, I was relieved that I didn't know the racist attitudes and stereotyping held by some people. Ignorance is bliss, as they say.

Another advantage was not being expected to conform or agree with pre-existing points of view. I formed and held my own opinions by listening and observing. In research terms I was a 'participant observer'. I participated in everyday life in Coonamble as I worked closely with the Aboriginal community. Yet I was an outsider, observing the interactions and attitudes. I joined in, but I was separate.

On a personal note, a huge downside to being an outsider is loneliness. I had prepared myself bringing videos, books and music, but they are no substitute for friends and a social life. Without Gail's friendship and her great sense of fun, life in Coonamble would have been unbearably lonely. She was an open-hearted and friendly woman and I enjoyed her company enormously, and was very grateful for it. In country towns where the population is stable, people form satisfying friendships groups and don't need or want more friends. I was fortunate that Gail understood what it felt like to be an outsider in Coonamble. She was a Queenslander from Dirranbandi, 300 kilometres north of Coonamble, not a born-and-bred local.

Coonamble Court House

As an outsider, certain situations that were taken for granted by the local population were a great shock to me. One of these was the divide between White and Black at the courthouse, where many Aboriginal people found themselves at the intersection of the police, law and the legal system.

Joanne, one of our new female participants, asked me to read a legal letter she had received. The letter told her to appear at the Court House and make an appointment to see the clerk. Apparently, when Joanne was in Sydney with her mates, they walked across a railway line at an unauthorised crossing. Unfortunately, they were seen by the police who gave them a hard time and issued them with fines. The girls had had a drink or two and let fly at the police with a few choice words. The police then booked them for using foul language and being drunk in a public place – a total of three charges. Joanne was very afraid of being sent to jail for her unpaid fines. This had been a relatively common occurrence in the recent past in New South Wales.

I had never previously been in a courthouse, let alone Coonamble's, but Gail, who had done a traineeship there, gave us instructions about where to go and what to do. The courthouse was only a short walk down the road so Joanne and I set off on foot. It was an imposing brick building with no windows. It's design looked more suitable for Norway in the winter than sun-baked Coonamble. Thank goodness it was air conditioned and cool inside. Joanne showed a staff member her letter and we were directed to an imposing counter. A rather snooty woman informed Joanne that she had unpaid fines from her Sydney railway crossing adventure. The encounter was starting to look uncomfortable for Joanne so I intervened and told the woman that Joanne was working at the CDEP and we would help her to have the fines paid off. Things became much more pleasant after that and Joanne was no longer in fear of being locked up. It took her a while, but with the CDEP deduction system, Joanne paid off all those fines.

Police station and courthouse in Coonamble, New South Wales
Mattinbgn, Wikimedia Commons

My next encounter with the courthouse was being asked to appear as a referee for Benny, one of our new CDEP participants. Benny was a small, intense young man. I didn't know him well and I felt slightly nervous about speaking on his behalf as he was facing a serious charge. However, I was more than willing to do what I could to keep him out of Bathurst or Long Bay jail.

On the day of his case hearing, I walked down the road to the courthouse as I had done with Joanne. I was surprised to see so many people milling about outside as it was a very hot day. The courthouse had been empty on the day Joanne and I went there, so I was completely unprepared for what I would see. The waiting area was full of people and almost all of them were Aboriginal. Coonamble was a White rural town, but here in the courthouse, it was a Black town. I felt like I had crossed over into apartheid. I was completely disoriented. I had witnessed this sort of situation in the Northern Territory, but it was the last thing I expected to see in Coonamble. I thought the courthouse would be representative of the town, but instead the Black and White divide was confronting me.

I don't remember how I lifted my feet as they felt frozen to the spot. I wanted to turn around and walk out of the courthouse and leave Coonamble, but I couldn't. Instead, I pulled myself together and found the legal-aid lawyer on duty. He told me what I had to do and where I should wait until I was called. As I sat there waiting, I felt completely alone in my shame of being part of this structural display of racism.

Finally I was called. It was the first time I had ever been in a working courtroom. It was a bizarre and surreal sight for me. Here in Coonamble, in the heat, dust and ordinariness of this boring little town, was a formal court setting with the robed magistrate and lawyers in suits. Outside, people were going about their normal business, yarning, drinking in the pubs and shopping. Here, inside the court, we were in another land. The land of law and justice. Justice?

Benny was convicted of the crime of sexual assault. My role, as his employer, was to present his record at work. According to the legal-aid solicitor, it would be touch and go whether Benny would be sent to Long Bay Jail.

I stood in the box and swore that I would tell the truth. The lawyers then questioned me.

'Do you understand the charges against Benny?'

'Yes, I do.'

'Can you tell us about Benny's behaviour at the CDEP?'

Although I didn't know Benny well, I was able to speak favourably about him being punctual and a valued crew member. I was the only person advocating on his behalf. I felt despairing for Benny, and other Aboriginal people who had no one to speak on their behalf at the court. Despite my efforts and those of the legal-aid solicitor, Benny was sent to jail. I felt disappointed and sad for him.

Benny's mother came into the CDEP office about two weeks later. She was a small, shy woman and I could see from her features that she was Benny's mother. I gave her a cup of tea and we sat down together. She was very grateful that I helped her son even though he was put in jail. I promised her that we would employ him again when he got out of jail. Many months later when Benny reappeared in town, we put him back on the CDEP, but it was no good. He couldn't fit in any more. I think his jail experience damaged him badly. Not that I was any expert, but I had noticed that men who had done time in the Walgett lock-up seemed to be okay when they got out, but not when they had been sent to Long Bay. It was the same for a couple of young boys who were sent to juvenile detention. They were hardened when they came back to town and wouldn't join the CDEP.

Over the next months, I became a frequent visitor to the courthouse either as a character witness or helping CDEP participants sort out their fines. The beneficial effect of the CDEP became well known to the magistrate and lawyers. Eventually, the need for my help diminished, until finally, I never had to appear again. The CDEP participants were staying out of trouble.

Not long after my first encounter with court day, Nick the new Coonamble Uniting Church minister, popped into the CDEP to introduce himself. He was a pleasant man, married with primary-school-aged children and keen to learn about the town. He was interested in the CDEP and asked quite a few questions about the type of work we did and how many Aboriginal people were involved. After that initial conversation, Nick dropped in regularly to say hello. I was most surprised when, during one of his visits, Nick confessed to me that he was troubled by his racism. He was keen to find a way for the Uniting Church and the CDEP to work together to overcome the embedded racism in himself and the town. His honesty and self-awareness were admirable and I promised to pass on any ideas he had for working cooperatively with the CDEP to our committee and workers.

It didn't take Nick long to return with a great idea – starting up a courthouse café with the Uniting Church and CDEP women working alongside each other to provide free tea and coffee to people attending court. Courthouse cafés in other New South Wales towns were very popular with both Aboriginal and non-Aboriginal people. In the alien environment of the courthouse, I could well imagine the positive difference friendly ladies dispensing free tea and coffee would make to people waiting for their cases to be heard.

I put the idea to Gail and we called a meeting of CDEP women. Initially they felt nervous about working with White women and said they needed time to think about it. Keen for the idea to succeed, Gail and I put our heads together. When we had worked out how the café would operate, we were able to persuade the women to have a go. The plan was that the CDEP women would ask waiting Aboriginal people if they wanted tea or coffee, and hand them the drink, while the Uniting Church women would ask White people. The church would provide the cups, coffee, tea and sugar and the CDEP would provide the urn and the milk. The courthouse would supply the tables. The Uniting Church negotiated the details with the courthouse and the Courthouse Café was given the green light for the monthly circuit.

The first café day arrived. Gail and I walked over to the courthouse with the CDEP ladies to meet the Uniting Church women. Everyone was feeling nervous. With Gail directing operations, it was not long before the café was set up and the customers were queueing for their tea and coffee. As soon as the women saw their happy customers, everyone relaxed and enjoyed themselves.

Most court days, I would go to the café to enjoy a coffee with the ladies and their customers. It was heartwarming to stand sipping a coffee and chatting with Aboriginal and non-Aboriginal courthouse customers. It felt like a miracle. Because Nick had acknowledged his racism, the Courthouse Café had been born and it now united both cultures. If only this could be replicated in all parts of the town. The CDEP and Uniting Church joint venture lasted for a year. It was a credit to the women from the CDEP and the Uniting Church for crossing the racial barrier and providing a much needed service to the courthouse.

The success of the Courthouse Café led to another CDEP undertaking. One of Gail's friends told her that the hospital was short of volunteers to deliver the weekly Meals on Wheels. Gail was inspired to become one of the volunteers and she persuaded two other CDEP women to share the duties with her. This was another first. Aboriginal people volunteering to deliver Meals on Wheels to White folk. It was an inspiring turnaround.

10 Woodwork, the Warrumbungles and art

From my first week in Coonamble, I had been writing regularly to my father, Bill. Bill had left Ali Curung a few years back and since then had roamed around working on cattle stations in outback Queensland and the Northern Territory. My letters describing Coonamble, the CDEP and the lives of Aboriginal people in this part of the world intrigued Bill and persuaded him to drive south to pay me a visit. I was overjoyed as my father was always great fun, ready for a chat and a laugh, day or night. He was also the perfect 'ear' for me to share my ideas and frustrations.

Bill decided to make Coonamble his base while he explored the Pilliga Forest, the Warrumbungles, Lightning Ridge and even out to Bourke. Bill had brought his woodworking equipment with him and found a cheap shed to rent. In between trips he would do a bit of woodworking on the side. The CDEP participants thought it was great my father was visiting me and were most interested to learn that he was a wood-turner, furniture maker, carpenter and builder. When it came to timber, there wasn't much that Bill couldn't turn his hand to.

When some of the participants approached him to teach them about woodwork, Bill was delighted. A couple of men wanted storage boxes so we scrounged offcuts and leftover materials and work started. With Bill guiding them, they did a great job and word spread. Some families brought broken furniture to the workshop for repair. Again word spread, the CDEP could fix broken furniture. Dog kennels came next followed by kids toys. As well as learning the practical skills of using electrical equipment such as saws, drills and planers, Bill taught them maths skills essential for measuring accurately as well as an understanding of angles.

Bill's part-time woodworking gradually became full-time. A small hobby became a CDEP program. The CDEP had been paying for the woodwork equipment from our income stream of council and gardening jobs, but this was not sustainable in the long term. A large shed was rented and successful ATSIC grants enabled woodworking equipment to be purchased.

There wasn't much Bill Jackson didn't know about woodworking. He helped develop the CDEP woodworking business and the men gained a high level of valuable skills.
Jackson collection, 1990

The men loved Old Bill and they were proud to be part of the woodwork team. The CDEP had been offered cypress pine timber free of charge from a Pilliga sawmill. This enabled Bill to expand his training program. Bill liked to boast that he'd been in the timber game for forty years and still had all his fingers. He was obsessed by safety and spent hours designing, fabricating and fitting safety features to the saws. During his time, there was not one accident. No one got cut or hurt in any way. He made sure that the men he worked with kept their fingers.

THE CDEP blokes loved working with Bill. He had a great rapport with the team. *Jackson collection, 1990*

The quality of the woodwork was improving every week and a few dog kennels and storage boxes had been sold. This encouraged Bill to consider developing timber products that could be sold as a CDEP business. His two main products were children's stick hobbyhorses and cutting boards. The hobbyhorses were cute with painted eyes, a rope rein and felt mane. The cutting boards should have been easy but Bill discovered that cypress pine was difficult to dry out properly and was prone to warping. To stabilise it, he decided to intersperse strips of cypress pine with another timber. This meant cutting thin lengths of timber, then matching and gluing them together. It made beautiful-looking cutting boards that were definitely good enough to sell.

The CDEP participants were growing in confidence as they mastered new skills and earned a good reputation around town. No longer were they dole bludgers. They were working for their money and developing skills in woodwork, council work and yard maintenance. One afternoon at the end of the work day, a bunch of CDEP workers piled off the bus and came into the office roaring with laughter. They told me the story. As they were driving along in the bus, they spotted a few young unemployed White blokes who had bad-mouthed them in the past for being dole bludgers. That afternoon the tables were turned! The CDEP lads stuck their heads out of the van windows and yelled at them.

'Lazy White dole bludgers!' What a great turnaround!

Bill loved a beer, and at least once a week Gail and I would join him at the Commercial Hotel after work. We would perch on our favourite bar stools and compete telling our funniest stories. When Rhonda, the funniest woman on the CDEP, joined us, we were told that our roars of laughter could be heard from the other end of Castlereagh Street. As well as Rhonda's storytelling ability, she added the actions. She would have made a great stand-up comedian.

After working on Aboriginal communities in the Northern Territory, it was a very different experience for Bill to work with the Aboriginal people of Coonamble.

Bill and I were having a counter meal by ourselves at the pub one evening and he was unaccountably quiet.

'Are you okay, Bill?' I asked. 'You're very quiet tonight.'

He nodded, 'Yeah, well, I'm having trouble working out these Aborigines here in Coonamble. They're not proper Aborigines! Not like in the Northern Territory.'

'Bill! How can you say that? Of course they are. They wouldn't have joined the CDEP if they weren't Aboriginal.'

'I'm trying to think it through, Barb. You know as well as I do, that some of your CDEP participants have got fair hair and blue eyes. How can they be Aboriginal?'

Although I had heard many variations of this theme, I was surprised to hear it from my father, but I realised that, as well as being a product of his time, Bill had lived with Central Australian Aboriginal people for many years, people with a very different history and colonial experience. To my mind, the variations of who is Aboriginal, all boiled down to one simple point, which I shared with Bill. 'Who has the rights and responsibilities of determining Aboriginality? Is it the non-Aboriginal outsider? Or the person who identifies as Aboriginal and knows where they come from and who their relatives are?'

Bill acknowledged the justice of this, so I pressed my argument further.

'Remember the story I wrote you about Rhonda meeting the young fair-skinned Aboriginal girl in Tamworth who was passing as a White person? Rhonda told her the truth. When you are Aboriginal, you are Black. It doesn't matter what you look like or what your skin colour is. It's your family. It's even more so in a small town like Coonamble rather than Tamworth. The Coonamble townies and cockies know the Aboriginal families. They know their family names. So even if they have blue eyes and blonde hair, they are Aboriginal.'

All this White preoccupation with denying Aboriginal people their own identity because they didn't look sufficiently Black drove me nuts. Being able to have a conversation like this with Bill was a testimony to our friendship. He was a man with a strong sense of justice and I hoped being in Coonamble would help him to understand the layers of complexity for Aboriginal people in this part of Australia.

My friend Heather arrives

In the days before mobile phones and emails, long-distance communication took place via letters or cheap telephone calls after 6 pm. As well as corresponding with Bill, I also wrote to my relatives and friends. I invariably added a PS invitation to come and stay with me. It was a happy day for me when my friend Heather from Bendigo decided to take up my invitation to visit. Instead of driving, she undertook a marathon twenty-hour bus journey from Bendigo through Shepparton, Cootamundra and Dubbo, then onto Coonamble. What a pal! It was wonderful to see her smiling face as she climbed down the steps of the bus dressed in her usual t-shirt and jeans.

'I could have flown to Los Angeles in less time than it took coming to Coonamble!' She greeted me with a laugh.

Heather was an open hearted, country girl who took to Coonamble like a duck to water. Inside my tiny flat, I turned on the fan, put the kettle on and showed her the single bed she would be sleeping on.

'I'm glad to see you've got a fan. I didn't expect it to be so hot in Coonamble,' she exclaimed.

'It's hot in summer and freezing cold in winter,' I replied. 'I nearly froze to death in the CDEP office my first winter here. The only heating we had was a frightful kerosene heater that stank to high heaven so we couldn't use it. I had to buy long johns, woollen gloves and a parka suitable for the snow! Then I was warm.' I laughed.

After a cup of tea, we drove back to the office so Heather could meet Gail and the women in the office. It was busy in the office as Gail was in her payroll clerk 'trainer' role preparing the wages for Thursday. It was an office highlight for Heather when Gail noticed one of the new workers struggling with her calculations about the days of the week. 'Okay, let's get back to basics,' Gail suggested. 'How many days are there in a week?'

To Heather's surprise, the answer promptly came back, 'There are eight days in a week! You know the Beatles song.'

We all laughed.

The next stop was the CDEP workshop for Heather to catch up with my father, Bill, whom she had met previously. Heather was mightily impressed with Bill's woodwork team, watching them as they measured, sawed, sanded and varnished a range of timber products. She declared the whole show impressive and an eye opener. For me, it was a heartwarming sight, watching Heather chatting away to Bill and the boys as she admired their work, and the boys laughing and joking and soaking up her praise.

The next morning I took Heather on my planned Coonamble 'walking-highlight' tour to take in historic buildings and the establishments I frequented. First on the list was the historic post office, constructed in 1881. Needless to say, Heather was not particularly impressed.

'Next,' she instructed.

'That would be the Commercial Hotel that was rebuilt in 1912.' I pointed across the road to the country-style pub with a veranda around it. 'We can have a drink there later if you're game.'

It was time to stroll down the main street to check the shops and look at the locals.

When we arrived at the Sons of the Soil Hotel, Heather was highly amused.

'Is that for real?' she exclaimed. 'How very earthy. My guess would be that farmers go to this pub. Is that right?'

The remaining tour highlight was the 7-kilometre levee bank. It was built in the 1970s to stop floodwaters from both Warrena Creek and the Castlereagh River. To keep fit, I had taken to jogging on the levee bank at dawn in the fresh, cool air. Heather agreed that the few metres in height of the levee bank gave a new perspective on the landscape of the Coonamble plains.

As luck would have it, there was a Rugby League footy match being played at Coonamble on Saturday. She couldn't believe she was going to a footy match between the Googars from Gulargambone and Coonamble Bears. For Heather it was a case of, 'Please pinch me, I must be dreaming. This is an Australia I didn't know existed.'

Sons of the Soil Hotel, Coonamble
Aussie Towns website

Heather and I are AFL followers so the Rugby League rules of scrums, tackling and tries went over our heads. Sitting on the bonnet of a car, and being accepted as part of the Aboriginal footy crowd, was what counted for Heather. The Googars won the match, which disappointed the Coonamble-ites, but it had been a great game.

At the footy, Heather got chatting with Lola, one of the CDEP participants she had previously met at the office. Lola suggested we get a small group together and go camping at the Warrumbungles. She had plenty of camping equipment and knew where to borrow some canvas tents. It was the long weekend, so we could drive to the Warrumbungles the next morning, camp overnight and head back to Coonamble on Monday morning. It was a great idea. In the end, eight of us went, including Lola, her husband, Keith, and stepson, Luke; Gail and one of her brothers; Tracker, Heather and me.

The land of the Warrumbungle National Park was previously home to the Kamilaroi, Wailwan and Wiradjuri people. In fact, the name Warrumbungle is an Aboriginal word from the Kamilaroi people, meaning 'crooked mountain'. Archaeological evidence suggests that Aboriginal people lived in the Warrumbungle Range for up to 17,000 years and there are caves in the ranges that contain hand stencils and engravings.[68]

The next morning, on the way to the Warrumbungles, we were somewhere near Gulargambone when Heather pointed. 'Look over there. That's weird! Do you see all those stumps in the paddock?'

I tooted the horn and the stumps suddenly turned into kangaroos when they put their heads up and looked at us driving by. There must have been twenty or thirty kangaroos in that paddock. We all laughed at Heather's stumps, but it was unusual to see so many kangaroos in one paddock, especially when we hadn't spotted any other kangaroos.

While Lola and Heather were busy chatting and setting up our camping area, Tracker headed off to climb one of the hills to find where his ancestors had camped in the past. He was joined by Gail and her brother, with me following behind. Tracker set a cracking pace and I was hard-pressed to keep up. After about thirty minutes, it dawned on me that I was an intruder and should not continue. Tracker was connecting with the past, and I wasn't part of that connection. It was a profound moment of realisation for me about the Aboriginal spirit in the land.

When I eventually returned to the camping area, Heather and the others were sitting on logs around a cheerful, crackling campfire. I joined them drinking a beer and enjoying the deepening dusk of the Warrumbungles. As I crawled into my sleeping bag later that night, Heather stayed at the campfire talking with sixteen-year-old Luke. Her heart went out to him as he told her that he didn't have a future, that he couldn't go anywhere because he wouldn't be accepted because he was Aboriginal. It was a conversation Heather never forgot.

The next morning was sunny, fresh and crisp. It was going to be a beautiful day. Lola was already up. She had stoked the fire and boiled the water for an early-morning cup of tea. We sat round the fire sipping our tea in companionable silence listening to the Warrumbungle birds.

Getting ready for a camp breakfast at the Warrumbungles
Cattanach collection, 1991

Tracker, Barbara and Luke looking over the Warrumbungles
Cattanach collection, 1991

Warrumbungles
Cattanach collection, 1991

'Time for ablutions, Heather. Come on, the bathroom and toilet block is over there,' I said waving in the direction. We gathered our toiletry bags and set off over the paddocks.

'Wait until we get back, we will pack up together,' Heather called out to Lola.

The water was icy so it was a quick hands and face wash. Although we were gone only twenty minutes or so, Lola had completely packed up the campsite.

'I can't believe it,' said Heather. 'How did you pack everything up so quickly? You should have waited.'

Lola smiled and said, 'I'm used to it.'

Having Heather stay with me in Coonamble had given me a real lift. I was sad to see her return to Bendigo, a town so very different to New South Wales country towns. Heather had loved the experience of being in an Aboriginal environment.

'I'll never forget my Coonamble holiday and being a part of the Aboriginal community,' she said. 'The people were so welcoming and friendly and we took each other for who we were. That was the best part.'

Art and craft

Several months previously, the Dubbo office of the Department of Education, Employment and Training had suggested the CDEP apply for a grant for an arts and crafts program. After a few weeks, we were delighted to receive notification of our success.

The company director was a highly experienced art coordinator who had been delivering art programs to Aboriginal communities throughout Queensland and New South Wales. She knew what to do and how to do it. Her name was Julie Verner and she was a friendly and confident woman in her thirties who was completely at home working with Aboriginal people. In fact, she loved it. The art program came in two parts – a short, introductory program which started the participants painting. If the CDEP agreed, a longer and more comprehensive program would follow. Part two of the program would include paper-making and linocuts as well as painting in water colour, oils and acrylic.

Women CDEP participants were at the front of the queue to sign onto the introductory program with around twenty-five participants signing up. It was incredibly pleasing to see our shabby workrooms turned into a large artist studio, with finished and half-finished paintings by our up-and-coming artists scattered around. Some of the artwork was very impressive, particularly as the CDEP artists hadn't painted since their schooldays. Julie told me that wherever she went, she had watched Aboriginal people painting creative, balanced and colourful works of art. Our Coonamble artists were 'naturals', Julie confirmed to us.

I was intrigued to notice quite a few of the paintings featured the White invasion of their lands. Some paintings depicted Captain Cook as a large, cruel man with Aboriginal people being shot by Captain Cook and his men. When I asked the artists about their paintings, they explained how Captain Cook went everywhere, hunting and killing Aboriginal people and taking over the land. Other paintings showed Aboriginal people being hunted across the New South Wales and Queensland landscape.

'There used to be a lot of Aboriginal people here, around Coonamble,' they said, 'but Captain Cook's men hunted them away. Some stayed though and ended up in Tin Town.'

There had never been a formal mission or reserve at Coonamble as there had been in Gulargambone, Walgett, Brewarrina and Bourke. However, until 1978 there were Aboriginal people living separately at Tin Town. Tin Town was in the DNA of Aboriginal history in Coonamble. It was their lived experience. As an outsider with a severe lack of historical knowledge of New South Wales, I struggled to understand the concept of Tin Town and the misery of a displaced people living on the margins of a comfortable, established town, disregarded by the White inhabitants.[69]

The paintings of the CDEP artists shone a light on the Aboriginal history of Coonamble and their interpretation of the White invasion of their land. They revealed the gulf between the Aboriginal and White perspectives that was so very evident in Coonamble in many other ways. Julie told me that she had seen Aboriginal interpretations of the Captain Cook story in other communities she had worked with. It was a powerful alternative story of invasion, vastly different to the mainstream, accepted, White Captain Cook story of settlement.

The arts and crafts introduction was very popular with the CDEP participants and the artists unanimously agreed to continue. It would be six weeks before the program would return, however, Julie made sure that our budding artists had enough supplies to continue painting. Although some interest did drop off, I was heartened to see the artists showing up every week until Julie returned.

This is Ted's powerful story about the invasion of Captain Cook. It depicts the Europeans travelling across the waves, White people coming to Australia, Aboriginal tribes and meeting places. Ted was a participant at the Coonamble CDEP.

11 Dark and light sides of Coonamble

With the arts and crafts program taking over the back rooms at the CDEP, we needed to find a permanent shed to store the smelly and dirty CDEP mowers, slashers and tools. It was a stroke of luck when we heard about a large shed available for rent not far from the main street. Despite it being run down, the supervisors decided the shed would be suitable for their needs. The CDEP supervisor, Frank, began arrangements to rent the shed.

Unbeknownst to us, a man called Frank Fish lived in the house next door to the shed. When Frank Fish heard 'the darkies' were going to rent the shed next to his house, he became apoplectic with rage. He repeatedly demanded of the shire that they rezone the shed land to prevent the CDEP from using it. The shire staff and councillors became worried about his health as his anger and frustration seemed to overwhelm him. Shire council management decided to approach the CDEP.

I received a call from the shire engineer asking me to come to his office. When I was seated, Jon very quietly and carefully told me of Frank Fish's vehement opposition to the CDEP renting the shed next door to his house. He said that the council was most concerned about Frank Fish's health.

'Mr Fish has no rights in this matter,' he explained. 'The CDEP is entitled to rent the shed. It's a free market and nothing to do with the council either. However, the council is concerned about the health of Mr Fish. Councillors and staff who know him, are afraid he might have a heart attack.'

'What do you want the CDEP to do?' I asked.

'We are asking the CDEP committee to please reconsider renting the shed.'

I put the council request top of the agenda for our scheduled committee meeting in two days' time. That afternoon, one of the local CDEP well-wishers who regularly popped in came to the office to have a word with me. He told me 'on the quiet', that rumours were going around town that Frank Fish had a gun and he was threatening to use it if the Aboriginal people rented the shed next to him.

It was a horrifying warning. I found it hard to believe that this level of visceral racial hatred could spew out in this small, normal-looking country town in New South Wales. It felt more like I was in an awful movie of lynchings and 'Strange Fruit' in the Deep South of the United States.

What were we going to do? A couple of committee members, including our president, Tracker, had come into the office.

'What about I phone Father Harry? Maybe Frank Fish is a Catholic. Even if he isn't, I reckon Father Harry will know him.'

The committee members agreed. I was relieved when Father Harry promptly answered his phone. I explained the situation and why I was calling. Then, finally, I put my question to him.

'Father Harry, what do you think Frank Fish will do? Do you think he is capable of shooting Aboriginal CDEP people?'

I waited for his answer with my heart in my mouth. There was a slight silence, then Father Harry cleared his throat, 'I don't know what Frank Fish would do, but I think that Frank Fish could do anything.'

A tremor of horror passed through me. I thanked him, put the phone down and repeated his words to the committee members. We looked at each other in silence as we felt the dark shadow of race hatred. Tracker made the first move as if to push the cloud away from us. He gazed at us, sadly shaking his head saying, 'I don't know what has got into that fella. I heard he had a "touch of the tarbrush" in him.' Tracker straightened his shoulders and said firmly, 'Well, we'll have to find another place – that's all.'

We widened our search to the industrial estate and fortunately found a better shed, larger and more functional. Over time, the malevolence of Frank Fish faded, but that moment remains etched in my memory.

The animosity towards Aboriginal people displayed by Frank Fish had a long history.[70] In the 1960s, the Coonamble townsfolk were split over whether land within the town should be made available to build houses for Aboriginal people. A group of local White people had formed an Aboriginal Welfare Association to assist Aboriginal families to attain secure housing. Members of the association included Bede Waterford, who was so very helpful to the CDEP nearly thirty years later, and his brother John. At that time, as well as being a solicitor, Bede owned the *Coonamble Times* newspaper. His brother was a grazier near Quambone, around 50 kilometres away.

In 1960, John Waterford quietly purchased three blocks of residential land in the town and informed the local council that the land would be transferred to the welfare association. When the town found out, 117 residents petitioned the council demanding the transfer be blocked. Frank Fish was an ALP alderman of the council at that time. He bitterly opposed the transfer of land on the grounds that 'the Aboriginal has yet to prove himself fit to live with the white man'. Another councillor insisted he 'would stop at nothing to stop Abos living among white people, [he] would even destroy their houses'. The Australian Workers Union who represented shearers, also strongly opposed the transfer saying, 'The Natives should be allowed to live well out of town'. Fortunately, there were people who supported the land transfer including the Country Women's Association, who insisted that 'our association makes no race, colour or creed distinction'.[71]

Eventually, widespread publicity of the fracas reached Sydney, forcing the Coonamble Council to hold a public meeting. On their way from Sydney to the meeting, journalists Helen Hambly and Cecil Holmes called into Tin Town at the junction of the Castlereagh River and Warrena Creek. Coming from the metropolis of Sydney, it must have been extraordinary for them to discover the makeshift Tin Town dwellings mostly made from flattened kerosene tins and bush timber with no electricity or water supply.[72] Upon enquiring, the journalists found out the Aboriginal people had not been invited to, or informed about, the meeting. As most of the Tin Town men were out working, Helen and Cecil invited six Aboriginal women to come to the meeting with them.

The first vote of the resolution to block the transfer of land was tied. At the second vote, Aboriginal woman Kathleen Boney spoke up, quietly saying, 'We do want to live in town, we do want our children to go to school, we do want to live in proper houses'. This time the Aboriginal women raised their hands to vote in favour of the land transfer and the motion was passed. Two years later when Helen Hambly returned to Coonamble, four Aboriginal families had houses built by the Aboriginal Welfare Board, but not Mrs Boney. As Hambly said, 'She never got a house. How dare she speak up and want something?'[73]

Before the 1970s, it could have been said that Coonamble was a divided town, with many Aboriginal families relegated to living in Tin Town at Warrena Creek. From the early 1970s, coincidently occurring with the progressive policies of the Whitlam government, racial segregation began to be overturned with a 'pepper pot' housing policy being introduced in Coonamble. The aim of the policy was to assimilate Aboriginal people by surrounding each Aboriginal family with White neighbours. As historian

Heather Goodall commented, 'the constant scrutiny and judgement from their neighbours must have been very stressful for the assimilating families'.[74]

With Aboriginal and non-Aboriginal families living as neighbours throughout the town, outward appearances indicated that racial antagonism was a thing of the past. But for Frank Fish, his extreme racism was unceasing.

The CDEP did not dwell on the ill will of Frank Fish. Instead they turned to the creativity of the arts and crafts program, woodworking and providing services to the town. With the mowers, brushcutters, assorted tools and cans of mower petrol moved out of the back rooms of the office to the new shed, the space was ample for the arts and crafts program.

With the return of Julie's arts and crafts program to Coonamble, the CDEP art students had transformed the back room into an art studio with their works of art in acrylic and oils, intricate linocut prints and handcrafted paper. The creativity and talent of the artists was clearly visible. In addition to works of art, a major part of the program was to create a lasting legacy for the Coonamble CDEP. Julie suggested that the CDEP be given a special name chosen by all the participants. The newly-named CDEP would be officially launched at an art exhibition. Julie provided us with a dictionary of Aboriginal words. Over the next ten days, the words were studied and debated by the CDEP until *Ellimatta* meaning 'our home' was unanimously chosen.

The linocut artists had the task of designing and printing the Ellimatta logo. The men were in charge of painting the interior of the office and back rooms. One of Julie's artist-workers erected scaffolding in front of the office. He then painted the linocut logo and our new name, Ellimatta, on the fascia of the shop front. He also painted trees around the windows. The Ellimatta design was huge and eye-catching. Coonamble was abuzz with the activity at the CDEP.

In the weeks leading up to the exhibition, Julie took us through the preparations. Deciding on the food was the easy part. It was drinks that gave the committee and participants much to think about. Everyone wanted the format of the art exhibition to be similar to regional or city art exhibitions with tasty nibbles, wine, beer and soft drink. Some of the participants, knowing their own drinking habits, were most reluctant to let this happen. The thought of someone getting drunk and spoiling the evening was too awful to think about. After much debate, the committee decided on a three drink limit for everyone, Aboriginal or non-Aboriginal. The plan was, when the guests came in, they would be given three raffle tickets to exchange for drinks. I was enormously impressed, in awe actually, when three of the participants who openly acknowledged their problem with drink, made the decision not to come to the exhibition at all. There was no way they would disgrace the CDEP.

The official opening of Ellimatta CDEP and the Arts and Crafts Exhibition was held on 2 April 1991. It was a 'glittering' evening. CDEP participants in their best clothes served nibbles and finger food to well-dressed townsfolk, who exchanged their raffle tickets for glasses of wine.

CDEP artists were excited and delighted to see the guests buying their paintings, handmade paper and linocut prints. The woodwork team saw their cutting boards and children's hobbyhorses sell as well as a coffee table. It was a wonderful moment for me, when I caught sight of one of the artists staring wide-eyed at the magistrate from the courthouse buying her painting for $90.

'He's a judge! He must be mad!,' she exclaimed.

'No, he just knows good art,' I replied, and her grin of sheer delight spread from ear to ear.

Committee President Tracker Robinson made the official welcome and opening speech. He described how the CDEP had given Aboriginal people in the town something to do, that they were learning new skills and were very, very proud of their CDEP. The clapping and cheering that followed his talk raised the roof.

It was reported in the local paper that 'the once dull building across from the Post Office has been [sic] risen from the doom and gloom and revitalised'. The article continued saying that the status of the CDEP 'has been accepted by all, as was witnessed by the huge roll-up of business men and women and members of the community that turned out to view the opening'. Ellimatta had arrived!

After the guests left, we turned off the lights, locked the doors and headed for the RSL to continue our celebration. There was a DJ that night and we requested Tina Turner's 'Simply the Best' over and over. It became the CDEP song as we danced and danced and sang:

> 'We're simply the best,
> Better than all the rest
> Better than anyone, anyone we've ever met.'

What a night! I felt like crying with happiness.

Coonamble Times

Wednesday, April 17, 1991

Registered by Australia Post
Publication No NAC0513

Recommended and Maximum price only
PRICE 60 CENTS

Member of Audit Bureau
of Circulations

Ellimatta Arts and Crafts Exhibition and Opening A Huge Success

Last Friday saw the official opening of Ellimatta, Coonamble's first Aboriginal Gallery Workshop.

The once dull building across from the Post Office has been risen from the doom and gloom and revitalised with a paint job and a complete new facelift inside and out.

Full credit to CDEP Co-Ordinator Barbara Jackson and her committee in their efforts to gain status in the community, a status which has been accepted by all, as was witnessed by the huge rollup of business men and women and members of the community that turned out to view the opening.

President of the CDEP Tracker Robinson welcomed guests to the opening and gave a short speech on their achievements to date.

Mr Joe Flick, Department of Employment Education Training (DEET), from Dubbo made the presentation of certificates to all the graduates, Julie Verner from Arrilla Training and Development spoke on the Training Program.

With the official opening of Ellimatta Gallery by Kevin Keady, Coonamble Shire President, the evening came to a close.

Turning a life around

Most CDEP participants were under thirty-five years of age. They were young and strong, and glad to have a job, but it was the older men who gave balance to the CDEP. They had work experience and understood the self-discipline needed to get through tasks. There were also a couple of great women who joined the work crews. Robyn was Gail's favourite. She was as strong as an ox and loved working outdoors. When Gail was planning the upcoming work schedule, she'd say, 'My best working man is a woman!' and made sure Robyn was on the team for a complex job.

The older men provided a steadying influence on the younger men.

They didn't get hot under the collar when equipment broke down, or claim unfairness when they were allocated to an unpleasant job. Mostly they didn't seek leadership roles. They just got on with the job. One of these steady men was Ron Williams, a man in his mid-forties with a young family. I always felt concerned about Ron as he looked unwell. His grey hair was lank, his skin was sallow and he looked plain worn out.

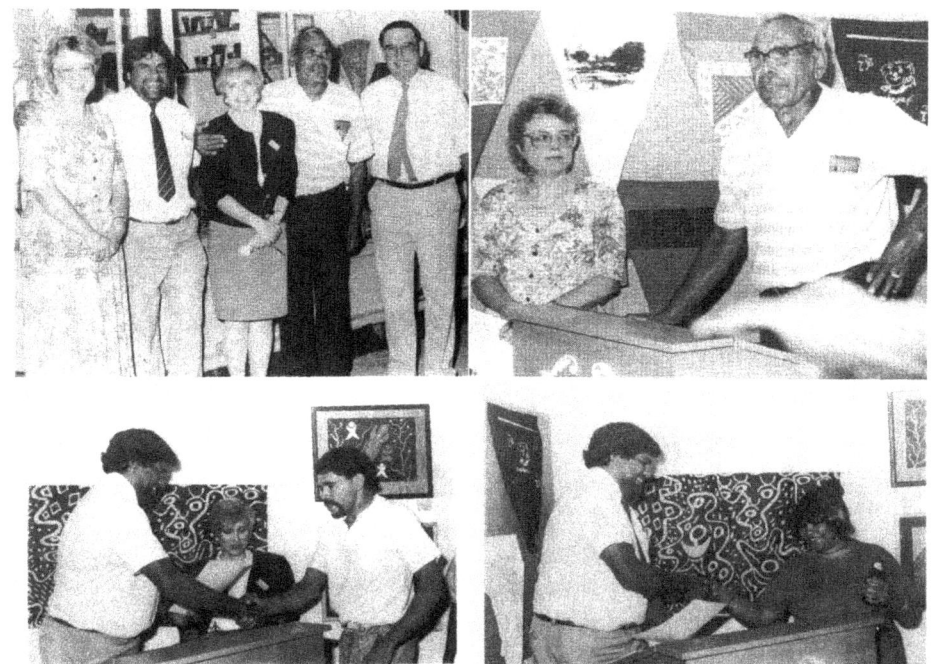

Clockwise from top left: Barbara Jackson, Joe Flick, Julie Verner, Tracker Robinson and Kevin Keady at the Ellimatta opening
Tracker Robinson welcoming guests to the Ellimatta opening
Joe Flick, executive officer from DEET presenting an award to Geoff Smith with Julie Verner from Arilla looking on
Joanne Dodd receives her certificate from Joe Flick

One afternoon, when work was finished for the day, Ron shared some of his life history with me. He told me his grandmother, who had lived in Walgett, was Aboriginal.

'Eric Fernando knows my grandmother,' he said, 'and the committee accepted me as Aboriginal.' Being Aboriginal allowed Ron to join the CDEP. He told me this was helping him to turn his life around.

'I am an alcoholic,' he told me, 'and I ruined my life and the life of my first family. The grog wrecked everything. I was always drunk and I used to hit them. They don't want to see me again.' Ron was silent for a few moments.

'But I've got a second chance now,' he said. 'I can turn my life around. I've got a second family with four children and I want to raise them as a proper father.'

He looked me in the eye and confessed, 'I was a meths drinker, but now I'm getting off the grog.'

'Good on you, Ron. You're a good man.' I smiled at him. 'I'm glad you are on the CDEP. Having older blokes like you is very helpful because you show the younger fellas how to work.'

As he got up to go, I stopped him and said, 'If there is anything I can do to help you, you just let me know. Okay?'

He nodded his thanks as he went out the door. Now I knew why his face looked so worn and tired.

What a hard life he's had, I thought. *Thank goodness for the CDEP.*

I truly loved working with the CDEP. It was the workplace heart of the community. A place of acceptance not judgement, inclusion rather than exclusion. A place for making friends, a place of action rather than boredom. I felt very grateful for the privilege of working with the Aboriginal people in Coonamble.

It was about six weeks later when Ron came into the office to share his progress in keeping off the grog. He had brought in a letter to show me.

'The pubs in town signed this letter saying they would refuse to serve me alcohol,' he announced.

I quickly read the letter and exclaimed, 'I didn't know they could do that.'

'Well, it's up to them,' Ron explained, 'but the police helped me with the letter so that made it easier.'

I felt immensely pleased for Ron. He looked very proud of himself. And so he should! 'How fantastic, Ron! It's tremendous what you are doing.'

Over the next weeks, I noticed that Ron's health was improving. He had more colour in his face and his eyes were brighter. I felt very happy for him.

Jon, the shire engineer, popped in a few days later to let us know that the current contractor who cleaned the cattle saleyards was retiring.

'Would the CDEP take over cleaning the saleyards for a few weeks while we prepare new tender documents?' he asked.

'Hmm, what a good opportunity. Thanks Jon. I'll take it to the fellas.'

Jon had given me the job description. I called a meeting of supervisors and interested men and we went through it together. There was a feeling of tension as we discussed the job. We knew cleaning the saleyards crossed the divide between the farmers and the Aboriginal community. This was something completely new. How would farmers react to Aboriginal people washing down the cattle yards?

By the end of the discussion, a crew of six men, including Ron Williams, had volunteered to clean the saleyards. They agreed that the work would have to be done to a high standard and on time. If it wasn't, they knew the CDEP would get a bad name. They also knew it was a good opportunity to gain experience when the time came for the CDEP to bid for the council contract. I typed up a letter to the shire, agreeing to their request. The CDEP would clean the saleyards for a period of three months at the stated rate.

Hosing down small mountains of cow manure was a dirty, smelly job. By the end of the second month, the young fellas had decided they weren't keen on the job. But Ron was! On the third month, he cleaned the saleyards by himself. He was thorough and had worked out his method.

The council released the tender document to the public. It was time for the CDEP to make a decision. I called the supervisors and the saleyard crew together to discuss it. There was much shaking of heads. The crew was not interested.

Then Ron spoke, 'If the CDEP doesn't want it, then I'd like to have a go at it.'

Everybody agreed. 'Good on you, mate, you have a go, and good luck!'

I helped Ron put his application together and he delivered it by hand to the shire.

I don't think there was a man more proud in Coonamble than Ron Williams when he received notification that he had won the shire contract to clean the cattle saleyards for twelve months. Ron was on his way in his new alcohol-free life.

The next time I saw Jon, I told him how delighted Ron Williams was to win the contract.

'I probably shouldn't tell you,' Jon said, 'but speaking confidentially, the council was pleased with the standard of Ron's work and admired him for having a go. They know he's had a hard life.'

Winning that contract changed Ron's life. It also nudged attitudes in the town. An Aboriginal bloke had been awarded a contract by the Coonamble Shire. To me, it was another CDEP miracle in the town.

12 Leaving Coonamble

It had been two years since I drove from Melbourne to Coonamble to start work with the Aboriginal community to set up their community development and employment program. As my contract was drawing to a close, the CDEP committee made the excellent decision to employ my counterpart, Gail Turnbull, as the next CDEP coordinator. My work was finished. It was time to hand over to the Aboriginal people who were more than capable of managing their enterprise. Not surprisingly, I found it a wrench to leave the CDEP, the friends I had made, and indeed, the town of Coonamble. Despite not fitting anywhere, over the previous two years I had somehow become embedded in the town.

The success of the CDEP was thanks to the overwhelming support it received from Coonamble's Aboriginal community. At the first community meeting, thirty unemployed Aboriginal people signed up immediately and within weeks the CDEP had eighty-four participants. That was a mighty impressive vote of approval.

The CDEP's success was also due to the practical support from the town. The commitments for work from the shire council and St Vincent de Paul were essential in getting the program up and running. The goodwill and support from Coonamble's townsfolk was also a large contributor. They had backed the CDEP by employing the participants to mow their lawns and help them do the heavy work around their homes. We also had my father, Bill, to thank for his untiring voluntary work with the woodwork team.

As I did my shopping around town or went to the cafés, clubs and pubs, townsfolk had told me how pleased they were that Coonamble had a CDEP and they wished the Aboriginal people good luck. As the profile of the CDEP grew, so did mine as the CDEP coordinator. I was asked to speak at Rotary and to be a prize-giver at the high school speech night. I must say I was startled to be asked to speak, but I recognised that it was not actually *me* they were asking, they were asking a representative of the Coonamble CDEP.

As a Victorian, I had initially thought Coonamble was a very ordinary and charmless town. It certainly was no Beechworth or Maldon. But it grew on me. The locals loved their town and when I asked them why, they said it was because people helped each other and it was safe. That was true. Not once had I ever felt nervous wandering home late at night from the RSL club or one of our uproarious sessions at the Commercial. That is certainly more than I can say about Melbourne.

From time to time I had pondered the layers and complexity of Coonamble, wondering how I might weave myself into the town. Eventually, I came to recognise that how we connect to place is more about ourselves and our adaptability than the place itself. My outsider status was different to other Coonamble Johnny-come-latelies. I had straddled both the Aboriginal and non-Aboriginal worlds, belonging to neither but interacting with both. In a way, I became somewhat of a bridge between the two spheres enabling me to form connections and relationships for the benefit of the CDEP and the Aboriginal participants.

Environment, history and economic opportunity give shape to towns and forge community attitudes. For both Aboriginal and non-Aboriginal people, Coonamble was *their* town, but their attitudes came from their different circumstances and layers. The town layers separated locals from outsiders, townies from cockies, rugby union from rugby league, and the White world from the Black world. From what I could tell, the main points of contact were through government institutions such as the schools, hospital, the council, courthouse and sport. Apart from that, they seemed to rarely interact.

Immersed in the CDEP, I was able to observe how the Coonamble Aboriginal people lived in the community. I admired the strength of their family bonds and the robust vitality of the family relationships and connections that wove their lives together. From my perspective, the Aboriginal presence was strong, although at that time, their history was not in clear view. The land of Coonamble that had been Aboriginal land 150 years previously, was now sheep, cattle and wheat land. The settler land-grab all those years ago was accompanied by disease, dispossession, violence and starvation of the original inhabitants. Instead of being equal, Aboriginal people were the minority, the poorest, excluded from jobs and their origins not even acknowledged. Perhaps the lack of acknowledgement of the past was the worst thing. Thankfully, the passage of time has changed perceptions and attitudes. Today the Wailwan people have been acknowledged as the traditional custodians of the area surrounding Coonamble.

It took me much longer to pack than I had anticipated as I had acquired mountains of clothing from the friendly op-shop ladies as well as accumulating household goods. As I drove out of town in my bursting car along the Castlereagh Highway towards Dubbo, I felt lonely and sad to be leaving.

Although I stayed in telephone contact with Gail who kept me up-to-date about the CDEP, it wasn't enough. Coonamble had filled my life for two years and I yearned to go back and reconnect with the CDEP and the town. Finally, after a year, I took the long drive back to Coonamble. As I drove into the town, I had the mixed feelings of an outsider coming home. My experiences and friendships had connected me to the CDEP, but I no longer had a place there. My wistful feeling fortunately vanished in the joyful moment when Gail and I hugged our hellos. As I gazed round the office greeting the admin women, I absorbed the feeling of being back in the office. Gail's office. It felt enormously satisfying. I had done my job well and now I was an onlooker at a successful, well-managed CDEP run by Aboriginal people.

The next morning I went to the office well before 8 o'clock so I could be there to meet up with the workers before they headed out for their day's work. It was great to feel that energy again and share in the laughter and jokes. Some of the artists turned up after the men had left for work. I stayed chatting with them as they showed me their work. I was thrilled that the arts and crafts program was continuing, albeit to a lesser extent. The woodwork program was also continuing although my father, Bill, had left town shortly after my contract had finished.

I enjoyed wandering down the main street, seeing the same shops, and nodding hello to people I knew. I spotted a couple of my favourite people, Joanne and her boyfriend Adrian. I crossed over the road to have a chat with them. Later that evening when Gail and I were having dinner at the Chinese restaurant, my old bridge-playing partner Geoff came over to our table.

'I knew it must have been you back in town!' he exclaimed. 'As I came round the corner into Castlereagh Street, I saw you talking to two Aboriginal people. It's the first time since you left that I've seen a White person talking to Aboriginal people.'

My few days in Coonamble reminded me how shallow my roots were in the town. My contacts, friends and acquaintances were all with the CDEP. I didn't have other friends to visit. No invitations to dinner. No coffees in the local café. Although I had felt embedded in Coonamble, it was through a long thin taproot with no supporting roots.

Over the next few years, the CDEP grew and prospered with more participants and expansion into profit-making ventures. Despite the wages remaining at the same abysmal rates of the dole, the Aboriginal people continued to work with enthusiasm for their families, their community and the whole town. As well as being a source of enormous pride to the Aboriginal population, the CDEP and its various enterprises brought increased prosperity to the businesses in the town. The CDEP was successful socially, culturally and economically.[75]

This happy state of affairs continued until 1996 when government policy changed. The CDEP of Coonamble would no longer be funded as the town was no longer deemed *remote*.[76] No doubt the decision had budgetary concerns somewhere in the mix and deleting a CDEP in far-off Coonamble saved Commonwealth dollars. It came at a terrible cost for the Aboriginal people and the whole town.

I returned again to Coonamble in mid-2021 when a gap in COVID-19 lockdowns enabled my friend Robyn and me to undertake the 2,000-kilometre round trip. Plentiful rains had turned the landscape into lush, verdant plains and rolling hills. Although the weather was cold, the sun shone and we revelled in the Australian countryside. The final few kilometres to Coonamble were exactly how I remembered them thirty years ago; the showgrounds, the Jehovah's Witness hall, the sporting fields, but the intersection at the entrance of the town was completely different. It was confusing and I felt a bit disoriented. There was now a smart, flower-covered traffic island at the corner of Aberford and Castlereagh Streets. But what had happened to the IGA supermarket where Gail and I had done the CDEP shopping? It was completely missing. Even worse, there was no CDEP building in Aberford Street. Instead we were looking at a derelict site surrounded by cyclone fencing. How strange! What on earth had happened?

Fortunately, at the Global Village Café across the street, we had the good luck to meet the delightful café owner. She explained there had been a fire in 2018 which had burned the supermarket and CDEP building to the ground as well as other buildings. Arson was suspected.

A walk down Castlereagh Street was a further shock to me. Years of drought, and perhaps general rural decline, had left the town a shadow of its former self. Many shops were closed and the Sons of the Soil Hotel, which had stood proudly midway down the main street, was also closed and shuttered.

The RSL at the end of the shopping block had closed down. There was no supermarket in the main street. There was scarcely any foot traffic and why would there be? No newsagent, supermarket or hotel to bring people to the street where they could catch up on the gossip with friends and acquaintances.

Poor Coonamble. Years of drought and rural decline. A fire destroying a section of their main street, and in 2021 a devastating mouse plague wreaking havoc on crops and infesting people's homes and personal belongings.

With no RSL, the place to go on a Friday night was the bowling club. We had just finished our roast lamb and three veg dinner, when one of the CDEP participants walked past our table. Although thirty years had passed, I would have known him anywhere. There were other CPEP participants at the bowling club that night and I saw them all. It was a happy evening and a gratifying way to close a chapter in my life.

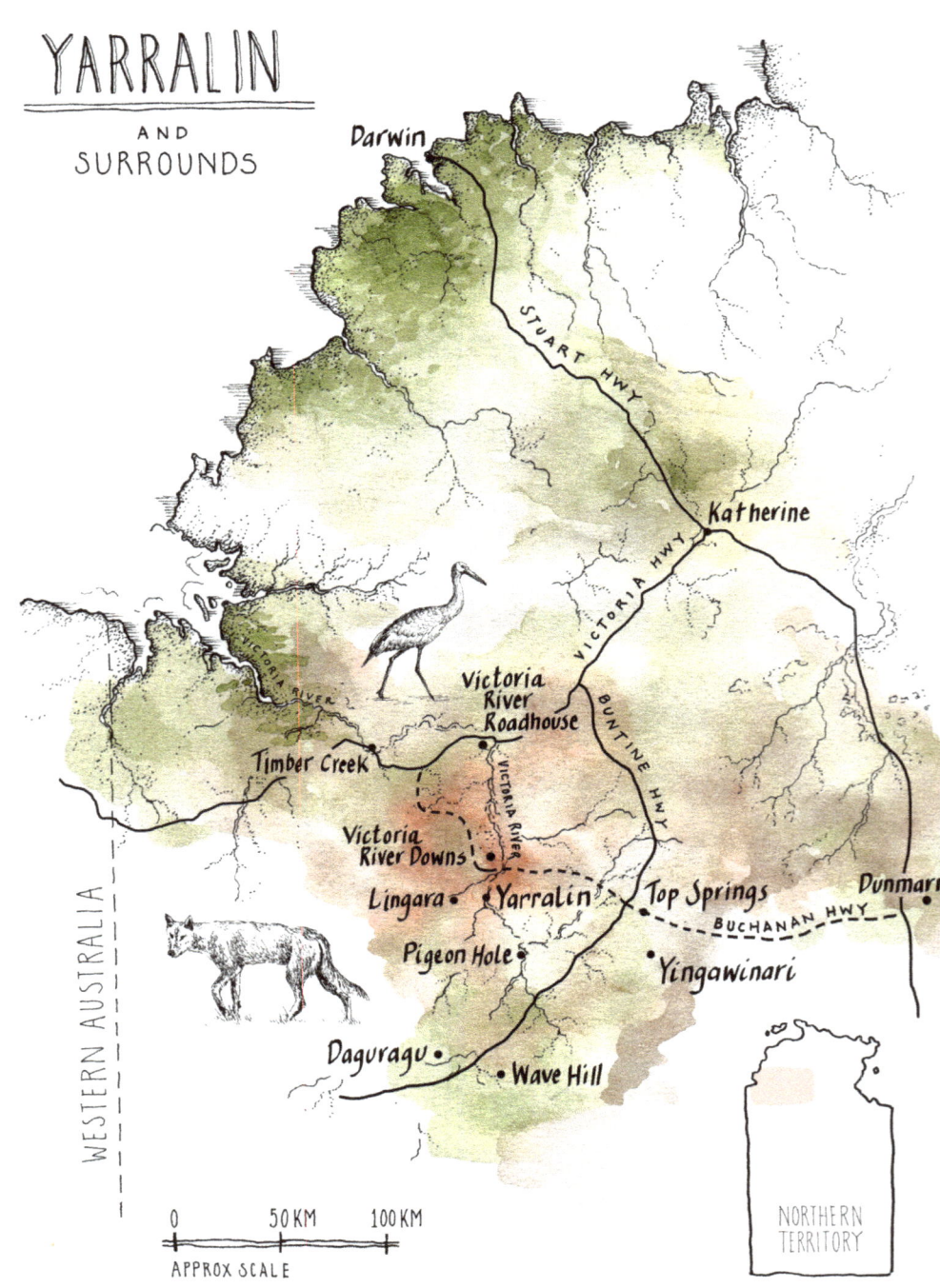

Part 3

Two Years in Yarralin

13 4,000 kilometres to Yarralin

'I'll come with you. It is too far to drive by yourself.'

I burst into a little dance and gave my best friend Margaretha a big hug. 'You are a lifesaver,' I declared. I felt thrilled and grateful that we would travel together to the Aboriginal community of Yarralin in the Northern Territory where I had accepted the job of council clerk.

'I'll take my car as well and of course my darling Samantha.' Sam was Marg's smart little dog, a maltese-shitzu-poodle cross. Definitely one of a kind. Marg grabbed her book of maps from the shelf. 'How many days on the road?'

I had already done the calculations and worked out it would take eight days to drive from Melbourne to Yarralin, a distance of 4,000 kilometres. We would change a time zone, cross the Tropic of Capricorn and move from Melbourne's temperate zone to the subtropical Victoria River region of the Northern Territory. It was extraordinary to think it was a similar distance to drive from London to Ankara in Turkey, crossing ten countries along the way.

A week later we set off at dawn in our two-car convoy for the first leg of our trip. I was driving my old Ford with Marg and little Sam following in her Holden Commodore. Our first day on the road was an easy 550 kilometres to Mildura on the Calder Highway. My car was packed to the gunnels with my precious computer, clothes, books, CD player and the basic necessities for setting up a house. Having worked in the remote locations of Papunya and Coonamble, I had a good idea of what I would need during my two-year contract as the Yarralin Council Clerk. Marg's car was also full as she was planning to stay with me in Yarralin for the first two or three weeks. After I had settled in, she would head off to Darwin for her unknown adventures.

Five days later, the lights of Alice Springs welcomed us when we pulled into the caravan park at dusk. The next morning, as we headed out of Alice Springs, we passed the well-preserved Telegraph Station of the Overland Telegraph Line which was established in 1872 to relay messages between Darwin and Adelaide.

The opening of the telegraph line led to the opening up of the Aboriginal lands in the desert regions of Western Australia, South Australia and the Northern Territory. Explorers were followed by cattlemen and miners, and the lives of Aboriginal people were changed forever.

About 20 kilometres up the Stuart Highway we passed the turn-off to the Tanami Road, on which I had driven so many times to Papunya. I remembered back to that challenging and never-forgotten year in 1982 when I had worked for the Papunya health service. It had been an important chapter in my life, and instrumental in my decision to work in Yarralin. We never know where the building blocks of our life will take us.

Tennant Creek, where we would stay the night, was a shortish 500 kilometres away. We were looking forward to making a stop at the spectacular Devil's Marbles, an amazing landscape of gigantic granite boulders south of Tennant Creek. The Aboriginal name is Karlu Karlu and it is a site of extreme cultural and spiritual significance. It certainly felt that way to Marg and me as we walked slowly around the amazing rock formations and sat in contemplation sipping our thermos coffee.

Karlu Karlu was a perfect place for contemplation and a coffee.
Jackson collection, 1982

The town of Katherine was our final stop on the Stuart Highway. It's a town of around 6,000 people and would be my local service town for Yarralin.

Katherine's main tourist attraction is the impressive Katherine Gorge. It was Marg's first time in Katherine and we had booked a Three Gorges Tour for the morning. Our afternoon would be devoted to food shopping.

The next morning, I awoke with a feeling of nervous anticipation, or was it trepidation? The big day had arrived. One more day of driving and we would be in my new workplace of Yarralin. I couldn't even imagine what my new life was going to be.

We gave ourselves six hours for the drive to Yarralin. Our first stop was Victoria River and the nearby roadhouse, which marked the edge of the Judbarra/Gregory National Park. This 13,000-square-kilometre park extended 50 kilometres beyond Timber Creek and south into the semi-arid areas of Tanami and Great Sandy Desert. The landscape was vast and varied, from the tropical savannah plains we were driving through, to the heart-catching glowing escarpments and rugged cliffs in the distance. We were in the Victoria River catchment area, where the Victoria River and its tributaries water an unimaginably large area of 87,900 square kilometres.[77]

About 30 kilometres before Timber Creek we turned off at the dirt road signposted 'Top Springs via Buchanan Highway'. This was our road to Yarralin via Jasper Gorge which runs through the flat-topped Stokes Range.

Water has surged through Jasper Gorge over a millennium of wet seasons
Allan Woo, Wooman Adventures

It was a slow, bumpy and exceedingly beautiful drive as the road wound through the gorge alongside Jasper Creek. The smooth worn rocks in the creek bed told of the volume and strength of the water that had surged through the gorge over a millennia of wet seasons. We pulled over and parked to immerse ourselves in the contrasting colours and wildness of dramatic ochre cliffs, silver green-grey eucalypts and the clear blue sky. As we stood still and listened, we could feel the quietness of the rocks around us. We could well believe that for Aboriginal people, the gorge was created at the beginning of the world when the great travelling Dreaming Walujapi black-headed python slid across Stokes Range, her body pushing up the curving sides of the gorge.

From Jasper Gorge the road headed across the plains. A small grass fire had passed through recently and to our utter delight and amazement we saw a group of brolgas dancing on the charred ground. It felt like an omen to me. We drove on and eventually reached the turn-off to Victoria River Downs Station or VRD as it was known. The cattle station was once famed as the 'The Big Run' when it was one of the largest stations in the world. The famous Australian billionaire entrepreneur, Robert Holmes à Court, purchased VRD in 1989.

Yarralin community, Northern Territory
Bushtel NTLIS Satellite Imagery, 2023

From VRD, it was only another 25 kilometres of dirt road studded with cattle grids to Yarralin. We knew we had reached the community boundary when we sighted the twin signs of Yarralin and 'No Alcohol Beyond This Point'.

I stopped the car and thought back over our trip from verdant green Victoria, across the Riverland of South Australia, the deserts of Northern Territory, and the magnificent country of the Victoria River region. My view was confirmed that the contrasts in the landscape, geography and climate of the 4,000 kilometres between Melbourne and Yarralin were much the same as between London and Ankara in Turkey.

I climbed out of my trusty Ford and walked back to Marg who had let her little dog out to experience her first smells of Yarralin.

'This is it, Marg, we're finally here.' She joined me standing on the dusty road as we took in the dry landscape, the hardy vegetation, the heat and flies. Marg gave me a sideways look, raised her eyebrows and said, 'Are you sure?'

'Apart from feeling scared to death, I'm fine,' I answered. 'Let's go!'

We crossed the cattle grid and entered Yarralin.

From the community mud map sent to me, I had a rough idea where the office was. To be sure, I called out, 'Where is the office?' to a young lad walking along the dusty road. He pointed to my new workplace 200 metres away. It was a shabby, corrugated-iron shed. We drove on and parked out the front. I got out and climbed the step to the office door. It was the beginning of my new life in Yarralin.

'Hello, I'm Barbara, the new council clerk,' I said brightly, as I entered the office. The few Aboriginal people in the office silently looked at me as I stood uncomfortably wondering what to do next. A White woman emerged from an office at the end of the shed.

'I'm Pam, the bookkeeper. Welcome to Yarralin. Glad to see that you made the trip safely. Did you have any problems?'

'It was a lovely trip,' I smiled. 'We came through Jasper Gorge, which was fantastic.'

Pam agreed saying, 'That's my favourite way, but in the dry season we usually go through Top Springs because it is easier.'

'Good to know. I'll go that way next time.'

An Aboriginal woman came out of an office and joined us.

'Here's Frances,' said Pam, gesturing towards her. 'She is our admin person who does the wages.'

'Welcome to Yarralin,' said Frances, smiling warmly.

'My friend Margaretha is outside waiting for me,' I told Pam. 'Would you mind showing us where the house is please? Marg will start unpacking the cars while I come back to the office with you.'

'No worries,' Pam replied, as she picked up the keys for the office Toyota and my house.

'Follow me.'

We jumped into our vehicles and headed off down the main road of Yarralin with Marg following.

Lucky Pam! Her bookkeeping office had windows
Pam Field collection, 1995

The house was a few hundred metres from the Yarralin office on a corner block facing Yarralin's main dirt road. It was painted pale grey and appeared to be relatively new compared to other houses in Yarralin. A quick look showed it was functional, furnished with the bare essentials and floored with vinyl tiles throughout for easy cleaning. By no stretch of the imagination could it be called homely. However, it was a vast improvement on the accommodation I had endured at Coonamble. I was very grateful.

A simple wire fence surrounded the large house block. The entrance was from the side street on a driveway made from car tracks. The large farm gate at the driveway entrance was obviously never closed as it was solidly stuck in the pale red sandy soil. There was a shed, but no outdoor improvements of any kind. No garden, no patch of lawn and no trees with the exception of a tall papaya plant next to the large veranda that ran the length of the house. The back door, which served as the entrance to the house, opened to the veranda. The actual front door, which faced the main street, was never used.

Fortunately, the kitchen was equipped with crockery, cutlery, pots and pans and there was even some bed linen and a few towels. I was most pleased with this as I had only packed odds and ends. I left Marg and her excited little dog to their unpacking and climbed into Pam's vehicle.

As Pam and I drove back to the office she told me that the house was allocated to the council clerk and no one else was allowed to live in it. Then she awkwardly asked, 'Did you get permission for your friend to come to Yarralin with you?'

'Oh my God! No, I didn't even think about it. What should I do?'

I was horrified that I had not even considered that.

'You should ask permission from the councillors as soon as you meet them.'

Aboriginal community councils and their community-elected councillors, were incorporated into the governing system of the Northern Territory. As the council clerk, I reported to the council.

'Thank you for letting me know, Pam. How stupid I am.'

'Don't worry,' she said gently. 'I'm sure it will be all right.'

Back at the office, Pam asked one of the men to let the councillors know I had arrived. She gave me a guided tour that took about two minutes, given the small size of the office. The office was a converted shed in which there was a large general office room with four small desks, a photocopier and a telephone. There were no windows, but thankfully there were air conditioners. Adjacent to the general office were four rooms, Frances's admin office, the council clerk office, the councillors office and a small storeroom. There were three paid staff at the council: two White people, Pam and me, and one Aboriginal woman, Frances. That was it! A quick look into my office revealed a dusty, dim and unappealing room. My heart sank a little. At the far end of the general office, a door led to the mechanic's workshop. I followed Pam into the workshop and she introduced me to her husband, Ken, the community mechanic, and his two Aboriginal assistants.

Frances had put the kettle on for a welcome cup of tea. Pam and

Frances explained to me that it was the end of the build-up which is what Territorians call the period between October and December. I remembered this pre-monsoonal season from my time working in Cambodia, when rain threatened but didn't arrive and the humidity rose unbearably. I was now to experience it in my own country.

As we sipped our tea in Pam's office, three older men came into the general office.

'Ah, here are the councillors,' Pam exclaimed.

Pam introduced me and we all shook hands. The councillors settled themselves at the office desks.

'I'm glad to be here and I look forward to starting work in your community,' I said, smiling. 'I hope we can work well together and that I can help you to implement the goals of your community plan.'

'Was your trip all right?' one of the councillors asked.

'Yes it was fine thanks. My friend Margaretha came with me and we drove through Jasper Gorge. It was beautiful.' I stopped speaking and collected my thoughts.

'I'm very sorry,' I apologised. 'I should have asked your permission for my friend Margaretha to come to Yarralin with me. She kept me company for the trip from Melbourne. Would it be all right if she stayed for a couple of weeks? After that she will be going to Darwin.'

The men looked at each other, then Billy Campbell, the council president, said, 'It's a long way from Melbourne and good you had company. But you should have asked us first. It's all right though. She can stay with you.'

Fancy making a blunder like that before I even began work. I was enormously relieved that I seemed to have been forgiven.

'I've read your five year community plan. It is a good plan. Is there anything you would like me to do straight away?' I asked.

Billy looked at the other councillors, then turned to me saying, 'Settle in first and get to know the community a bit, then we can talk about the plan.'

The phone rang. It was for Billy. He got up to answer it and the other two councillors also stood up saying they 'gotta go'. I wondered if they felt as uncomfortable and tongue-tied as I had.

By this time it was late afternoon and I decided to discover more about my workplace the next day. I thought I would to walk to my new house and have my first experience walking through my new community.

'I'm going home now, Pam. I'll see you at nine o'clock in the morning.'

'Good idea,' she replied. 'You've got heaps of unpacking and sorting to do. See you in the morning.'

I walked from the office to my house slowly to absorb the look and feel of this remote Aboriginal community. There was one main road and a couple of side roads with around fifty dwellings. The roads were unmade with overgrown roadside verges. I noticed a couple of people sitting outside the shabby store and nearby a few young boys were kicking a ball around. Here and there people were sitting under shade trees outside their houses. I gave them a wave as I walked by and received an occasional small acknowledgement in return. The houses were mostly faded dark green or red metal cladding with iron roofs. The fences around the house blocks were square chicken wire. Out the front of every house was a forty-four-gallon drum that was used to burn off rubbish. Quite a lot of the rubbish had escaped from the bins – no doubt helped by the roaming dogs. Although I knew better than to judge a community by its rubbish, I was a bit shocked to see how much litter was lying around.

In the midst of the dusty pale ochre of the road and verges, I was surprised by a blindingly green patch of well-watered grass and an enormous stand of shady bamboo. It was a small park that was obviously highly valued by the community.

As I glanced up a small side road, I saw buildings that looked somewhat like demountables behind a barbed-wire fence. It was the primary school.

Although I knew Yarralin had a health clinic, it eluded me on my stroll home. I later discovered there was a health clinic demountable a short distance from the rear of the office. As I walked, I soaked up the feel of Yarralin's slow pace of life and the quiet of the untamed landscape. It took me back to my first experience of an Aboriginal community in Ali Curung where I visited my father, Bill. Yarralin, however, was smaller and more forlorn.

As I turned the corner and saw Marg's car parked next to mine, I breathed a great sigh of relief knowing I had a friend waiting for me. I climbed up the couple of steps onto the veranda and opened the screen door. One look at Marg's face told me she was exhausted, hot and sweaty. 'You've been cleaning all afternoon haven't you? You must be stuffed, you poor thing.'

'All the kitchen benches and cupboards were covered in dust and the fridge needed a jolly good wipe-over,' she moaned. 'I couldn't put anything away until it was all clean. It's my Dutch heritage. Everything has to be super clean.'

'I'm home now. Let's have a cool drink and then I'll get dinner. I wish I could offer you a cold beer.'

Marg rolled her eyes at me. 'So do I but I'll have to get used to being in a dry community with no alcohol. How did you go at the office?'

I didn't dare tell her that I'd forgotten to ask permission for her to come to the community. She would have felt mortified. The council had okayed her stay so I decided the best thing to do was to let sleeping dogs lie. One look at her little dog Sam dozing on the couch convinced me.

'I met three of the councillors. I don't know what they made of me and it was all a bit awkward. I think it will take time for them to get used to me. Thank goodness I have the community plan to follow.'

The rest of the evening was devoted to sweeping, making the beds and finally our well-earned dinner of steak and salad.

I woke the next morning both excited and apprehensive about my first day in the office. Thanks to Marg's hard work the previous day, I enjoyed a breakfast of tea and toast in a splendidly clean kitchen. Although it was still early, I could feel the humidity on my skin and smell the dry grass and dusty earth through the open doors and windows. As I sipped my tea and crunched into my toast, I reflected on my motivation to work in Yarralin. I remembered the tingle of excitement I had felt when I saw the job advertisement for a council clerk in the Saturday job's pages of *The Age* newspaper. As I read the job criteria and description of the community, I knew it was a fit. I had previously worked in the Aboriginal community of Papunya and started a Community Development Employment Project (CDEP) with the Aboriginal community of Coonamble. Yarralin was a small community that suited my level of experience. It was located in the Katherine area which I knew relatively well. It was a job where I could support a community to make the changes they wanted for their future.

As I rinsed my breakfast dishes, I thought about how fortunate I was to be able to accept the job in Yarralin. I was always a do-er rather than a talker. As far as I'm concerned, we can talk about injustice until the cows come home, but nothing changes unless we get out there and actually do something to try and make changes for the better. I was sure that some people felt sorry for me because I was single with no children. However, I considered myself to be fortunate to be a completely free agent living a life very different to most people's. My desire to contribute to justice for Aboriginal people and willingness to throw routine and security to the wind, meant I could pack a few belongings into my car and head off to a job in the outback. It was a privilege that not many people have.

It was 1995 and I was the first council clerk to be appointed to the newly established Walangeri Ngumpinku Community Government Council of Yarralin community. Around 450 Aboriginal people lived in the four communities of Yarralin. Approximately 290 people, mostly Ngarinyman, lived at the main community of Yarralin. Pigeon Hole, with 110 mostly Bilinara people, was on unalienated stock-route land about 95 kilometres south-east of Yarralin. Around fifty people lived at Lingara outstation, a 4-square-kilometre block of land near the old Humbert River homestead, 30 kilometres west of Yarralin. At that time, no one was living at Top Springs (Yinguwunarri) outstation, which was 120 kilometres away. Each of the communities of Yarralin and its three outstations had representatives on the Walangeri Ngumpinku Council.

The land of Yarralin was an excision from the adjoining Victoria River Downs Station. Yarralin's land was classed as a 'community living area' and quite bizarrely the title was held by the Department of Consumer Affairs. Sadly, it would be another two decades before the Yarralin people would claim their land under land rights legislation.

Yarralin community lies alongside the picturesque Wickham River, a tributary of the mighty Victoria River, one of the longest rivers in the Northern Territory. The Victoria River and its tributaries change from vast unimaginable quantities of water in full flood in the wet season to a series of picturesque waterholes in the dry season that are perfect for swimming and fishing.

Walking along the dusty road to the office, I wondered what my first weeks would bring. Settling into a new job always has its challenges but I suspected Yarralin would be a 'doozy' of a challenge for me.

Pam was already in her bookkeeper's sanctum when I walked through the door. After some good morning chitchat, Pam handed me the keys to the office troopie saying, 'As the council clerk, the council said that only you are allowed to drive the troopie. And you have to make sure it always stays in good condition in case it is needed for emergency transportation.'

'My first actual council clerk responsibility. How unexpected!' I smiled as I took the keys from her.

'Ken will make sure the maintenance is kept up to date. It would be good if you could let him know when you are going out of the community,' Pam said with a smile, as she turned back to her work.

When Ken and Pam came to Yarralin, Pam had vowed she was finished with bookkeeping. However, as well as being an expert bookkeeper, Pam had a very warm heart. When the council asked her to step in on a temporary basis to bookkeep after the previous administrator left, of course she agreed. I was made aware of Pam's wish to step away from bookkeeping at the time of my interview and thought it best to raise the issue with her at the beginning.

'I remember, Pam, that you wanted to leave the bookkeeper position. Have you changed your mind about that?' I asked.

'No I haven't but there isn't a solution right now. To employ a bookkeeper, the council would have to provide accommodation and there isn't any spare accommodation in Yarralin.'

Pam went on to say, 'The council accountant, John, is coming from Katherine in a couple of weeks. I would appreciate you and John keeping my request in mind if there is any chance the budget can stretch to providing accommodation.'

I assured Pam we would do that. Unfortunately for Pam, her desire to leave bookkeeping was not destined to be fulfilled during my time as council clerk.

With the accountant due next week, the sooner I sorted out the mess in my office the better it would be for both of us.

'Do you have dusters and cloths?' I asked. 'I'm going to start the office clean-up.'

As she handed them to me, she smiled and said, 'Good luck.'

The council clerk office had not been used for months and I had no idea when the previous administration people had left, or what they had done. Layers of dust, unopened envelopes, letters and documents covered every surface. Over the next days, I dusted and cleaned, binning the obvious junk and sorting the correspondence for future scrutiny. Gaining a semblance of order, I turned my attention to the row of four-drawer filing cabinets with the immediate goal of finding the council minutes. I needed to know the previous topics of council discussion and what policies or decisions had been passed.

Most Australians are familiar with their shire or municipal council. Council trucks pick up household rubbish and council workers repair footpaths and maintain sporting facilities. Kids play in council parks and playgrounds and we've probably all attended a council-run carols by candlelight or gone to a community festival.

While the legal status and authority of remote Aboriginal community government councils is the same as their municipal or shire cousins, they operate in a different reality. Yarralin, like many community government councils, was a major employer. The difference was that municipal and shire councils have a rate base to employ the staff providing rubbish-collection services and infrastructure maintenance. Yarralin's workers, on the other hand, were paid the equivalent of unemployment benefits under the CDEP 'work for the dole' scheme.

Not having a rate base meant that Yarralin's Community Government Council was dependent on both the Northern Territory and Commonwealth governments for every dollar. Following the adage 'he who pays the piper calls the tune', it was the government that decided what infrastructure and facilities Yarralin would have, including housing. The lack of housing was a chronic and perennial problem for most Aboriginal communities and Yarralin was no exception. Other facilities such as sporting grounds were funded at the discretion of the government. For example, the sports ground at Yarralin had no spectator seating, lighting or change rooms. Indeed, if I hadn't been told where the sports ground was, I would not have even noticed it. It was a bare paddock, albeit with goalposts.

Similar to most remote Aboriginal communities, the Commonwealth and Territory governments provided universal services to Yarralin, such as the primary school, health clinic and the supply of power and water. Like most Aboriginal communities and cattle stations in the Northern Territory, Yarralin had its own airstrip, which was occasionally graded when a grant was available. The twice-weekly mail plane used the more serviceable airstrip at Victoria River Downs, a twenty-five-minute drive away.

The council office was the hub for Whitefella business. The council and council clerk were responsible for the myriad of interactions with Territory and Commonwealth government departments. They were also responsible for the management of budgets and grants, purchasing and payments, management of the CDEP and community administration for Centrelink.

It didn't take long for me to discover that the council was also a personal resource for the community when they needed help with problems. The office staff were often the link between the community member and their service provider such as their bank, Centrelink, aged care or a hospital. There was a never ending stream of people needing assistance with their banking and money issues, medical appointments, completing bureaucratic forms and organising transport.

Yarralin Council did not have the well-lit, clean, efficient yet comfortable accommodation of most shire and municipal councils. Instead, it was an uninsulated corrugated-iron shed with a windowless general office. When a fuse blew from the inadequate power supply, the council office would be plunged into inky blackness. The power failure would knock out the air con and within a few short minutes, the office would be furnace-hot.

The council filing system was another example of difference. As I progressed through the drawers of files in search of council minutes, I was intrigued to discover the same documents again and again in different files. It dawned on me that my predecessors, whoever they were, had erred on the side of caution, storing copies of documents in every conceivably related file for safekeeping. I eventually found the file of council minutes. My jubilation was short lived as the file was incomplete and, much to my despair, none of the information seemed to be useful to my settling-in period.

As I trawled through the files, I felt disheartened that many of the documents made little sense to me. However, one interesting find was a copy of a grant approval for a community garden filed separately under grants, finance, purchasing, garden, and tools. Eventually I found the original grant application which included a beautifully designed permaculture garden with the obligatory central tyre pond for growing chestnuts. I went back to the approval form and saw that the project started about eighteen months previously. A couple of keen gardeners had obviously come to Yarralin with their bright idea and had a go at teaching sustainable gardening. I could well understand why someone would have thought a community garden was a good idea as the vegetables at the store were stale and expensive. I had been thinking of the idea myself as a possible CDEP activity.

I wondered where this garden was and took a walk to find it. All that remained of the permaculture garden were some enormous zucchinis and straggly tomatoes in a fenced-off area with a tap. I asked a passer-by if I could pick one of the monster zucchinis and was given a wave of permission. I took it home and sliced it up for dinner. Never again. It was tough and tasteless with a lingering bitterness. I later learned that overgrown zucchinis are only good for being stuffed.

The next day I asked Peter, the Aboriginal CDEP supervisor, about the garden. Did anyone still work there? After a long silence, he shook his head. I went into Frances's office and asked her what had happened with the garden.

'It didn't last too long,' she said. 'I don't think people were very interested.'

I regretfully scrapped my own idea of creating a vegetable garden.

The council office was a busy place and the phone rang incessantly. I quickly learned that the office phone was also a community phone. Although Yarralin had a well-used phone box for outgoing calls, incoming calls came to the office, not the phone box. I tried to avoid answering that wretched phone as much as I could. It was a nightmare for me as I had no idea who the caller was or who they wanted to speak to and, in addition, my ear was not tuned in to the Yarralin way of speaking.

Prior to my arrival, a community expert had consulted extensively with the Yarralin Council and community and developed the five-year community plan that was my bible for action. Although councillors appeared at the office nearly every day to make phone calls and have chats together, I felt uncertain about how I should approach them about the community plan. I didn't want to be pushy, but neither did I want to spend all my time in filing cabinets.

I needed to know what their priorities were so I gently buttonholed a few councillors asking, 'I've read the community plan. Are you able to tell me what you'd like me to do first?' I felt quite despondent with their responses of 'later' or 'tomorrow'.

Being able to debrief with Marg at the end of the day was a godsend.

'I can't imagine, Marg, what the councillors are thinking about me,' I began. 'I don't know how to communicate with them. I have been asking them what they want me to do and they never tell me anything. I feel so awkward and uncomfortable.'

Marg consoled me saying, 'Don't worry, Barb, it is always like that in new jobs. People are expecting you to perform when you haven't got a clue where to start.'

'That's true,' I agreed. 'But this job has the added zinger of the communication hurdle of trying to work within two cultures and two world views. What have we got in common to bridge the gulf? I don't have kids or a family to talk about. Maybe I'll have to learn about fishing and football.'

Marg laughed, 'Yep, you are a foreigner here, that's for sure. In fact, I feel like we are both aliens who dropped into Yarralin from Planet Melbourne.'

I sighed, 'If only there was a "cultural guide" like I had with Gail in Coonamble, or a helpful government officer like Andrew from the Department of Aboriginal Affairs. Gail helped me to understand the community and Andrew gave Gail and I guidance and support as we started up the CDEP.'

Marg agreed. 'I would have thought it should be par for the course. Governments have been funding Aboriginal communities for decades. It is bizarre they haven't put in a system to support new arrivals in communities.'

Yarralin CDEP

In Yarralin there were close to one hundred part-time workers on the Community Development Employment Project or CDEP as it was called. As well as being council clerk, I was also the manager of the CDEP. It was written in the community plan that the CDEP needed to be improved. CDEPs had been operating in remote Northern Territory communities since the late 1970s and were well established and extensive. The scheme was designed to operate as both a community-development program and an employment program. In Yarralin it was to be managed by the local council. As well as receiving the 'dole' money to pay participants, CDEPs received a loading for on-costs and capital support. CDEPs were the most extensive programs in the Aboriginal policy arena.

When the CDEP workers came to the office to sign on in the morning, I set about introducing myself to them and offering to help if they had any problems or questions. Mostly they were very shy but I was pleased to be meeting some community members.

It was Frances who paid the fortnightly wages and she held most of the CDEP information. Frances was a kind and caring woman and I enjoyed chatting with her.

'I hope you won't mind if I ask you a few questions about the CDEP?' I asked.

Frances welcomed me into her office saying she was happy to tell me anything she could.

Each participant was expected to work twenty hours a week. I couldn't imagine how there would be enough work in Yarralin to keep a hundred people occupied for twenty hours a week. My doubts were confirmed when Frances showed me a list of CDEP tasks which included working with Ken the mechanic, doing home maintenance, picking up rubbish and carting it to the Yarralin tip. The women worked at the preschool, cleaned the office and did home duties. Yarralin CDEP was very different to the Coonamble CDEP where I had worked previously. I would have to adjust my expectations.

I had the CDEP sign-in book with me and had noted that not many participants signed on and off each day. Frances explained that the payroll was relatively straightforward as all employees were paid the same regardless of whether they worked or not. She explained her method of calculating the wages and making up the pay envelopes and said that Pam always gave her a hand on the wages day. A complicating factor in Frances's work was terminating and restarting workers who had moved in and out of Yarralin from other communities. Leah from Centrelink gave Frances assistance with this. Leah's role was to ensure that the residents of Aboriginal communities were receiving their correct entitlements. Frances spoke very fondly of Leah and I was looking forward to meeting her.

Every government officer I had met to that point was an 'Anglo' Aussie, so it was a welcome surprise to meet an Aboriginal officer. Leah was a tall woman, athletic and energetic with a sharply intelligent face. She explained that ensuring participants received their correct entitlements could be complicated and she tried to visit Yarralin every month to help Frances. Leah was an absolute pleasure to work with. Nothing was too much trouble and she genuinely wanted to help. I left Frances and Leah with their administration work and returned to my latest project, which was the grubby but satisfying task of cleaning out the storeroom.

After completing her work with Frances, Leah needed to stay around to check the entitlements of several people. I offered her a cup of tea. As we drank our tea together, Leah asked me how I was going. She was so friendly and understanding, that I started to share my woes about not being able to talk to the councillors.

'What about I stay overnight and we can have a good chat,' she suggested.

'That would be wonderful. Please do,' I begged. I knew Margaretha would be thrilled to have a visitor as well.

As Marg, Leah and I cooked and ate our dinner that evening, I unburdened my feelings of discombobulation on Leah. She had visited many communities and was highly experienced. In addition, her Aboriginality gave her insights into communities that I could only dream about. The most valuable piece of advice she gave me was to seek help from one of the strong women in the community. She suggested I visit Marie, one of the Traditional Owners. I was very grateful for her understanding and support.

'You aren't like any public servant I've ever met before. Thank you so much.'

Leah look pleased.

Marg and I were interested to hear Leah's personal story. She was originally a Queenslander. As with many capable and ambitious Aboriginal young people, Leah's path to employment was filled with 'Aboriginal-designated' traineeships for six or twelve months. She had been trained in administration at a high school, the law courts, a hospital and state government. It had been a frustratingly circuitous journey for her to eventually find a permanent position with Centrelink. That evening was the beginning of my four-year friendship with Leah.

Leah was the first Aboriginal person Marg had met socially and they got along famously. In fact we all got along so well that Leah ending up staying the weekend. Although no alcohol was permitted in the community, we could hear the results of Saturday-night drinking at the fence. We were glad of Leah's calming presence when she explained that the sounds of shouting and fighting were not nearly as scary as they appeared.

On the Monday, I took Leah's advice and walked down Yarralin's main road to see Marie and ask for help. Marie looked surprised and a bit uncomfortable to see me at her door.

'Sorry to bother you, Marie, but I need to talk to you. I would like your help,' I stammered, feeling very uncomfortable myself. 'I've come here as the council clerk, but no one is telling me what they want me to do,' I blurted out. 'Can you help me? Can you ask the councillors what they would like me to do?'

Marie looked at me, and nodded her head slightly. 'I'll talk to them.'

'Thanks Marie.' I saw there was going to be no more conversation so I nodded back and said, 'Okay, bye.'

Leah's suggestion had worked. A couple of days later, when I once again approached a councillor to ask what I should do, he said, 'We'll hold a council meeting.'

Hurrah. Thank goodness for Marie and Leah.

As my first meeting with Yarralin Council convened, I felt nervous as the men straggled into the office and found themselves a chair. There was no meeting room so we sat scattered around the desks in the main office. As it turned out, it was an easy and friendly meeting. We introduced ourselves and I felt relieved to have finally met all the councillors properly. Their main agenda items were to get the CDEP working better and tidy up the community.

I was relieved to hear the council express concern about the CDEP and that participants were paid regardless of whether they worked or not. Over the next few days, I spoke with some of the older men and said that we needed to draw a red line on the attendance book at 8.30 am. If participants hadn't signed on by that time, they would be docked one hour's pay. I waited a couple more days hoping that the sign-on information had percolated through the community. At the beginning of the next week, I plucked up my courage and at 8.30 am I drew a red line in the book. I wasn't sure what would happen but I didn't have to wait long to find out. The red line had created a minor uproar.

There was a barrage of: 'Who did I think I was?' 'What right did I have to rule off the sign-in book with a red line?' 'You can't do that!'

The council didn't actively support me, but neither did they oppose my red line. I decided to keep going. Not every day, but often enough so people would realise they actually had to turn up for work, even if they didn't have anything to do.

The red line created the beginning of change in the CDEP. Interest in working for the CDEP stirred. More rubbish began to be collected. It was a slow process, but over time, working for the CDEP became a viable alternative to doing nothing.

14 An old man is dead

Riley was the Traditional Owner and 'boss' of Lingara, a small community outstation that lay between Victoria River Downs and Humbert River Station about 30 kilometres from Yarralin. He was a delightful man with a ready and open smile, a twinkle in his eye and a shock of snowy white hair. He was dedicated to Lingara and his community of around fifty people. Riley was a councillor and I had been introduced to him in my first few days at Yarralin. I took to him immediately. It was only a week later that I came to know Riley in a very different way.

It was a Saturday and Margaretha and I were having a morning cuppa at the kitchen table when our chat was interrupted by a vehicle skidding to a stop in the driveway. This was quickly followed by the sound of feet running up the steps to my back door. It was Riley and he was in great distress. I ushered him in and offered him a chair, but he was too upset. At first I couldn't understand him because he was talking too fast.

'Please slow down, Riley, slow down. What has happened?' we asked.

'The old man is dead, the old man is dead,' he repeated over and over. 'He's been shot.'

It was unbelievable. An old man shot? Dead?

I asked again. 'An old man has been shot?'

'Yes. Yes. You come with me. You have to come! He's dead. You come now!'

'Where is he?' I asked.

Riley told me the location near a creek but of course I had no idea where he meant. At that stage I'd scarcely even seen the Wickham River right next to the community.

'We'll go there in your Toyota,' said Riley as he was heading to the door. 'Come on!'

An old man was dead and we had to come with him. Right now. Somebody was dead. Not far away. Near a creek. Shot.

Riley's panic was contagious and I could feel it rolling over me. I was at a complete loss as to what to do. I looked at Marg and I knew she had even less idea. Riley was wailing, crying and insisting that we come with him to the old man. Thoughts blew through my mind like sharp gusts of wind. If I was in Melbourne, I would have determined the location of the dead man and called the police. But here, in my first weeks, I had only the vaguest notion of a police station in Timber Creek and I had no idea of the phone number. In any case it was a two-hour drive from Yarralin to Timber Creek.

Ken, the mechanic, had been living in Yarralin for some time. The sensible idea would have been to rush to his house and ask for help, but ridiculously that didn't enter my mind. Instead, we were swept up in Riley's fear and distress. Marg and I put our shoes on, grabbed a bottle of water and piled into the troop carrier with me driving and Riley directing us south-west out of the community on a road that was completely new to me.

We drove in silence for what seemed to be forever, but in reality was only fifteen or twenty minutes. Riley started to wail when we came closer to the area of the old man's death. He wasn't certain of the exact place so he instructed me to drive here and there over the rough land until we found the place. I climbed out of the Toyota with Riley leading the way and me following. Riley pointed at the body on the ground and then turned and hurried away, leaving me standing there staring. The old man was lying on his back. For all the world he looked as though he was sleeping peacefully in the shade of the leafy paperbark trees. Then I saw the gun lying near him. It was a rifle.

The peaceful and picturesque setting under the trees contrasted surreally with the body of the dead man. I gazed down at him feeling completely bewildered. The shocking reality of this tragedy hit me and I emerged from my cocoon of confusion. I went back to the vehicle where Riley and Marg were sitting waiting.

'We have to drive back to Yarralin and get in touch with the police. Ken the mechanic will know what to do. Let's go.'

'No,' Riley wailed, 'someone has to stay with the old man.'

We to'ed and fro'ed, with me insisting we all should go and Riley wailing that one person must stay. I thought it was my job as the new council clerk to go with Riley to Yarralin, but Riley didn't agree. He demanded I should stay with the dead man and he would go back with Marg. I was far too out of my depth to know the appropriate course of action so I gave in and agreed. I handed Riley the keys and he and Marg drove off leaving me to bear witness and guard the old man.

They were gone for what seemed to be hours. I had left the water bottle in the vehicle and now I was thirsty, hungry and very ill at ease. The old man looked very peaceful. I could hardly believe he was dead. I kept thinking he might wake up. Maybe he was just unconscious. I crept over to him feeling utterly foolish but I had to be sure. I stared intently at his chest hoping in vain that I would see a tiny movement of breath. I put my cheek near his mouth, but there was no breath and no movement. The poor man remained perfectly still.

The sight of the gun completely unnerved me. It was awful to see the weapon of death lying next to the old man. It was like an insult. Sacrilege. The weapon that caused his death should not be next to him. I really don't know what got into me but I picked that gun up and put it behind the tree so I couldn't see it.

I was more than relieved when, finally, I heard the sound of vehicles coming closer. As it turned out the police had been relatively close to Yarralin. Riley had found Ken, told him the story and Ken contacted the police. The cavalry had arrived. The police allowed me to return home and I thankfully left my guard duty and jumped into the Toyota with Riley to shakily drive home.

Much later, when the police and Ken came to my house, they were horrified when I told them I had moved the gun. Ken looked at me as if I was mentally deranged. Almost with one voice, and in utter amazement, they exclaimed, 'Haven't you watched police shows on television? You never, never touch the evidence.'

I felt totally humiliated at my utter foolishness and looked down at the floor.

The police filled us in on the awful story. The gun had a faulty trigger and it was the old man's grandson who had shot him. The boy had picked up the gun to play with and that's how the accident happened. I felt viscerally distressed for the child. He would be scarred for life with this tragedy. Worse still, a few weeks later, I overheard a woman say, 'He was the son of _____ Like father, like son.'

I grieved for the boy. Everyone knew what he had done, and who his father was. The accident would never be forgotten and he would be tarred with his father's brush. But perhaps, over time, it would be forgiven. I hoped so. The Yarralin community was in mourning and the sadness was palpable.

Life went on, however. My workload had increased and I was feeling more comfortable in the council clerk role. I was sorry that Margaretha had made her decision to leave Yarralin and head to Darwin, but I understood she felt it was time to move on. Our food cupboard was empty and the office was almost out of stationery. Marg and I would both drive to Katherine where we would share our last weekend together and I would do supermarket and stationery shopping. This time we chose to travel via Top Springs. It was nowhere near as beautiful as Jasper Gorge, but a much easier drive.

We stayed in a cabin at one of Katherine's caravan parks and it was a welcome sight after the long drive. That night we treated ourselves to a delicious restaurant meal and a couple of glasses of surprisingly cold red wine. Territorians never drank red wine at room temperature I learned. After all, who would want to drink wine that is 30 degrees or more? I was sad to see Marg drive off on her way to Darwin but very grateful for her friendship and support during my first weeks settling into Yarralin. Especially for being by my side during the tragedy of the old man.

Pigeon Hole

Yarralin had been the total focus of my work since arriving in the community, but it bothered me that I had not found time to visit the outstations of Pigeon Hole, Lingara or Yinguwunarri. I was keen to see and meet people in their own communities and observe their living conditions. Little did I know that an opportunity would present itself for me to visit Pigeon Hole, but not in the way I wanted.

I heard a man's voice asking to speak with the council clerk. I popped my head out of my office door and saw a middle-aged Aussie bloke standing there.

'I'm Barbara, the council clerk. Can I help you?'

'G'day, I'm Max the housing consultant. There are a couple of houses at Pigeon Hole that I need to talk to you about.'

I was vaguely aware that houses were being constructed at Pigeon Hole. I gazed at him, trying to remember what I knew about the two houses. As I scrabbled through my overloaded memory banks, I recalled being told there had been funding for two houses. After a long period of waiting, the Pigeon Hole community had been overjoyed that finally, a government grant had been approved and the small community would get some relief from their overcrowded housing.

I invited Max into my office, transferred a pile of papers from the visitors chair to the top of a filing cabinet and asked him to sit down.

'I don't really know anything about the houses,' I confessed. 'You'll have to fill me in.'

'Everything has been going well up to now, but we have hit a problem,' Max said. 'There's not enough money to finish the houses. Prices have gone up and the builder informed me last week that there isn't enough money to finish them.'

As I looked at him, I felt lost for words. Yarralin was on a tight budget and I knew there was no money to inject into the Pigeon Hole housing. I couldn't imagine what I was supposed to say or do.

'I don't know what to say,' I admitted.

We looked at each in silence. Eventually a thought came to me.

'Have you spoken with the NT Housing Department?' I asked.

'Yes I have. They told me there is nothing they can do,' he replied.

I had a dismal vision of two half-built houses deteriorating over time.

'What's your suggestion then?' I asked.

Max shifted in his seat and said, 'The builder suggested that we can save money by not insulating the houses. Later, when the council can afford it, you can put the insulation in.'

With today's high level of awareness of climate change and energy costs, it seems strange that until that moment in 1995, I'd never given a thought to insulating houses.

'Do most houses have insulation?' I asked.

'Yes, but not always. It depends on the money,' Max said. 'I think we both should drive over to Pigeon Hole and take a look.'

I was excited to visit Pigeon Hole for the first time, but sad that it was to give the community the news there would be no insulation in their new houses. I explained the situation to one of the Yarralin councillors and asked him to come with us. It was a two-hour drive to Pigeon Hole on a rough dirt road. Fortunately it was the dry season as the road could become unpassable in the wet. We went in the council troop carrier so I got to drive.

I found it somewhat stressful being the driver with such experienced passengers watching me as I carefully steered our way through the potholes and corrugations. As we drove into Pigeon Hole, I saw immediately it was much smaller than Yarralin, a hamlet rather than a village, with less than a dozen houses. When we pulled up and climbed out of the vehicle, I took in a deep breath and felt the peaceful atmosphere of Pigeon Hole. With its shady trees, it looked cooler than Yarralin. Max pointed out the two new steel-clad houses and I was heartily relieved to find my vision of half-built houses wasn't true. Both houses looked neat and clean and ready to move in. A Pigeon Hole leader and a couple of younger people came over to join us. Max explained the money problem again and led the way into the houses for an inspection. To my inexperienced eye, it looked as though there was only finishing off to do. It was a nice house – open plan and full of light.

As we stood in the small kitchen, Max explained that because the government would not increase the grant to cover the cost of insulation and the council didn't have any funds, there was only one option. The houses would have to remain uninsulated. Reluctantly we all agreed for the builder to complete the work without insulation.

The daily temperature in Yarralin averages around 35 degrees. In the hot season it can be in the low 40s and doesn't get much lower than 23 or 24 degrees at night. I was to discover much later that during a school experiment, when students were asked to measure the ground temperature in the heat of the day, it was 75 degrees. The Pigeon Hole houses were not insulated and I was fairly sure Yarralin houses weren't either. The heat, lack of fans and lack of insulation rendered many of the houses in all the communities almost uninhabitable. Our bookkeeper, Pam, had a thermometer on the wall of her kitchen. In the hot months it read 56 degrees. Unbearable. She deserved a medal for cooking in that hot box.

The Pigeon Hole insulation story fortunately had a good ending as funds were eventually made available and the homes got their long-awaited insulation. Such a relief for them and me.

Jackie Anzac from Pigeon Hole

A knock at my office door was the first indication that Pigeon Hole was to become a feature in my life. I looked up and saw a tall, handsome Aboriginal man wearing a large akubra stockman's hat. It was Jacky Anzac from Pigeon Hole. I had seen Jacky around the community but this was the first time I had spoken with him.

'Come in, Jackie, how can I help you?'

Jackie settled himself into my visitor's chair. He gazed at the floor for a few moments as he collected his thoughts.

'I've been over to see Jim at Victoria River Downs. He's the manager there. I asked him for a job to run a droving team. He wants to talk to you about the job. Can you phone him please?'

Of course I agreed. I was puzzled and intrigued by the request. Why would the VRD manager want to talk to me? I also felt a slight tingle of excitement as I had never been on a cattle station before. The mystique of the cattle industry in the Northern Territory, fed by the iconic outback stories of *We of the Never Never* by Jeannie Gunn and *Kings in Grass Castles* by Mary Durack had fascinated me for decades. Gunn and Durack told their truths and wrote their facts as they saw them. They were stories of their time that were inescapably coloured by the prevailing societal views and available knowledge. Storytellers, song writers, historians and anthropologists have since written their truths and facts and added more layers to the continually unfolding history of the Northern Territory and Victoria River region. Now that I was living in Yarralin, I had learned there was a very dark side to the cattle industry. Nevertheless, I was chuffed to be invited to The Big Run to meet the manager.

I gave Jim a call and we set up a meeting. The day arrived and Jackie came to the office to collect me, looking like the fair dinkum stockman that he was. We set off to VRD, 25 kilometres away. As we drove in the main gates of the station, I was surprised at how many buildings there were. Jackie directed me past the 'big house', where the station manager and his family lived, and past the VRD store to a largish building where we pulled up. Jackie led the way to Jim's office, which had a closed door. We knocked and were invited into a large timber-lined office, very masculine and businesslike. Jim gestured to the visitor chairs at his large desk.

Jim explained to me that he was considering a proposition Jackie had put to him. He went on to tell me that Jackie Anzac had been the head stockman on VRD. It was Jim's respect for Jackie that he was willing to give him a go at building a droving team that would be used to drove and quieten wild cattle. Apparently Heli-Mustering was successful at finding and mustering cattle, but the animals needed to be quietened down before they were trucked to Darwin for shipping to Indonesia in the live-cattle trade. If Jackie succeeded in getting his team together, then Jim guaranteed he would provide Jackie's team with droving work. My role was to apply for a grant that would pay for horses, some fencing, equipment for the team and training. There was one condition. The current president of Yarralin Council was not to have any control over the project. If he was, the deal was off. I was a bit taken aback but said, 'If Jackie can manage to sort that out, I certainly won't invite or involve the president in any way.' It was an exciting offer for Jackie and the men who would join his team. We made the deal.

On the way back to Yarralin, Jackie told me there was around $50,000 unspent grant money from a cattle project that hadn't gone ahead. This money would kick start the new droving contract. Jackie had already spoken with the aforementioned council president who had agreed for Jackie and his project to use it. As soon as we were back in the office, I phoned the accountant who confirmed that the grant could be reactivated. He agreed to set it in motion when I faxed our side of the paperwork to him.

15 A fraught history

The relationship between Victoria River Downs Station and the people of Yarralin and its outstations has a fraught history of massacre, murder, exploitation and dispossession of Aboriginal land.

It wasn't until I came to write this book in 2022 that I gained an understanding of the painful and chaotic history of the people of Yarralin. Their history of suffering is embedded in the history of the cattle industry. It was their unpaid labour and exploitation that helped to build the pastoral industry, which today contributes 65 per cent of the total value of the Northern Territory's primary industry.[78]

The following is my distillation of the history of Aboriginal people who lived and worked on Victoria River Downs Station. My primary sources were *Hidden Histories* by anthropologist Deborah Bird Rose and *A Wild History* by historian Darrell Lewis, supplemented with information from a variety of websites. For readers who wish to have a fuller understanding of the past, I thoroughly recommend delving into the books by Bird and Lewis.

In 1879, wealthy financiers and pastoralists Charles Fisher and Maurice Lyons leased 41,155 square kilometres to form Victoria River Downs (VRD) Station.[79] This enormous area of land, equivalent to 60 per cent of Tasmania, was initially stocked with 20,000 head of cattle overlanded by Nat Buchanan in 1883. This heralded the clash over land and resources which resulted in the murder, massacre, dispossession and exploitation of the Victoria River Aboriginal people who had been living on their lands for tens of thousands of years. It was also the beginning of the environmental degradation of the lands for which the Aboriginal people were custodians.

The invasion of Whites and their cattle became what anthropologist Deborah Bird Rose called a violently brutal 'death-space' 'where Aboriginal people were treated like game to be hunted, vermin to be exterminated, as slaves of sexual and murderous violence'.[80] Riley Young from Lingara told Rose that when he was a boy, his family told him to behave carefully around Europeans because 'they shoot you like a dog and just let you burn on the fire'. Riley said that 'the white man been coming here stealing the land from blackfellow. Wasting blackfellows, shooting blackfellows from land'.[81] As Bird stated, the advice Riley received marks a moment somewhere between the days when people were routinely shot, poisoned or beaten to death, their bodies burned, and the day they stood up and walked off the land.[82]

The Victoria River people did not submit quietly to the invasion of their lands. They fought back, spearing the cattle and stealing the White man's goods. In the 1890s, the Aboriginal people on VRD were reported as being 'excessively troublesome'. However, the guns and violent tactics of the White men smashed the resistance. As the historian Henry Reynolds stated, 'Aborigines were confined to ever-smaller areas of rough, resource-poor country.'[83] Retaliation was certain for spearing livestock or stealing goods. There was also fighting between rival clans. It was a murderous and chaotic time and life in the bush became increasingly hazardous. Eventually Aboriginal people had to choose between two evils, 'staying out' or 'coming in'.[84] Many Victoria River people chose to come in, and in October 1900, the Wickham Blacks camp on VRD was established.[85] As the Aboriginal people learnt basic English and developed station skills, they became a ready pool of unpaid labour under the control of station Whites. In 1900 VRD was purchased by Sydney Kidman and in 1909 it was bought by Bovril Australian Estates, an English absentee-owner corporation.

The conflict did not cease for those who had come in, or those who stayed out. There are stories of bush people sneaking in to see relatives or claim women and being captured or shot. As told by Anzac Munnganyi of Pigeon Hole, whose father worked at Gordon Creek police station, when Aborigines who were forced to work decided to run away, they were tracked and brought back. Some were chained and others shot.[86]

During the following decades, station Blacks suffered from inadequate nutrition, poor housing, a lack of medical treatment and brutal treatment at the hands of Whites. On VRD in 1967, Aboriginal housing was described by a writer as 'dirty little humpies [that] look as if a good push would knock them down. Sheets of old corrugated-iron serve for beds, supported by empty oil-drums; a few rags of clothing are flung over bits of string attached to nails in the wall, strips of sacking make the doors'.[87]

Infant mortality was extremely high and housing and sanitation ranged from non-existent to substandard. Work-related injuries and disease were compounded by malnutrition. VRD Aboriginal people assert that Europeans settled on the blood and bones of the Aborigines they killed.[88]

Despite their hardship and difficult living conditions, many Aboriginal people became skilled cattle-station workers proud of their ability. Doug Campbell, a Ngarinyman Traditional Owner, and Anzac Munnganyi, a Bilinara Traditional Owner, told of their expertise in mustering, droving and handling cattle. They spoke of hard days with wild cattle to deal with and no yards or fences. Branding cattle was particularly hard and dangerous physical work with none of the cattle crushes used today to control the animals.

In the early days, the women were also used in mustering and droving but later their duties were confined to domestic servitude. They worked just as hard as the men, starting before dawn and working late into the night. They cooked for the station, washed clothes and dug vegetable gardens from the hard soil. They carted all the water from the river in buckets.

Classified as wards of the state and as inmates of cattle-station 'institutions' until the 1967 referendum allowed them to become citizens in their own country, the Victoria River Aborigines' rights were massively restricted, their voices largely unheard. 'Neither their bodies, nor their children, nor their labour, nor the fruits of their labour were their own'.[89]

In the 1930s there was a conference on wages for Aborigines and 'half-castes', chaired by the Protector of Aborigines to determine whether they should be paid.[90] After several days of discussion, the resolution was to exempt stations from paying wages as long as they were providing 'food, clothing, tobacco, medicine and other reasonable requirements in kind' for employees and dependents. Pastoralists and missionaries voted for the resolution; union representatives voted against.[91] The food provided was generally flour, tea, sugar and salt, meat, but no vegetables. Clothing and poor-quality boots were issued for the mustering season. At the end of the season, the Aborigines had to hand back their clothing and boots when they were turned off to go bush.

In 1943, Patrol Officer Sweeney reported that 'cattle stations are generally unable or unwilling to bear the full responsibility for the dependent women and children and old people on their stations. The result of their policy has been the decreasing native population and stagnation for the natives that remain on their holdings'. Four years later he expressed concern over the few births of 'full-blood' children. He noted that VRD, 'the largest station in the Northern Territory' had only seven births of 'full bloods' in the preceding three years.[92]

This was corroborated by Deborah Bird Rose who said many women she spoke with about the issue told her of having lost their children in the first year of life. Some had no children and many older women had no surviving children.[93]

Although the killings diminished, over the following decades death still bore heavily on VRD Aboriginal people. By the mid-1940s, Aborigines seemed to be dying out and labour was becoming a problem for the cattle industry. Anthropologists Ronald and Catherine Berndt were hired by Vesteys at neighbouring Wave Hill cattle station to investigate. Their report recommending food, housing, sanitation and medical care was rejected in favour of the strategy of bringing in more 'wild blacks'.[94]

After World War II, wages were introduced for Aboriginal workers. Yet, in spite of unionists' arguments for equality, they were paid well below the minimum award wage, which did not keep pace with inflation in the 1950s.[95]

In 1951, Welfare Patrol Officer Evans tried to improve working conditions for the Aboriginal women carrying buckets of water up the very high and steep banks from the river to the homestead. Evans noted that the women would spend an average of two hours daily carting water and that each load weighed 80 pounds. At Gordon Creek outstation (now Yarralin), the water was carried about 250 yards, then up a bank about 35 feet high. At Pigeon Hole the distance was about 450 yards and the bank climbed about 25 feet high. He approach the manager Mr Magnussen who said that 'in his opinion the work occasioned no distress and was a fit duty for lubras'.[96]

The disregard and neglect of the children was also evident as the Aboriginal children on VRD were not educated. The VRD manager stated the view in uncompromising terms, 'This school has always been restricted to White children – educating the Aboriginal children is against our policy.'[97] Until 1953, children of mixed ancestry were taken from their families and placed in institutions. After being 'educated', they became cheap labour pools in towns and in the bush.

The mismanagement, neglect and abuse of Aboriginal people on the vast cattle station was replicated in the neglect and mistreatment of the cattle and the environment. Bovril owned VRD from 1909 to 1955. They maintained a capital-starved open-range system of running overstocked cattle with little fencing and very few bores. In 1936, Gordon Buchanan wrote, 'It is safe to say that the Bovril company loses from ten to fifteen thousand head of cattle yearly for the need of bores and the necessary equipment to give them a drink.'[98] Fifteen years later Gerry Ash, a stockman who worked on VRD in the early 1950s, described VRD as having 'the largest uncontrolled herd in the world'.[99] Needless to say, a serious lack of capital combined with huge herds of uncontrolled cattle severely degraded the banks of rivers and springs, trampled native flora, set up large-scale erosion sites and changed the natural environment, probably forever.

The appalling treatment of Aboriginal people and the environmental degradation continued through the following ownerships of VRD, that of Buckland in 1955, Hooker Corporation in 1960 and Peter Sherwin in 1984. The long-term pattern of abuse of Aboriginal people and land degradation stopped with the current owners, Heytesbury, who purchased VRD in 1989. Over time, the cattle station land has been whittled down until today it is 8,900 square kilometres. The Heytesbury company is researching and implementing a sustainably managed grazing system.

The conditions suffered by the Aboriginal population on VRD were the same, or worse, than those suffered by the Gurindji on Wave Hill Station, privately owned by the UK Vestey Group. On 23 August 1966, Vincent Lingiari, a Gurindji man, led around two hundred of his people in a strike that became known as the Wave Hill walk-off. The strike was more than a demand for wages and working conditions. It was the reclamation of their Country and of their home. In 1967 they petitioned the governor-general to grant a lease of 1,300 square kilometres around Daguragu stating, 'We feel that morally the land is ours and should be returned to us'. This was the first claim for traditional Aboriginal land in Australia.[100] It should be noted very clearly, that wages and land were not the only motivations for the walk-off. In the petition of April 1967 to Lord Casey, the Governor-General of Australia, the Gurindji people stated the walk-off was also to 'protect our women'.[101] Given the physical and sexual abuse of Aboriginal women over the decades of White settlement, it is extraordinary that this demand is not generally well known.

Lord Vestey offered to surrender 90 square kilometres of Wave Hill Station to the Gurindji people. The land was acquired by the Aboriginal Land Fund Commission and, on 16 August 1975 at Daguragu, Prime Minister Whitlam gave the deeds of leasehold title to the Gurindji, symbolically pouring soil into the hands of Vincent Lingiari saying; 'Vincent Lingiari,

I solemnly hand to you these deeds as proof, in Australian law, that these lands belong to the Gurindji people.'[102]

The Wave Hill walk-off set the scene for the VRD walk-off in 1972 when people from VRD and the adjoining Humbert River Station joined the strike and moved to Wattie Creek with the Gurindji people. The day after the people left VRD, in a truly vindictive act, the Hooker Corporation manager on VRD ordered 'that their homes be razed and bulldozed into gullies'. As Jack Doolan, the Regional Welfare Officer said in January 1972, the Aboriginal camp on VRD was 'appalling' and 'shocking', nevertheless they had been the people's home for all of their lives. In Rose's words, 'If VRD people were in any doubt prior to the strike about their vulnerability, the manager's reaction should have convinced them'.[103]

In October 1973 Hooker agreed in principle to return 240 square kilometres to the VRD Aboriginal people. Most Aboriginal people were not satisfied with the size of this offer, but were prepared to regard it as a gesture of goodwill. On 25 November 1973, a group of Ngarinyman people returned to VRD, settling at the old Gordon Creek outstation which they named Yarralin.[104] The Bilinara people went to Pigeon Hole and the Humbert River people went to Yarralin and from there moved to Lingara outstation near the old Humbert River homestead.

Two years later, Justice Ward, the Interim Land Commissioner, heard the land rights case for Yarralin. He wrote to the Federal Minister for Aboriginal Affairs stating that the Aboriginal land claim had been 'effectively and mutually settled' between Hooker of VRD and the Ngarinyman people of Yarralin. He further wrote, 'all that remains is for your own department and that of the Northern Territory to complete the legal formalities'. Tragically, the recommendation of Justice Ward was never followed by the Australian government and no reasons for the lack of action were ever made public.[105]

The combined population of Yarralin and Lingara was 170 relatively permanent residents. By 1981 government agencies had provided Yarralin with thirteen one-room corrugated-iron shacks with a water tap in the yard, four communal pit toilets and three shower blocks. There were two water tanks fed by diesel bore pumps. The people of Lingara built their own shelters which were functional in that they provided shelter from the sun and rain. Both communities had outdoor bush kitchens with no storage facilities. Apart from a generator to supply electricity to the school, there was no power available for the people.[106]

Delivery of food was fortnightly. Because there was no refrigeration, only small amounts of fresh vegetables and fruit were available and these were consumed within a couple of days. Fresh beef, which was plentiful, was supplemented by bush tucker. Apart from meat, the standard diet consisted of white-flour bread, tea, sugar, milk, tinned fruit and vegetables, and juices. The food was shared, which meant no individuals or families went hungry.[107]

One of the most significant achievements for Yarralin was a school that took children through to year six. It was a two-way school where both European and Aboriginal subjects were taught. Local people were employed as teachers for the Aboriginal lessons as well as providing teaching assistance with the European lessons.[108] For reasons unknown to me, the two-way education was not continued. Instead, primary-school teaching came to be delivered solely in English.

In 1984, twelve years after the VRD walk-off, the Northern Territory Government finally decided to hand over a 140-square-kilometre excision. This was 100 square kilometres smaller than had been agreed with Hooker. Furthermore, the land was not transferred under the Land Rights Act. Instead, the title was given to the Ngarinyman Yarralin Community Incorporated. A second block north of Yarralin of 355 square kilometres was transferred to the Northern Territory Development Land Corporation. This was a Northern Territory government tactic to thwart land being claimed under the Land Rights Act. After twelve years of strikes and negotiations, the Hooker Corporation relinquished about 4 per cent of its land. Yarralin Aborigines got title to 1.2 per cent and the Northern Territory Government got title to about 2.8 per cent.[109]

Unfortunately, the road ahead would not be smooth. Deborah Bird Rose said by the time it got title to the Yarralin block, the Ngarinyman Yarralin Community Incorporated had 'begun to pile up debts through what appears at best to be mismanagement of funds', and in 1985 the title to their land was held by a bank in Katherine as security against a massive overdraft.[110]

In the mid-1990s, shortly before I arrived at Yarralin to take up duties as the council clerk, Ngarinyman Yarralin Community Incorporated was dissolved. Because it was an incorporated body under Northern Territory legislation, the Northern Territory Commissioner for Consumer Affairs seized the title to the Yarralin block, which it held until 2016.[111]

Yarralin's luck turned when a surveying oversight was discovered. A 3,100 hectare slice of land south of the Yarralin block had been left unalienated. The Northern Land Council took advantage of this oversight and lodged the 'Wickham River Land Claim' in 1983. At the hearing, the Northern Territory government conceded that there were indeed Traditional Owners and the claim should succeed. This enabled the Wickham River claim to be parcelled with the other two claims. All three claims were scheduled as Aboriginal freehold land under the Land Rights Act.[112]

Another thirteen years passed, but finally justice was delivered as Yarralin was handed back to traditional owners after forty-four years, on 14 June 2016. Hundreds of Yarralin residents gathered for a momentous celebration of the handback of their land. Federal Indigenous Affairs Minister Nigel Scullion handed over the title deeds for the 50,310 hectare Wickham River land claim on behalf of the Commonwealth.[113]

Deborah Bird Rose was present at the ceremony. She spoke of the people who had walked off VRD and then waited decades for the land to be returned, and who were still waiting when they died. She said it was a time for reflection to remember those old people on the handback day. Yarralin never gave up the fight – land rights is another step in the long struggle for justice.[114] (See also Appendix 2 Victoria River Downs.)

Traditional Owners of Yarralin with Indigenous Affairs Minister Senator Nigel Scullion hold a framed copy of the title deeds.
Photo supplied by Northern Land Council, July 2016, Issue 3

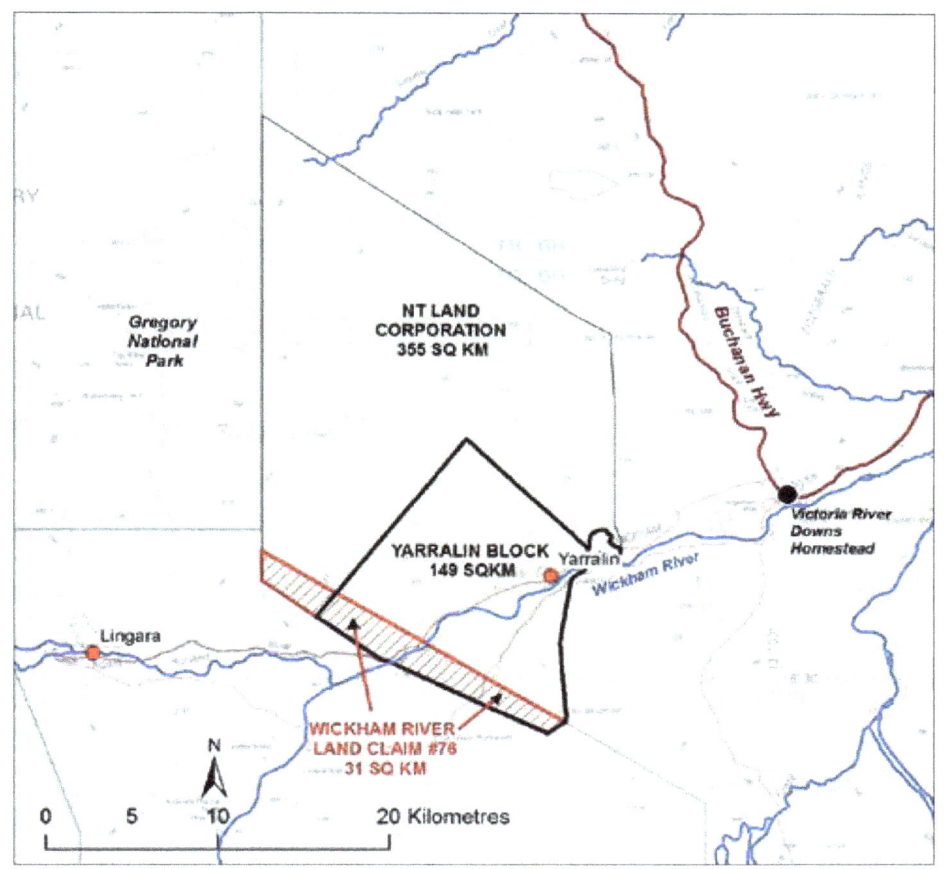

Wickham River Land Claim Title Deed Handover 14 June 2016
Supplied by Northern Land Council, July 2016, Issue 3

16 Mistakes, achievements and failure

Jacky Anzac had vanished from my view for a few weeks. My settling-in period was over and I was caught up in a myriad of tasks from dealing with government to requests from community members. I was also learning about the differences between my mainstream White culture and the Aboriginal culture that surrounded me. I recognised obvious Aboriginal culture such as men's or women's business, having strong family ties and not looking people directly in the eyes. But there were situations that I had thought of as normal, when in fact they were only normal to me with my cultural perspective.

Until I lived in Yarralin, I had no idea that 'small talk' was cultural. I thought it was something that everybody did. Being a friendly person and wanting to connect, I started making small talk with the people in my new community. I did the small talk thing about the weather. You know how it goes, 'It's hot today', or 'Do you think it will rain?'. That sort of nonsense. And then there were the inane questions I asked councillors and CDEP workers to make casual conversation: 'How are you?' 'Have you had a good day?', or 'What have you got planned for the weekend?'.

The responses I received varied from a one-syllable reply, to silence, to a mystified look. Even when someone did reply, 'Good', to my 'How are you?', there was no question back to me. I was engaged in one-sided conversations. At first I thought people were shy because they didn't know me. Then I thought maybe they didn't speak enough English, or perhaps they didn't like speaking to White people. Finally it dawned on me that my brand of small talk was something not done in Yarralin. My small talk was White culture, not Aboriginal culture.

My next cultural awakening was about questions. I was forever asking questions. When was this? Why was that? Who was there? What happened? How did it happen? For all my incessant questions, I was often left none the wiser. Another dawning of consciousness arrived as I realised that I rarely heard an Aboriginal person asking a question. This was completely bewildering to me.

How can they learn things or know things? I pondered silently to myself.

Over time I learned that I needed to wait for information to be revealed to me. My questions were another manifestation of my White culture.

It was Riley Young from Lingara who taught me another invaluable cultural lesson. I had previously worked in rural Cambodia where raising chickens was a way of life, and in some cases, a stepping stone to a better life. My friend Saman, who had founded her own non-government organisation in a very poor province, was passionate about chicken-raising and I caught some of her passion. When I received notification that community grants were available, chicken-raising leapt into my mind.

What a wonderful idea for Lingara and Pigeon Hole, I thought excitedly. *They could raise chickens for meat as well as eggs! Great nutrition for the children, and perhaps they could sell chickens to the store.*

The next time Riley came to the office I put the idea to him. He listened very politely to my enthusiastic idea.

'What do you think Riley? Do you think it is a good idea?' I asked excitedly.

Riley pondered for a few minutes and then said, 'Might be a good idea.'

Hmmm, that doesn't sound like a yes or no, I thought.

'Okay then, you have a think about it and I'll talk to you next week,' I replied.

As I thought about Riley's response, realised I hadn't fully explained the chicken-raising concept. I decided to put that right the next time he came to the office.

I saw Riley at the store a few days later and enthusiastically invited him back to my office. 'I've got more to tell you about chicken-raising, Riley,' I told him eagerly, and launched into my stories about chicken-raising in Cambodia and how good it had been for the villagers.

Poor Riley. He is a very polite and an altogether lovely man. My chicken enthusiasm was overwhelming for him. How was he to say 'No'? At the end of my explanation, he agreed to try chicken-raising. Happily I headed to the computer and completed the grant application. I was determined to make this grant worthwhile. By the time I added up the cost of the materials for a very handsome chicken house, installation of a nearby tap, fencing and netting material and tools, I managed to inflate the grant to $17,000. I immediately faxed it to the government department.

It was probably about three weeks later I received notification the grant was approved. I was astonished at the speed of approval and quite chuffed that the bureaucrats had been impressed by the marvellous innovation of chicken-raising. I immediately told Riley the good news and asked him to make some time to discuss putting the project into action.

Time went on and Riley was always too busy to work with me. Then out of the blue he appeared at my office door. 'I've been thinking about the chickens,' he started. 'Sorry but we can't do it. Snakes will come for the chickens and a snake might bite a kid. The people would blame me.' That threw me for a loop. Snakes! I hadn't factored snakes into my idea.

'Of course, Riley, I understand. Don't worry. We'll find another worthwhile project for the money.'

As Riley's objection sank into my head, I slowly realised what I had done. My enthusiasm for my idea had overridden a basic community development fundamental. The community must lead. Instead, I'd foisted a Cambodian idea onto an Aboriginal outstation leader in cattle country. Riley had known all along it wouldn't work but he needed to find a way to convince a 'Whitefella' to hear his objection. As I reflected on the end of the chicken project, I could clearly see that the idea would never have worked. This was a completely different culture in which chicken-raising simply didn't feature. In practical terms, it would not have been possible for Riley to have kept the kids and dogs out of the chicken house. I had just relearnt an old lesson and gained a new cultural perspective. Indeed, I had already learned this lesson in Cambodia where people often say 'Yes' so they don't offend. I now had to apply it in Yarralin.

I phoned our accountant and explained the 'changed circumstances' of the $17,000 grant.

'Can we keep it for a while to see if there is another project that would be more suitable?' I asked. 'I'm sure we can spend the money well. There is so much need here.'

John reluctantly agreed with me. 'Okay. Ask the council at the next meeting what they want to do and I'll go along with their decision.'

At our next council meeting, I explained the situation and they unanimously decided to let the money sit in the bank until a good solution was found. I put the grant to the back of my mind where it could await a good project for activation.

Some time later, George from Yinguwunarri outstation brought a tale of woe to the council meeting. He desperately needed funds to improve the infrastructure at his community. His community members had moved to Daguragu where there was a larger community and many more services. Poor George wanted to attract people back to Yinguwunarri and was having no luck.

At the next council meeting, Riley took the floor. He commiserated with George's financial issues and lack of community people living at the outstation.

'To help you, George' he said, 'Lingara will give you the $17,000 grant. We don't need it. Your people do.'

George was stunned as were the other council members and I. The council president looked at me and asked, 'Can Riley do that?' I had no idea. 'I'll phone the accountant after the meeting and check,' I replied.

I felt quite overcome by Riley's generosity. What an amazing man to gift his $17,000 to an outstation that had more need for the money. The accountant gave the okay and advised me to submit a grant amendment to DAA before he made the paper transfer to Yinguwunarri.

I called George into the office to start the grant application. The main problem for the community was a lack of power and insufficient water. The community also needed a more robust vehicle to get in and out of Yinguwunarri community. These items would cost substantially more than $17,000 but we decided to have a go. Between us we documented the sorrowful case of trying to provide transport, lighting and water to an outstation to encourage families to live there permanently.

A couple of months had passed when George from Yinguwunarri appeared at my office door. 'We don't want Lingara's money anymore,' he announced. 'Just leave it like it was.'

I was most surprised and asked George what had happened. But George was a man of few words and there was no more information. I sent a note to DAA withdrawing the Yinguwunarri grant application and copied it to the accountant. The $17,000 was transferred back to Lingara. When I informed the council, there were mutterings directed at George followed by helpless shrugs. The money was relegated to the 'too hard' basket for the time being.

Riley took his responsibility for the $17,000 grant very seriously. He didn't want it wasted and he didn't want it to be sent back to the government. It was community money now. He turned up at my office with his next offer.

'Pigeon Hole is a good community with good people,' he stated. 'The money should go to them. They'll spend it the proper way.'

'Okay, Riley. We'll raise it at the next council meeting,' I replied, and put the item on the agenda.

By the time the meeting came round, Pigeon Hole had heard about Riley's plan and had discussed it thoroughly. Although they appreciated Riley's offer, they knocked it back. I was most surprised at this. After all, it is not often that $17,000 is offered to you. But as I reflected on it, I realised that, on the one hand it was quite a lot of money, but on the other hand, not nearly enough for what was needed. Pigeon Hole needed more houses, they needed a better road, they wanted a new health clinic. Riley's gift would not actually help with the things they wanted.

With all three outstations rejecting the grant, the $17,000 had not been spent within the financial year. This was very annoying to DAA, which had to carry over the grant into the next financial year. I received warnings that we must spend the grant or return it.

With Pigeon Hole turning down the grant, it was now up to the council to decide what to do. In the end, it was unanimously decided by the three outstations of Lingara, Pigeon Hole and Yinguwunarri that the money should go to Yarralin housing. This was a very easy grant application for me to write. All I had to do was ask Phil the builder what he wanted and he had a list as long as his arm. He consulted his Aboriginal team of workers and after much discussion they decided to put the bulk of the money into house repairs, buy more tools, and allocate nail bags and overalls to the workers. It was a great outcome that pleased everyone.

I had thoroughly enjoyed the saga of the $17,000 grant and was in awe of the careful thought and consideration that the outstation Traditional Owners and council had given to this money. They were determined that the windfall would not be wasted. It had to used properly for the people.

Those chicken-raising dreams of mine had turned out to be concerning and disturbing for all of us. I vowed to myself that I would never again write a grant application unless I was completely sure that it was wanted and agreed to by all those concerned.

The stockmen team

Jacky Anzac had been very busy over the past few weeks as he started building his stockmen team. He had regained the Yarralin saddles borrowed by the Daguragu community. With the horses the VRD manager had lent him, Jacky had enough saddles and horses to start a droving team. A couple of the men were relatives from Pigeon Hole and others were older men he had worked with in the past. Most of the men were already employed on the Community Development Employment Project (CDEP). For those who weren't, we did the paperwork and got them on the program. As well as having experienced men on his team, Jacky wanted to train a team of young men for the future.

Jackie was starting from scratch and he worked tirelessly. He'd teamed up with the highly experienced cattleman Bill Fordham, who helped him to negotiate his contract with VRD. The contract was to move cattle for fifty days over a six-month period. Jackie's plan included developing a team of young Pigeon Hole and Yarralin men to be the stockmen for his droving contract. The lads needed to be trained and Jackie wanted Bill's company to do the training.

Bill was the first Aboriginal person to become a registered training provider in the Northern Territory.[115] Bill and his wife, Shirley, had purchased King Valley Station and set up their training company, Broken Spur, to train young Aboriginal men who wanted to work in the cattle industry. It was a thirteen-week course in the basics of stock-horse riding, horseshoeing, fencing, occupational health and safety and communications.

A few weeks earlier, Chris, an officer from the Department of Education, Employment and Training (DEET) in Katherine visited Yarralin to introduce DEET's foundation skills and vocational training. He urged me to call if I had questions or training ideas I wanted to run past him. With Jackie's need for training, this was the perfect time, so I dug out his card and phoned him. I explained Jackie's contract with VRD and the need to train the stockmen. Chris jumped at the chance to be involved.

'This is right up my alley,' he said. 'I'll come out to Yarralin next week and we can work it through with Jackie. There's no problem about Broken Spur. It is an accredited training provider and DEET can provide funding for the course.'

That was the start of our three-way partnership, Jackie, Chris and me.

We met many times to work through the requirements of training a droving team. Jackie's team was morphing from a great idea into reality.

Jackie's first completed milestone was getting the horse yards built. The Yarralin, Pigeon Hole and Lingara communities turned up in force to celebrate the horse yards with a community barbecue. I felt a bit out of place as there were very few women at the barbecue but I wouldn't have missed it. Notwithstanding the long history of exploitation and hardship working on VRD, the Aboriginal people had been highly skilled stockmen and were proud of their abilities. Since the VRD walk-off in 1972, there had been few opportunities for Yarralin men to continue working in the cattle industry. Jackie Anzac wasn't aiming at a single contract, he was pursuing a new future for young men, offering them employment, purpose and pride as stockmen.

I was at the table getting my steak sandwich when the new council president, George, walked over to me. He was holding a lump of very fatty meat in his hand.

He looked at me and asked, 'Why do you think I'm eating this fat?'

I shook my head, silently telling him I didn't know.

'It's because this is the rubbish meat that Vestey threw on the ground for Aboriginal people to eat. I got used to it.' Then he turned calmly and walked away.

My foolish mistake of a couple of weeks ago had come back to bite me. Somehow or other, Daguragu, Wave Hill and Vestey had come into a conversation I was having with George in my office. Before I could stop myself, I had blurted out that when I lived in England I had shared a house with Lord Vestey's great nephew. What a clanger!

I knew I would never forget that moment at Jackie's celebration barbecue, when an experience from my working holiday in England many decades ago crashed into my present. Being confronted with my foolishness took some of the gloss off the celebration for me. Shortly after I returned to the office. Another lesson learned.

Education failure

My house had a common boundary with the Department of Education house where the primary-school principal lived with her son. In my first few months, I had seen Pat on the weekends when she worked in her garden, but I had not yet met her. I was a bit surprised that she had not come to the council office to introduce herself, but I shrugged it off, thinking she was probably too busy. I was keen to learn about the primary school and hoped that we could form some sort of working relationship. One Saturday afternoon I decided to climb the chicken-wire fence between our properties and meander over to her house. Pat was in her fifties and I knew from my office colleagues she had been teaching in Yarralin for a couple of years prior to my arrival. Pat was a small, trim, grey-haired woman who looked very much at home in her garden. I smiled my greeting as I walked up to her.

'Hi there, I'm Barbara the new council clerk and I live just over there,' pointing to my house.

'I'm Pat,' she replied. 'The principal at the primary school. I heard there was a new council clerk. Are you settling in okay?'

'Yes thanks, there is a lot of work to do, but I'm enjoying it.'

I had expected that Pat would be neighbourly and offer me a cup of tea or cool drink. Instead, she remained silent. Awkwardly, I tried asking a few friendly questions.

'How long have you been here?'

'Are you a long-time Territorian or from somewhere else?'

Pat was certainly no conversationalist. In fact her brief answers bordered on rudeness.

I thought I better cut my losses before it became embarrassing.

'Okay, I can see you are busy, I'll get going. Perhaps we can have a cup of tea together one day?' I suggested.

Social etiquette gave Pat little choice but to agree, 'Yes, we'll have a cup of tea one day.'

My hopes of friendly relations were dashed, but my interest in the primary school was not going away. I decided to wait a little while and invite her over to my place for a cuppa. My expectation was that the school community could somehow be integrated with the broader community. I hoped Pat and I could work together on community or school issues and do 'feel-good' community-development projects together.

A few weeks later when I spotted Pat in the garden, I climbed the fence again and suggested we have that cup of tea. This time she agreed and asked me to come back in a couple of hours when she finished her gardening for the day.

Her house was much 'homier' than mine with comfortable furniture and pictures on the walls. She had prepared some afternoon tea and we settled down to have a chat. Pat was a very experienced teacher and said that she enjoyed teaching at Yarralin. She seemed to be fond of the children and pleased with their progress. At that time she was the only teacher at the school, although a beginner teacher was to join her a bit later in the term.

'Would it be all right with you if I visited you at the school one day so I could see the children in the class?' I asked.

Pat reluctantly agreed saying, 'Yes, but you mustn't stay long as I don't want the class disrupted.'

Of course I agreed and we made a time for the next week. It was a bright and cheerful classroom with the children's pictures decorating the walls. Pat introduced me to the children and I took a seat while she continued teaching. It only took about five minutes of Pat ignoring me for me to realise that she did not want me to be there. I stood up and waved a small goodbye to her and the children. I continued to wave to Pat when I saw her in the garden, but there were no more invitations. I gave up. There were not going to be any *feel-good* projects and I was not going to be a friend of Pat's.

Over the next months, it became very clear to me that quite a few Yarralin children were not attending school. Pat may well have been pleased with the progress of the children who did attend school, but what about the children I saw hanging about the shop or playing with their friends? In the Northern Territory, children aren't required to start primary school until they are six years of age. By my reckoning, I thought there should have been thirty to forty children attending primary school. On the day of my visit I counted around twenty children and they all seemed to be young. Because the school went to year 6, there should have been at least ten children in the eleven- and twelve-year-old age bracket, however, I only recall seeing a couple of older children in the classroom.

I knew that some of the parents were not supportive of education. Indeed, one of the councillors told me, 'I didn't go to school and I did all right. No need for school.'

Despite this, I knew in my gut that a combined education and council community development approach addressing the benefits of going to school would help to increase attendance. However, with Pat's attitude, and the general lack of interest by the Education Department, that was not going to happen. What a pity.

In their homes and community, the people of Yarralin spoke the languages of Ngarinyman, Kriol and Aboriginal English. When dealing with White people, many but not all spoke functional standard English while some spoke fluently. To my knowledge, Pat did not speak any of the community languages, although of course her teacher assistants did. I wondered how much the children understood of the lessons delivered in English when they were surrounded by their own languages outside the classroom. I thought it very sad that the current primary education contrasted so dismally with the Yarralin two-way school that was started way back in 1981 when both European and Aboriginal subjects were taught.[116]

As I wrote this story of my failed hope for integrated community education projects, I realised I needed to try and understand why the schooling system failed Aboriginal children in remote communities. In the literature I scanned on the internet, the blame for the failure of remote education was levelled at a lack of full-time teachers, a lack of Aboriginal teachers, the quality of teaching, inadequate teaching materials, curriculum problems and lack of attendance. Blame was also directed at communities and parents, albeit acknowledging that overcrowding, hearing loss in children and cultural responsibilities for ceremonies and funerals contributed to attendance issues.[117] The problems were frequently labelled as 'intractable'.[118]

What was so disheartening and frustrating for me was the lack of Aboriginal voices in the millions of words I scanned. I wanted to hear what Aboriginal people thought about the education system and why their children didn't go to school. It wasn't until I finally found a body of work produced in 2016 by the University of South Australia *Red Dirt Education: A Compilation of Learnings from the Remote Education Systems Project*, that I heard the voices of Aboriginal people in communities.[119]

Not surprisingly, Aboriginal parents and communities wanted their children's education to be related to their culture and to maintain strong links with their local language, kinship and stories. They wanted their children 'to be strong in both worlds', with their children learning how to engage in their own culture and be confident engaging with western culture. They wanted their children to speak both English and Aboriginal languages. Clearly, the frame of reference that mainstream Australia understands of education being linked to employment, economic participation, housing and health did not respond adequately to the needs of remote communities.

For Aboriginal parents in the Red Dirt surveys, both Aboriginal and

Western language and culture are at the heart of education in remote communities. For the education system, teaching and learning in the English language is fundamental to the Australian curriculum and the education of Aboriginal children. Over the decades, teaching approaches of bilingual and two-way education have had considerable success, only to be later discarded or defunded. In a recent approach of teaching English as an Additional Language (EAL/D), ironically and hypocritically, teachers in remote schools were not required to have this important EAL/D qualification. In teacher training, there is a critical lack of mandated or promoted programs and approaches that support language teaching and learning in remote schools.[120]

The Red Dirt research pointed to the known correlation that when Aboriginal people were employed at the school, attendance increased. The employment could be as teacher assistants, gardeners or drivers, it didn't seem to matter. The point was, the school was not an almost exclusive domain of White people and their White ways. Unfortunately, despite this being known by the Northern Territory Education Department, employment of Aboriginal people in schools is not mandated or funded adequately.

From my community-development perspective, there were a myriad of ways that schools and communities could be integrated. Sports days, teachers and students going bush, a community pizza oven on school grounds, community stalls, elders being invited to the school to give cultural talks and demonstrations … the list was endless. The only things that stopped this happening were the top-down approach, not listening, or listening without action. What the community wanted was not officially acknowledged or respected by the Department of Education.

I discovered that in 2016 only 19 per cent of the 7,800 children in remote Northern Territory communities attended school at least four days a week. This dropped to 14 per cent in 2019.[121] The lack of literacy and numeracy visible to me in Yarralin all those years ago was still apparent more than two decades later. My naive view of school and community integration was a pipedream back in 1995 and for most school children in remote communities, it remains so today.

Thank goodness for Annie Pollack and the creche, as it was known. It was the community and educational highlight of Yarralin. It's real name was Yarralin Children's Services and it was a combination of playgroup, childcare and kindergarten. It was, and is today, a warm and welcoming place for children and their mums. Annie, the founder, overflowed with her love and care of children. She loved her community and was passionately determined that Yarralin children would have a good start in their educational life. The creche certainly achieved that as children were able to much more easily transition to primary school.

When I was in Yarralin, the creche was well supported and funded and Annie was superbly competent. The creche cruised along not needing council input or funding. I loved seeing Annie come into the office, usually with a child on her hip. She was great friends with Pam the bookkeeper and it warmed my heart to see them chatting away in Pam's office. Annie brought the creche into the office with drawings from the children decorating the walls of Pam's office. The bright pictures lightened my day every time I needed to discuss an issue with Pam.

Annie was both a Bilinara and Ngarinyman woman so she kept her finger on the pulse of both Pigeon Hole and Yarralin communities. From time to time, when Annie joined a council meeting, it was usually to raise an issue on behalf of women or childcare. But for Annie, it was never about politics, it was all about service to the community. Yarralin Children's Services has gone from strength to strength and are now partners with the non-profit One Tree community services provider.

The health clinic was next on my 'getting to know you' list. The health situation in Yarralin seemed to be much better than Papunya in Central Australia, where I had worked thirteen years previously. I was heartily relieved about that. I was keen to hear about the general health of the population in Yarralin and the outstations, and I wanted to learn how the council could help support the health needs of the community.

I headed over to the clinic to introduce myself to the nurse. I knew she was there as a few people were sitting outside waiting to see her. I went inside the clinic and stood waiting. One or two people were sitting in the clinic but I couldn't see the nurse. I guessed she was in the treatment room. When she finished with her patient, she came to the door of the treatment room and called in the next person who got to their feet. The nurse glanced at me standing there, but despite my smiling look of greeting, she said nothing, turned away, and went back into the treatment room.

Well, thanks for nothing, I thought grumpily, as I went back to the office. I tried again a couple of weeks later. This time I managed to say hello before I was curtly told 'I'm too busy to talk now, you'll have to come back another time.'

How deflating that the nurse wasn't helpful, and seemingly not community-minded either. In any case, I was darned if I was going back there again to be ignored and receive rude treatment.

I found it extraordinary that the three main services on the community, the council, the school and the health clinic, seemed to have no communication channels between them. Why was that? After all, we were all working for the betterment of the community so surely we could share our successes and work together to solve any issues. Was it because education and health department staff answered to the Northern Territory government and not the community? Was it because Yarralin Council was the political arm of the community and government staff were advised to keep their distance? Whatever the reason, I was very disappointed. It reminded me of Papunya where the health service, school and council operated in separate spheres with little contact between them.

I had so much pressing work that, for the time being, I abandoned my pursuit of the council connecting with education and health. Instead I decided to wait for a good opportunity to present itself. Unfortunately, it never did.

Yarralin health clinic
Pam Field collection

Yarralin creche, 1995
Pam Field collection

Yarralin Primary School, circa 1995
Pam Field collection

Employing an office girl

My workload included a myriad of small tasks such as ensuring we had sufficient stationery supplies including paper, pens, scissors and in particular photocopier toner. This sounds like an easy task, but of course it wasn't as there were no shops nearby and stationery had to be purchased on trips to Katherine or Darwin every month or two. Another small but time-consuming task was sorting out the storeroom which was invariably a mess. Then there was opening and distributing the community mail. If I wasn't in the office when the mail plane arrived, the letters could go anywhere. Answering the phone and taking messages was another tiresome task as the council office had one of the few telephones in the community. We were forever answering the phone, then trying to find the person to relay the message. And of course, dusting. A heavy coating of Yarralin dust lay on everything.

The council office needed an admin assistant and I was delighted when a young woman came into the office and asked for a job. I asked Frances our payroll officer if she would give her some training. It took only a couple of days to find out that this keen young woman was barely literate and unable to carry out any of the easier office tasks. Unfortunately, we had to let her go. She was the first of many young women who wanted to work in the office but did not have sufficient literacy or numeracy to do the work. There was still the dusting and running around the community giving people their phone messages, but quite understandably, these tasks were not particularly appealing.

I had not realised the level of literacy required to address an envelope, make a list of stationery supplies, or transfer the names of the CDEP workers from the attendance book to the payroll. They were simple office tasks but quite beyond the level of education these young women had achieved. We could not employ them in the council office and that was a tragedy. I felt desperately sad for the girls as they loved to sit in the office in the air conditioning. If only they had sufficient education, we could have trained them. But they needed to have a good primary-school education at the very least.

At that stage, I had no knowledge about the education system. With a primary school based in Yarralin, I had the expectation that Yarralin children would have received the same education as any Australian child would receive. With our failure to employ an admin assistant, I wasn't sure who I should point the finger at for the lack of numeracy and literacy.

How was it that these young women had attended primary school but could barely read or write? In a couple of instances, they were able to read simple instructions but were not able to enact them. I discovered that in general, the young women could add and subtract, but they were not able to multiply or divide.

Despite our early failure, the council was keen to have a local girl employed in the office and I was in complete agreement. We were starting to despair when Hazel ventured into our office looking for a job. Hazel was a very bright young woman who had managed to gain a primary-school education and attend secondary college in Darwin. Hazel became our star. She knew how to multiply and divide and she could read and write. She also came to work every day. Frances was looking forward to taking a few days off every now and again and she worked hard to train Hazel in the payroll system.

The end of June rolled in. We had to prepare the group certificates and get the payroll done as well. It was all hands on deck: Pam the bookkeeper, Frances, our wonderful Hazel and I. Hazel was a trooper. She'd never worked so hard in her life and she stuck at it. When the last pay was done, she let out a whoop of delight and shouted 'What a week!'

She'd got it. The joy of working and getting a job done.

One of the nicest houses in Yarralin at the time
Pam Field collection, 1996

17 Upskilling Yarralin's young workers

Yarralin's accountant had tracked down the grant money which allowed Jacky to start buying equipment and more horses. This drew me into Jacky's orbit on a weekly and sometimes daily basis. Because Jacky had never been to school to learn how to read and write, I was his purchasing officer. We spent many hours together as he taught me about the items we needed to buy and where I should buy them. I learned about saddles, stirrups, headstalls, snaffles, clinches, gauges, and mysterious horseshoeing tools such as nippers, picks and rasps. From time to time, when I struggled to understand what piece of equipment Jacky wanted, I would unthinkingly ask, 'How do you spell that?' He would give me a wry grin and say 'You know I don't read and write.'

'Oh, sorry,' I would say. 'I forgot.' And I'd write down whatever I thought it might be and hope that the chaps at Katherine's Dalgety Stock and Station Agency could work it out.

The trainee droving team had grown to sixteen young men and DEET had approved the six-week Introduction to Stock and Station Skills training with Bill Fordham. The students lived at King Valley from Monday to Friday undertaking practical skills training in horse riding, mustering cattle, building stockyards and maintaining stationary engines such as bore pumps and power generators. It was a momentous experience for the young fellas to learn about the world of work, sharing the domestic tasks of a stock camp and experiencing mateship around the campfire at night. They also had to learn to get up on cold mornings at 4 am. Of the sixteen young men, only two dropped out.

While the young men were away at training, Jackie and I were busy buying horses. I drove him all over the Top End to cattle stations where Jackie inspected the horses and bought what we could afford. I had thought only one horse would be needed for each stockman but Jackie told me that a droving team horse plant should have three horses per man. But good horses were expensive and our grant funding only allowed for two horses per man.

Jackie would hear about a horse for sale and it was my job to phone the cattle station to make the first enquiry. If the price was manageable within our budget, Jackie and I would drive to the cattle station to check out the horse. Often, when we found cheaper horses that were within our means, they were not of a suitable quality. Nonetheless, Jackie had no choice but to buy them. We had to drive far and wide to find horses, even into Western Australia. It was a great adventure for me but frustrating and sometimes disappointing for Jackie as we saw some excellent horses that were far beyond our reach.

One of my funniest phone calls was to Fitzroy Station. The telephone book was forever disappearing so I would phone the telephone directory service which was 013 back in those days. I asked for 'Fitzroy Station' and was put through to the Fitzroy police station in Melbourne. My confusion turned to laughter when I realise the directory service operators were national not local.

We were well into the wet season. The dry season waterholes of the Wickham River bordering Yarralin had disappeared under a fast-flowing river that gave the pandanus its annual soaking and allowed the fish to escape from the waterholes. With an abundance of water and food, it was breeding season for the birds. As the run-off from Jasper Gorge and the surrounding hills found its way into the Wickham, the water rose to a flood. As Sandy Creek near Yarralin rose, it flooded the causeway between Yarralin and the Victoria River Downs Station. The road became impassable, cutting us off from the mail-delivery plane to VRD. No mail for a few days mattered little to me. It was less of a headache actually as there were no complications from the myriad of government departments Yarralin had to interact with. The wet season also prevented public servants from visiting many remote communities, including Yarralin, due to their concern at being stranded if one of the rivers went up quickly.

The floodwaters filled the Humbert River system cutting off the small community living at Lingara outstation. Lingara didn't have a community store so I hoped they had stocked up with the basics to wait out the flood. Apparently not, as the next day, Riley, the community elder and leader, phoned me. He instructed me to hire a Heli-Muster helicopter from VRD to fly him to Yarralin store in order to buy groceries. The mustering helicopters are great fun to take a ride in. They have only two blades and are small, fast and very manoeuvrable. The big bubble canopy in front gives a panoramic view, good for mustering and terrific for a little jaunt. Heli-Muster set up a base at VRD in 1976 when VRD started using helicopters to muster cattle after the Yarralin walk-off in 1972.

After ensuring that the Lingara families would foot the bill for their helicopter taxi service, I phoned Heli-Muster and booked a flying bubble to pick Riley up from Lingara, deposit him at Yarralin to do the community shopping, then take him back to his community. I was highly amused, intrigued and in awe of Lingara people who, wanting to buy groceries, ordered themselves a helicopter to do their shopping. Fantastic.

I loved the wet season in the Top End: sharp cracks of lightning, crashes of thunder followed by downpours of rain that cleared magically into blue sky. I won't ever forget a trip driving back to Yarralin from Darwin watching great thunderclouds moving over the vast landscape. In the distance, I could see hazy patches connecting the clouds to the pasture. At first I was puzzled by the patches, then I understood. The hazy patches were great scattered dollops of tropical rain. Out of the blue, I found myself driving through one of these heavy rains. I was quite unnerved as I struggled to find the wiper knob. The rain was sudden and unexpected and for a long moment I was driving blind. Thankfully I managed to grab hold of the wiper knob and the windscreen cleared as the blades wiped off the rain, bugs and grime and I could see again.

It took only a couple of days for the Sandy Creek flood to subside. The road was open again and the council vehicle chugged its way through the quagmire of a road to collect the mail. Black soil holds water and turns into a sticky, heavy, bogging clay. One morning the council driver didn't show up for work. My spirit of adventure rose up and inspired me to become an outback heroine and drive to VRD airport myself. It was a terrifying 25-kilometre journey. Not that I would have been hurt or anything. My terror was of becoming bogged and needing to be towed out. The humiliation would have been unbearable.

I knew the theory. Stay in the wheel tracks. Drive slow and steady. Never stop. Don't panic. I don't think there has ever been a steering wheel gripped with such steely determination. I made it. There and back. While I don't think I would put my hand up to do it again, it was an experience that holds me when I doubt myself. It was an 'I can do this' moment.

Sandy Creek in flood, closing the road to VRD
Pam Field collection, 1996

Jackie's stockmen project was not the only thing keeping me busy. The state of Yarralin's deplorable housing was of great concern to the council and the residents. Although the houses had been handed over to the council, thereby technically giving the council ownership of them, financially the council didn't have the means to maintain them. Most people did not pay rent, which was a significant contributor to the housing dilemma. Unfortunately, due to particular circumstances, the council was not able to evict the residents who did not pay rent. As a consequence, there was no local fund to undertake the necessary repairs and maintenance. Instead the community had to rely on an allocation of repairs and maintenance funding from the Northern Territory government, which was totally inadequate to the task.

Plumbing was always a problem. Whenever a housing or plumbing consultant turned up, I would take them on a tour of the houses, usually in the hottest part of the day. On this particular occasion, the consultant seemed to be genuinely interested in the community and its housing problems. I rewarded him by taking him around the community early in the morning when it was cool.

At the first house we visited, he poked around the stink pipe from the bathroom, known more technically as the drain-waste vent. He showed me that the pipe had been stuck in the ground and was not connected. 'A common practice to save money,' he explained. After a couple more house inspections, I saw he was to be trusted and left him to go around on his own.

A couple of hours later he came in for a chat. He told me he had seen old plumbing parts that hadn't been used since the 1960s and that Yarralin was like a museum. His guess was that money-making contractors had dug out the parts from leftovers or demolished houses and used them in Yarralin houses. More money made by contractors and a shoddy job for the community.

Yarralin's housing woes received a lift when the mail plane brought long-awaited good news. A grant application put in months ago had finally been approved. Yarralin was to receive housing funding and wages for a builder. Fortune smiled and the council appointed Phil, a highly experienced and committed builder. Phil was married with three kids but he started work immediately, contracting a team to help him build his house. As soon as it was finished his family joined him. What a good man!

Phil realised straight away that Yarralin urgently needed a plumber. The council agreed and another advertisement was placed in the papers. Some fancy accounting and understanding bureaucrats gave us approval to purchase a portable house for our new plumber.

Batchelor College foundation skills

When the new plumber arrived, Yarralin would be employing three tradesmen: the plumber, a builder and a mechanic. Embedded in Yarralin's plan was the goal for the younger generation to gain qualifications to do the work White people normally did in communities. Yarralin wanted to manage their own community and have their own people qualified and employed in jobs. Young CDEP participants were already working as offsiders to the local handyman and mechanic. More young men were keen to work with the builder and new plumber. They wanted to learn trade skills in carpentry, plumbing and car mechanics so they could hold these positions in the future. However, if Yarralin's young people were to gain qualifications, they needed remedial education in literacy, numeracy and foundation skills before they could move into apprenticeships or gain starting-level jobs in administration. The glaring inadequacies of the Northern Territory education system were clearly exposed yet again.

Fortunately for Yarralin, by the mid-1990s Batchelor Institute, or Batchelor College as it was then known, had extended its curriculum from training teaching assistants to become qualified primary teachers to include a range of courses and certificates. This included Yarralin's much-needed foundational skills. One of my treasured contacts at Northern Territory University was certain Batchelor College could help us and advised me to get in touch with them.

Our luck was in. Batchelor College was willing to help the young people of Yarralin to re-enter the education system. My job was to compile a list of students who would commit to attending classes on a small Yarralin campus. If I could do that, a teacher from Batchelor College would come to Yarralin to teach them. I gave the council the good news and we pieced together a list of young men and women who were willing to give further education a go so they could get a proper job. I sent off the names of eight young people and their goals to Batchelor College. The college agreed to hold foundation classes on Yarralin and contracts were signed on the condition that Yarralin provide safe and secure accommodation for the teacher.

Now I had two portable homes to buy. One for the plumber and one for the Batchelor College teacher. Following some interesting conversations held between funding bodies, Yarralin's accountant and the council, there was agreement to purchase the two demountable homes. I set about the task with gusto!

In those days with no internet or 'google', it was Yellow Pages, phone, fax and snail mail. Getting quotes was instructive as each supplier asked different questions and their portable homes had variations in design or materials. I had to learn fast. The enormity of this purchase was daunting as each one-bedroom portable home cost around $18,000. It doesn't sound much today, but back in the mid-1990s, it was a lot of money. Although the designs were similar, I didn't want to make a mistake. I eventually decided on the most suitable design which included a small veranda at the front door. For a cost comparison, I entered the quotes into an Excel table to ensure the pricing was clear to the councillors who had to make the final decision. The main points to consider were the cost, size, design, layout and the strength and durability of the structure. The homes needed to withstand the shaking they would receive as they were be transported by truck over the dirt roads leading to Yarralin.

In the end, four companies competed for the business: an agent in Katherine, two manufacturers in South Australia and one from Mt Isa in Queensland. The freight cost put Mt Isa out of the picture. As I expected, the Katherine agent's price was much higher than the other quotes. That left the two Adelaide companies competing. They both had good-quality houses with similar layouts, fittings and fixtures. In the end, it was an easy choice for the councillors – the cheapest price won the day. I filled out the purchase order right then and there at the meeting, obtained the appropriate signatures and we all watched the order being faxed to the Adelaide manufacturer.

A few weeks later the manufacturer phoned me to say the houses were on their way to Yarralin. Almost a week later I was walking back to the tin shed council office when I saw in the distance, through the shimmering heat, what looked to be two trucks carrying a load of containers. They were heading slowly towards Yarralin on the dusty pot-holed road. As I walked along, I stared at them wondering what they were. Then I realised.

'They're here!' I shrieked to the empty street. 'The demountables are here!'

What a beautiful sight. I had never actually seen them but I knew every inch of them, as I had studied the drawings, read their specifications, poured over the photographs and chosen their fittings, fixtures and colour. I had also helped to measure and prepare the ground they were heading to and chosen the furniture that was wrapped up in heavy plastic waiting for them in the workshop.

These portable houses were heralding a new era for Yarralin. As soon as they were set up on site, two major projects would get underway. The Batchelor College teacher would come to Yarralin to teach Foundation Studies and we would employ a plumber. This meant housing program delays would largely be overcome as we would have both a plumber and a builder living and working in our small township of Yarralin.

These thoughts were swirling in my head as I watched the trucks with their clouds of white dust coming closer and larger. I took off at a run to the office. There were no windows in the awful council office so nobody in the office could see these wonderful houses drawing nearer. I raced through the doorway into the office and cried out to everyone sitting there, 'Quick, come and see, the houses are nearly here.'

Everyone jumped up and ran out of the office to stand and watch the lumbering trucks laden with Yarralin's harbingers of change. Word had got around and I could see people appearing from everywhere to watch the houses arrive. It was an exciting milestone for Yarralin. The council president and the builder went out together to the road to greet the truck drivers and give them directions to the sites where the houses would be positioned.

Our building team had already laid the foundations. It was now just a matter of sliding the houses into position. I couldn't imagine how they were going to do it, but in the end, it just happened. Yarralin had two more small houses in position and the trucks drove away.

It was one of the best telephone calls I ever made when I phoned the head of Batchelor College and said, 'You can send your lecturer Sherrill down to Yarralin now. We have her accommodation waiting for her.'

Yarralin's motel for guests on the left and Batchelor College classrooms on the right
Pam Field collection, 1996

Dates of birth are complicated

Leah continued to visit Yarralin regularly to support Frances and ensure Centrelink payments were kept up to date with the changing participation in the CDEP, particularly with the changes in Jacky's stockmen team. When time permitted, Leah stayed overnight at my house and our friendship deepened slowly. Leah was a private person and trust didn't come easily to her.

I would let Leah know when I was visiting Katherine and we usually had dinner together or met up on Friday night for a few beers and laughs at the back bar of the Katherine Hotel. Generally speaking, I didn't like the pubs in Katherine but the Friday night back bar was one of the few places where Blacks and Whites mixed freely without an atmosphere of racism. There was usually a country-music band and a bit of dancing. It was fun and I enjoyed meeting the locals: Aboriginal people that Leah knew, ringers, office workers, tough blokes who worked at the abattoir and a few stray tourists thrown in for good measure.

Yarralin Council with its unceasing tight budgets meant that I usually stayed at the cheapest caravan park in Katherine on my visits. One day, Leah invited me to stay at her house whenever I came to town. I was very touched by her offer and equally thankful to ditch the caravan park. A trip to Katherine became a double pleasure. It was great to get out of the community for a break, and even better to stay with a friend in a comfortable house. Leah lived in a typical Katherine suburban house on stilts with louvred windows in every room to entice an air flow. Over the following months I met her mother and a couple of her brothers. I really enjoyed being a guest in an Aboriginal home. I realise as I write this how far apart our cultures and lives are in Australia. It really shouldn't have been novel and vaguely exciting for a Melbourne-born-and-bred woman to stay in the home of an Indigenous woman.

During our mealtime chats, I asked Leah about her work. She was an Aboriginal liaison officer with responsibility for several remote communities requiring many 'out bush' trips with masses of office work after each trip. She was a busy woman. Leah also had to participate in meetings at which decisions were made that affected Aboriginal communities.

Through Leah I had met some very capable and competent Aboriginal people who could have been doing my job as a community council clerk. As I headed into Katherine at the end of a tough week, I was determined to ask Leah a question that had been bothering me for ages. 'Why are we Whitefellas in charge in communities and not Aboriginal people?'

I put the question to her as we settled down for a cool drink on her veranda with the fan blasting us. It set her back for some minutes, but eventually she answered. 'I think it's because we're all related or connected to community people. We would find it too hard to say no to all the demands.'

As I thought about her answer, I realised all the difficult demands and decisions of the job came about because of the White colonial system in the first place. Aboriginal people had to endure the lack of inclusion in designing programs and implementing policies that were supposed to serve them. Top-down decision-making by White bureaucracies equated to disempowerment of Aboriginal people. I had to ask myself the question, 'Why would Aboriginal people want to be in charge of a system that disempowered their people?'

Leah was sharply intelligent, hyper-observant and her radar caught bullshit and hypocrisy mercilessly. I admired her and was in awe of her. I was also a bit scared of her catching me out when I inadvertently exposed my unknown assumptions and casual racism that was hidden in my cultural upbringing.

Leah was well versed in the disempowerment of Aboriginal communities and individuals. As an Aboriginal liaison officer she witnessed government policies and processes that did not acknowledge the need for Aboriginal input and agreement. She saw firsthand the incorrect assumptions and disempowerment that resulted from a lack of consultation.

Leah invented her own particular brand of clear and cutting feedback which she usually gave to offenders privately and casually, but I felt certain it was devastating. Leah's public feedback was saved for the meetings she attended in her official liaison role. I remember one night at her place when we had finished dinner and were having a cup of tea. I asked idly, 'Anything exciting happen at work today?'

Leah gave me a wicked grin. 'We had an inter-agency meeting this morning with a bunch of Whitefellas talking about what they thought would be good for Blackfellas. They never once asked for my opinion. They didn't even look in my direction. I stayed quiet and let them dig themselves into a great big hole and then I let them have it.' She stopped.

'Go on,' I urged. 'What did you say?'

'I said to them, "If you haven't noticed, you've got a Blackfella sitting right here at the table. Don't you think it would be a good idea to ask my opinion?"'

'So what did they say?'

'They were full of apologies and how remiss of us. So I gave them my feedback! You can bet they won't do that again in a hurry.'

Fearless Leah. She was never going to be a token Blackfella.

Little by little, Leah helped my eyes and ears to open to disempowerment hidden from view by Australia's colonial 'White superiority' past and present. In fact I can testify that disempowerment can hide in plain view. I found it in the most unexceptional place: dates of birth. This happened when two teenagers came into the office to enrol for the Community Development Employment Project. Although I had been inculcated into the common belief that Aboriginal people did not know their date of birth, I did the boys the courtesy of asking them if they knew their birthdate. As I expected, they didn't know so I phoned the Yarralin health clinic. Birth dates are central to our identity and for Aboriginal people in the Northern Territory, health clinics and hospitals were the holding-bays of their dates of birth. The clinic nurse on duty searched their records to no avail. She told me I would need to phone the Hall's Creek clinic because the lads had been living in Western Australia. I got the number from her, made the call and documented their date of birth on the CDEP enrolment form.

When I met up with Leah the next week, I related the story to her. She exploded.

'That's how they keep us as children.'

I had no idea what she was talking about. I had reached a 'sort-of' conclusion that maybe Aboriginal people couldn't remember numbers. After all, from my early primary years I had known my age and my birthday. From my perspective, it wasn't difficult. It was normal. This did not seem to be the case in Yarralin or other Aboriginal communities. Although the children lived in remote locations they still went to school and they should know their date of birth. Ergo, there must be another reason they didn't know their birthdates. It's easy to see that my understanding was flawed and frankly quite ridiculous. But that is one of the dangers of loose cultural assumptions.

Leah saw that I didn't get it. With subdued fury, she told me that only a couple of years ago, during a visit to the doctor, the nurse didn't ask her for her birthdate. Instead, she checked past records to find the date. Leah glared at the nurse.

'You're looking up my birthdate aren't you?' Leah asked accusingly. 'You don't have to check. I can tell you. I do know my date of birth.'

Now it was my turn to cop the glare. 'You Whitefellas judge us about that. We're ignorant, or stupid, or too lazy to remember! And then there's that myth that Blackfellas can only count up to three.'

I was starting to feel a bit sorry for the nurse.

'Okay. I see that I got it wrong. So what do I do, Leah? For those boys.'

'You teach them, so they know forever.'

I had a great time teaching those boys. I called them into my office and asked them if they would like me to teach them their birthdates. They were very shy and didn't look at me as they nodded their agreement. I gave each boy a piece of paper with their age and birthdates written in three combinations: 25/4/1978; April 25th, 1978; 25 04 1978.

Over the next few weeks, each time I spotted one of the boys, we played the birthday game. We had a lot of laughs.

What's your birthday?

How old are you?

What's your date of birth?

What year were you born?

What day of the month were you born?

What are the months of the year and what are their numbers?

What is the fourth month of the year?

Those boys were so proud when they could answer all my questions. I knew they would never forget.

I was astonished at the complexity of a birthdate. It was a humbling experience for me. Whatever was I thinking that Aboriginal people couldn't count or remember numbers? A birthdate is embedded in our western time-bound conceptual notion of the world. We have seconds and minutes, days, weeks, fortnights, months, years, calendar years, financial years, decades – the 60s, 70s, 80s, 90s. It's a numbers game that is second nature to our society. Babies' weight gain is measured over time. Young children are vaccinated at dates set from birth. Children start school according to their date of birth. There is an age for teens, a working age, a drivers-licence age, a drinking age, twenty-first birthdays. Then down the track there's the retirement age, seniors, the pension.

Our identity is proven by our date of birth. You can't have a conversation with your electricity provider, your bank, your insurer or any service without giving your date of birth. If you don't know your date of birth, then who are you? If someone else holds your date of birth, what happens to your rights? If you don't know your date of birth, you remain childlike, not responsible. It was a learning experience I never forgot.

18 A council clerk is never bored

Being the council clerk of Yarralin was a hands-on job requiring multiskilling – from day-to-day administration to the Housing Infrastructure Project; from Jacky's droving project to Yarralin's on-site Batchelor College classes. Fundamentally, however, my job was directly and indirectly about government funding, that is applying for and acquitting grants. I had to ensure the money was spent according to the guidelines and policy direction on housing, transportation, CDEP wages and various community expenses.

All major decisions regarding government money had to be made by the Walangeri Ngumpinku Community Council, and on occasions, the community people as well. This meant bringing councillors together endlessly to authorise expenditure and make this or that decision. Even more difficult were the decisions that required agreement by the whole community. For these decisions, I had to call a meeting in the park and then drive round the community pleading with people to come to the meeting. If we got fifteen people to a meeting it was a good day. Bringing councillors and community together was not easy as people were often away visiting relatives, or in Katherine or Darwin. The government-required compulsory meetings became the bane of my life.

One day when I was walking past the park, I saw perhaps 200 people sitting on the well-watered grass in the shade of the bamboo stand.

'Wow, what is going on?' I wondered.

When I got to the office I asked around and was told it was community business about people marrying with the right skin group. This meeting was about Aboriginal business and they were enthusiastically right into it. What a contrast to all the boring Whitefella business that I foisted on them week after week. It was little wonder that the community saw council business as 'Whitefella' business. The policy directions, government grants, government systems and processes all belonged to the White culture. Rarely did Aboriginal people actually get what they really wanted in a process of their own making.

There was one piece of council business where I gained full cooperation from the entire community. One of the Yarralin residents had complained to me that they couldn't sleep because cockroaches were biting them. As you can imagine, I was horrified. I didn't even know that cockroaches bit people. A few more enquiries informed me that there was indeed a huge problem with cockroaches.

I phoned a couple of pest-control companies in Katherine and found that cockroach infestation was a relatively common problem. I got three quotes and selected the company that sounded the least racist and whose price seemed to be reasonable. I booked them to come to Yarralin in three weeks.

I discussed the issue with the council and took their advice. I was to personally go to each house and ask them to prepare to move everything out of their houses the day before the pest people arrived. Off I went each morning, trudging around the dirt roads to give each house the news. The response was very low key and I had no idea whether my request would be followed or not. I kept up the effort, telling everyone who turned up to the office about the pest-control visit and asking them to spread the word.

The day before the visit, I saw bedding, clothes and furniture piled up in front of the houses. My goodness I was surprised. I knew then that cockroaches were indeed a huge problem for the community. I also realised that my home visits had been one of the best things I did in the community. I got to meet and talk with everyone on their turf, not in the office. In fact I had loved making the home visits.

The next morning the pest people arrived with a small truck towing a tank with spraying equipment. It took them two days to spray every house. It was both horrifying and satisfying at the same time, as the team told me that it was one of the worst infestations they had come across. They said that thousands of cockroaches had come out of the walls of the houses. Awful. But thank goodness I had brought the pest-control company into the community.

It was such a bad infestation that the company said they would need to come back again in three months to repeat the process. I went through the same procedure of notifying everyone. But this time, only half the houses put all their belongings on the front lawn. I guessed, with relief, that the infestation was nowhere near as bad this time.

Cockroach infestation was not Yarralin's only environmental health problem. I had been summoned to an on-site meeting about septic tanks. It was probably my least favourite topic. According to those who know, septic tanks should be pumped out every two to five years. Considering the overcrowding in Yarralin houses, the low end of every two years was probably about right for pumping out. As far as I could make out, the septic tanks had never been pumped out for the simple reason there had never been any funding. The sewage had become a health hazard for everyone, particularly children.

As well as cockroaches, septic tanks, plumbing and housing maintenance, Yarralin's water supply took my attention when I noticed that a bucket of water I had left on my veranda had turned bright green. I was horrified and became very suspicious about the Yarralin water supply.

Yarralin's water and power supply was under the jurisdiction of the Power and Water Authority (PAWA). At the next visit by a PAWA representative, I told him about the bucket of green water and questioned him about the safety of Yarralin's drinking water. He airily dismissed my concerns saying it would have been the copper pipes in my house that turned the water green. When I suggested that it might be algae from the holding tank, he shook his head and told me 'it wouldn't be that'. His offhand manner was quite galling and did nothing to lower my suspicions about the quality of Yarralin's water supply.

I remembered that I had found some previous correspondence in my shambolic filing cabinets asking PAWA for the water supply to be tested.

Aha, I thought. *That's what I'll do ... I'll put in a request for water testing.*

What a saga that turned out to be! PAWA told me there was no need to get the water tested as it was artesian water, treated with chlorine and therefore clean. They may well have been correct, but I wanted the water tested and I wasn't about to be flicked off like that.

As it turned out, water testing was a complicated procedure without PAWA's cooperation. A series of water samples had to be collected from taps around the community. The samples had to be kept cold, transported to Katherine by aircraft, picked up at the airport and taken to PAWA. This was beyond my resources to organise. I felt sure the PAWA representative could have collected the samples himself and taken them to Katherine in an esky, but there was always a reason why he couldn't. I wondered repeatedly to myself, would the same attitude have occurred if it had been a White community rather than Black?

I bided my time as the months went by. Finally, my repeated requests hit the mark and a test was authorised. When the results finally came, they rewarded my persistence. There was indeed faecal contamination in the water supply. This really confounded the PAWA people. According to them, there was no way there should have been any faecal contamination.

It was our plumber who found the reason. He climbed up to the top header tank and found the tank lid had been moved and the water tank was full of frogs. I climbed up to the header tank myself to see. And sure enough, there were heaps of frogs in the tank, some dead and some alive. It was surprising and quite yucky to see all those frogs. Until then, I had never heard about frogs climbing ladders, and I don't think anybody else had. Weird.

With proof of contamination, the dismissive, patronising PAWA did an about face and swung into action. Within days, the header tank had been drained, cleaned and refilled. I must admit to an extreme case of smug satisfaction and had no hesitation is saying, 'I told you so,' to the PAWA representative. He had the grace to chuckle and agree.

Coonamble's water supply
Pam Field collection, 1996

More than twenty-five years later, PAWA seems to take its responsibilities more seriously. They have published a very smart-looking document about Yarralin's water which informs residents how the water supply works and how safe it is.[122] All I can say is, thank goodness for that.

I had always been confused by the terms sewage and sewerage, but in Yarralin it didn't really matter because there were both sewage problems of the waste being discharged, and sewerage problems with the septic tank infrastructure. Whichever term was used, there was a problem. Yarralin is in black-soil country and its rock hard soil was unforgiving to septic tanks. Seepage from the tanks didn't disappear into the soil. Instead, it rose to the surface. In the wet season the sewage spread further. A nightmare health hazard for the barefoot children who roamed free to play where they chose. What Yarralin needed was a fair dinkum sewerage system and even more so because the seepage ended up in the Wickham River a few hundred metres away.

It was the build-up and I was sweating my way down the road looking for the latest septic meeting. The distant rolling sound of thunder held the cooling promise of rain, but not yet. We would have to put up with the heavy humidity and heat for another couple of weeks. As I wiped away the sweat from my eyes, I spotted a couple of councillors and the local handyman staring down at the latest septic quagmire. I joined them for another fruitless discussion about potential costly solutions. In the end, we agreed to chuck some old corrugated-iron and branches over the sticky mud and I'd write a follow-up letter to the grant application I'd made a few weeks ago.

Yarralin's dire sewage situation proved to be a blessing in disguise. The Health Infrastructure Priority Project (HIPP) was underway in the Northern Territory and Yarralin's sewerage and infrastructure problems fitted neatly into the HIPP criteria of large-scale environmental health infrastructure. As well as Yarralin's sewage woes, HIPP would also address water supply, priority housing, internal roads, drainage and dust controls, all delivered in a whole-of-government approach.[123]

But first, Yarralin had to get on the HIPP list of communities. The field officer from the Department of Housing and Community Development advised the council to arrange a meeting with bureaucrats from the Commonwealth Department of Aboriginal Affairs and the Northern

Territory Department of Health, the Power and Water Authority and the Department of Housing and Community Development. This was truly 'whole-of-government' taking an interest in Yarralin. The council's mission was to tell the 'septic' story as well as the unworkability of the office and mechanics workshop, the overcrowding and lack of housing.

The exciting meeting day dawned and I piled into the council vehicle with four of the councillors. My role was to make the introductions and then be quiet until someone asked me to say something. As it turned out, I didn't need to speak at all. It was an historic meeting charged with passion and determination. The government mob were there to listen to the Yarralin community, to hear their story with genuine respect and decide how they could help. The councillors told them about the endless problems with septic tanks, the lack of housing and the plumbing issues. They told the government that their community had waited long enough. Too long in fact. Yarralin was a sick place and it was time for the government to help them. The bureaucrats were right on side. They all knew the history of Yarralin and the neglect the community had suffered. By the end of the meeting, the government agreed to fund a $50,000 feasibility study to get the HIPP process underway. I was thrilled by the outcome of the meeting. As we drove back to Yarralin, I think we all felt hope that finally there would be a change and Yarralin would get the help it so badly needed. All we had to do now was wait for the feasibility study to be completed. I felt sure we had a strong case for HIPP funding, but it was a nervous couple of months to wait.

By this stage, Jackie's project had developed to the point where it was necessary to construct portable stockyards for the horses. Jackie's droving team needed training in welding. Once again, the Department of Education, Employment and Training was able to help. There was an accredited welding program that could be run at Yarralin and they were looking for students to fill the current program.

Chris from DEET drove Dave the welding instructor out to Yarralin the next week to discuss the training process and the tools and equipment that Yarralin would need to provide. Jackie had already gained council approval for the program and the training contract was signed on the spot.

Dave gave me a list of equipment to purchase and businesses I could approach in Katherine and Darwin. Once again, I became a purchasing officer as I priced and ordered welding helmets, gloves, pliers, hammers, brushes and jigs. Most of the material for the stockyards had been supplied by Victoria River Downs Station. We only needed a couple of extra panels and a gate and we were set.

Dave the trainer arrived and our young stockmen team was raring to go. Dave was a great fellow and mightily impressed with Jackie's program.

'This is no Mickey Mouse project,' he declared. 'It's the real thing.' He loved working with Jackie and the team. We were all sorry to see Dave go when the training was completed.

Jackie Anzac's planning had come together. The team was kitted out with stockmen clothing, boots, hats and swags. The horses were in pretty good shape. The portable yards were built and ready to go. We just had to wait until VRD was ready for the droving team.

A couple of weeks had passed when Jackie appeared at my office door with a huge grin spread over his face.

'The job's starting in a couple of days,' he told me.

It was great news. Exciting news. I was so happy for Jackie and his team. It was an awesome moment for the whole community.

A few days later I drove out to see the droving team in action. A mob of cattle had been Heli-Mustered and it was the job of the stockmen to walk the cattle quietly from the mustering yard to the trucking yards where they would be loaded onto cattle trucks and transported to the port of Darwin. It was like being on a movie set. The cattle were mooing and moving slowly along in the heat over the open plains. Aboriginal stockmen wearing big akubras were quietly riding alongside them. Occasionally there would be a whistle and a couple of cattle that escaped the mob would be rounded up and brought back. It was quieter than I expected. Jackie explained to me that the cattle had been running wild and were afraid of humans. The slow walk would gradually ease them into a calmer state while getting them used to people. These cattle were part of the live cattle export trade to Indonesia.

Jackie Anzac was a remarkable man. An extraordinary stockman and a true leader of men. To have achieved the position of head stockman on one of the largest cattle stations in Australia was an extraordinary accomplishment in an industry not noted for treating Aboriginal people well. His success in reviving Aboriginal employment in droving for VRD was a result of his sheer hard work, dedication and total commitment. This first droving job in 1997 initiated by Jackie Anzac was the start of a long-term successful Aboriginal contract stockmen team.

Jacky Anzac, master stockman and boss of the Aboriginal stock team
Darrell Lewis collection, 1995

Damper for dinner; stock camp near Pigeon Hole
Darrell Lewis collection, 1995

Stock team moving cattle, Pigeon Hole area
Darrell Lewis collection, 1995

Aboriginal contract drovers moving cattle, Pigeon Hole area
Darrell Lewis collection, 1995

In 2009, the Jackie Anzac Contractors were going from strength to strength
Kent Saddlery, 2009

Lily and her dogs

Lily was one of my favourites. She was a slight woman who always had two or three dogs walking with her. She had the sweetest smile, gentle and brimming with friendliness. My spirits lifted when Lily passed me by with her smile and soft greeting. Earlier on, I'd thought she was rather old, but it didn't take me long to realise she was probably only in her fifties.

I was close by the office on my return after lunch and saw Lily coming from the store. As usual she had her dogs with her.

'Your dogs love you, Lily,' I said and gave her a smile.

'They're good dogs.' She nodded as she headed back to her house.

I think every Yarralin family had dogs, but Lily's dogs seemed especially attached to her. I was still smiling to myself as I entered the office.

'I've just seen Lily and her dogs,' I commented to Frances. 'I don't think I've ever seen her without them.'

'That's true,' she replied. 'She loves her dogs very much. Everyone in Yarralin loves their dogs.'

That is also true for the millions of dog-loving Australians who treat their dogs as part of the family. In Yarralin's case, however, their relationship with dogs is a continuum that goes way back in time to the arrival of the dingo from South East Asia, which scientists believe was around 5,000 years ago. Over those thousands of years, Aboriginal people incorporated dingoes into their Dreaming and they became part of their rituals, songlines and stories. According to anthropologist Deborah Bird Rose, Yarralin people think that dingoes are very close to humans. Indeed, the dingo is 'what we would be if we were not what we are'.[124]

I must confess I really didn't understand what was meant by that, but I did understand that while dingoes remained wild animals and had never become domesticated, they provided companionship for Aboriginal people that had never before existed. Like the dogs of today, dingoes responded to them by coming when called, helping in the hunt, sleeping with people and learning to understand human words. The dingoes became part of the family, were given names and fitted into the wider kinship structure. Like dingoes, Yarralin's dogs also provided company and protection and were fitted into the wider kinship structures. But unlike urban dogs, they were allowed to roam freely and by the size of them, I could see that some were often not fed sufficiently. Nevertheless, the dogs in Yarralin, particularly Lily's beloved dogs, were in much better condition than the poor animals I remembered from Papunya.

I would never hurt an animal, let alone anyone's pet dog. I was devastated when, driving home very late one night, I ran over a dog that was sleeping on the road. It was even more terrible for such a thing to happen in Yarralin where dogs are so special.

I was on my way back to Yarralin after a busy day in Katherine with meetings and purchasing. I usually left Katherine early afternoon so I could drive mostly in the daylight and get home at a reasonable time. But on this day, with so much to do, I didn't leave until around 6 o'clock at night. I knew that I had close to a five-hour drive ahead of me with much of it in the dark. I was not a happy woman!

The first 130 kilometres on the Victoria Highway were uneventful. It was the next couple of hours on the Buntine Highway to Top Springs that unnerved me. There were wallabies everywhere. Reluctantly I slowed down, even though I knew it would add extra time to my trip. Then I heard an awful bang. Damn. I'd hit a wallaby. I stopped to see if there was any damage. Of course, in my forgetful way, I hadn't put a torch in the vehicle. With only the light from my headlights, I wasn't able to see if there was damage. I couldn't even see the injured or dead wallaby, so there was nothing to do but climb back into the Toyota and keep driving, hoping it wouldn't happen again. But it did! A second *bang* occurred, but this time I didn't even bother stopping. I just kept on driving, feeling very sad about injuring wallabies.

The thought of a cup of coffee at the Top Springs pub filled my mind. It took a long time coming, but finally I could see the lights of the pub. What a welcome sight! I drank my coffee slowly to recover my equanimity before heading out onto the dirt road for the final one-and-a-half-hour journey to Yarralin. After driving steadily for about an hour, I arrived at the causeway at Victoria River. *Thank goodness*, I thought. *Not long to go now.*

There was water flowing over the causeway so I carefully eased the vehicle onto the concrete strip and started driving through the water. To my astonishment and horror I saw the flicker of a Johnstone Crocodile in the far left vision of my headlight. I couldn't stop. Then I felt my wheels run over it. Ker thunk, ker thunk. My heart sank. I stopped the vehicle when I got through the causeway to the other side, but of course I couldn't see a thing. I felt very remorseful and hoped that the poor little crocodile had been able to swim away, a bit bruised and battered, but still alive.

This murderous trip didn't finish here. It was all quiet in Yarralin as I drove into the community. Although my headlights cast light on the dusty road, there were shadows from the potholes and corrugations and I didn't see the sleeping dog until too late. I had run right over the top of it. I braked hard and skidded to a stop in the dust. I could hear it yelping loudly, then all was silent. The dog had been sleeping in front of Lily's house.

'Oh no! Oh I've driven over one of Lily's dogs!' I was mortified.

'What a dreadful night,' I moaned. 'I've hit two wallabies, run over a crocodile, and now I've hit a dog.'

I swore I'd never leave Katherine so late ever again. I would stay in town and come back early the next day.

First thing next morning I went to Lily's house and was relieved to see that she was already up and about.

'Lily,' I called out. 'I have come to see if your dogs are okay. When I came back to Yarralin late last night, I think I hit one of your dogs with the Toyota. Your dog was sleeping on the road.'

'Oh, don't you worry about that one,' she said. 'He sleeps on the road and always chases cars. He's a nuisance dog. Anyway, I saw him this morning. He's all right.'

Thank goodness for small mercies. I was highly relieved that I hadn't hurt Lily's dog. My day brightened considerably with that news.

19 The Health Infrastructure Priority Project begins

It had been a nervous and impatient wait for Yarralin to learn that the community had been accepted for the Health Infrastructure Priority Project (HIPP). It was great news, but none of us had much idea of the scale or process of the project. It would prove to be much bigger and better than we could have imagined. ATSIC had out-sourced the management of HIPP to the world-renowned engineering firm, Ove Arup and Partners, to manage the program and coordinate the various government departments.

It was an exciting day for Yarralin when the Ove Arup HIPP team flew in from Darwin. Following introductions, there was a town walk-around directed by the Yarralin councillors. I was very happy to be tagging along behind and leaving it to them. HIPP was a whole-of-government approach and also a whole-of-community approach. Environmental health infrastructure was to be targeted in a holistic way requiring a proper town plan. There had obviously been a town plan made many years previously, but with HIPP, the council and community were to be involved in the design of their town. Radical.

A few months back, Yarralin's mechanic, Ken, and his offsiders had been mightily relieved when Yarralin received a long overdue grant to construct a new mechanics workshop. Ken and the young men who worked with him should have been paid a hardship allowance for working in the hot and pokey mechanic's workshop tacked onto the office. Ken was a top-notch mechanic and a patient and skilled teacher and it was a credit to all of them that they kept Yarralin's vehicles on the road despite their dreadful working conditions. The discussions on the location of the workshop had been before my time. With no town plan, it had been sited in the only available area close to the office. Under the supervision of the local handyman, the site had been excavated and the foundations laid for the workshop. It was fortunate that a consultant on another project had wandered over to the construction site and taken a good look around. What he saw horrified him and he immediately came to my office.

'I'm afraid you'll have to stop the construction of that workshop,' he told me with a concerned look on his face. 'The foundations are no good. They are not stable.'

I was startled. 'What do you mean? What's wrong with the foundations?'

He realised I needed some tuition in construction and proceeded to draw diagrams to show the problem.

Not much the wiser, I said bravely, 'Leave it with me. I'll work out what to do.'

As luck would have it, I overheard some of the Elders talking about the shed being sited too close to the men's business area. When I asked the president, George, what the problem was, he told me that the men were worried that women would be coming to the mechanic's workshop to get petrol and they would be too close to the men's area.

Aha, my solution had appeared.

'George, one of the consultants told me that the foundations of the workshop are not stable. He believes the shed should be pulled down and built somewhere else. If you and the elders don't want the shed there, we can pull it down and put it somewhere else.'

George called a meeting of the elders and asked me to repeat the story about the shed.

'What about the government? They'll be angry if we do that,' one councillor said.

They all looked nervous.

'Bugger the government,' I replied. 'It's what you fellas want that is important. You can do whatever you think is best.'

It didn't take long for the elders to make their decision. They instructed the handyman to pull the building down and store the materials.

This drama over the workshop had taken place before the HIPP feasibility process. When the councillors told the HIPP team what had happened, the HIPP team pulled out their drawings and said, 'We'll include a new site for the mechanics workshop and petrol station in the plan. Now where do you think it should go?'

And with that, the problem was solved. Fantastic!

There were regular meetings over the next few weeks and I was extremely impressed by the knowledge of Yarralin elders about their infrastructure. Yarralin was their place and they knew the location of every tap, pipe and septic tank and how long ago they had been installed. It was a delight for me to watch from the sidelines as the community was planned from a new starting point. I felt privileged to be part of this process.

The small township of Yarralin was sited parallel to the Wickham River with one main street. As you entered Yarralin, you would turn left to visit the store, office and workshop and turn right to the community housing. The current layout allowed limited room for expansion of the town.

Through the HIPP town-planning process, the council and Elders were led gently to the idea of a complete redesign of the community. The planning included sites for additional housing and public facilities such as the primary school, preschool, health clinic, sportsground and council office. There were also sites for community services such as the petrol station and mechanics workshop, motel and store as well as a future police station. The town plan also included the utilities of the water supply, power station and sewerage system and took the topography into consideration.

The town planning became a wonderful experience for the whole community. Instead of making do, their minds turned to what could be. This led to the new mechanic's workshop being built near the entrance to the community. Completely logical considering that is where the petrol was to be sold. It also led to a new spacious and well-designed office being located in a better position. And of course a proper town sewerage system would take the place of the toxic septic system.

Planning for future housing caused much puzzlement and discussion. Where should the new houses go? Gradually, the location revealed itself. The most suitable site for additional housing was the current site of the old primary school. The council was aware the Education Department was planning to rebuild Yarralin's school in the existing area. This did not sit well with the council. Instead, they proposed to site the new school in the public facilities zone.

Yarralin's next step was to meet with the Education Department, which had some form of infrastructure lease over the land. When council requests to meet with the Education Department were ignored, the council approached the Yarralin Aboriginal School Council. Although the school council agreed with the idea to move the site of the school, they could not override the wishes of the department.

When the school council was told that Education Department officials were coming to Yarralin to meet with the school principal and school council, they immediately informed Yarralin's councillors. The council instructed me to contact the department and invite them to a community meeting to be held on the day of their visit. The purpose of the meeting was for the Education Department officials to hear the wishes of the whole community.

The day of the meeting arrived. The education officials flew into Yarralin and went straight to the school. The community gathered in the park and waited. Over an hour went by, but the officials didn't show. By this time there were close to a hundred people in the park waiting. Nobody left despite the heat. It became too much for me so I strode over to the school determined to bring them to the community meeting. I found the bureaucrats, principal and school councillors conversing in the classroom. The officials completely ignored me. But not for long.

'You might think you are having a meeting here, but the *real* meeting is in the park,' I barked. 'The council is there and about a hundred people from the community. They are all waiting in the heat for you to turn up. We expect you to come now to talk to us.'

With that, I strode out of the classroom back to the park.

About fifteen minutes later the officials turned up. There were no chairs for them to sit on and I stood up to find them some. The council president shook his head at me. 'No, let them stand in the sun,' he said.

I was happy to obey.

William Gulwin, a highly respected leader and usually a quiet man, moved to the front of the crowd and let fly.

'We're the people here. We know what we want and you have to listen to us. We want the school to be moved. We remember why it was built there. No one asked us. Now we are telling you. We're not a bunch of myalls[125] that you can fool. We are the people of Yarralin and we are doing the planning of the community.'

The bureaucrats just stood there, stony faced. They hated it, and I loved it. *That's telling them, William*, I thought to myself. *Good on you.*

Finally, one of the education men came to the front. He told the crowd that they had listened to the community and would let Darwin know. But they had no commitment to the new location. It wasn't up to them.

It would have been too much to expect the department to cave in to an Aboriginal community. Over the next few months, there was a resounding silence from Darwin while Yarralin refused to concede to the department's plan. The stand-off became political. Councillor Billy Campbell and I were both interviewed on the radio. Aboriginal self-determination was up against political intransigence.

In the end, Yarralin won and I loved seeing their quiet pride in taking on the government and winning. There should be more of it.

Family violence

The Timber Creek police had come to Yarralin early in the morning. They were in the office talking to a couple of councillors when I arrived a bit before 8 o'clock. I was surprised to see them at this hour of the day.

'What brings you to Yarralin so early in the morning?' I asked puzzled.

'We got a call from Lily from the public phone box about three in the morning. She was very upset, saying we had to come straight away.'

Sweet gentle Lily. 'My goodness, what happened?' I asked, 'I didn't hear any disturbance.'

'Well, as it turned out, it wasn't what we had thought. We thought she said that she had been raped. But what she actually said, was that she had been 'raked'.

I was startled. 'Thank God she wasn't raped. But what did she mean by raked?'

'Apparently her nephew was angry that she wouldn't give him any money, and he hit her on the head with a rake. It's a nasty wound but she'll be all right.'

Poor Lily, I thought. I couldn't imagine what I would be feeling if one of my relatives had hit me on the head with a rake.

Mostly Yarralin was a peaceful community but from time to time violent incidents occurred. Particularly when there had been too much drinking at the boundary fence and the drunkenness spilled into the community. The 'raking' incident of poor Lily was the first time that a woman I actually knew suffered from family violence. I had heard of other incidents in the past, but with gentle, sweet-natured Lily the violence came more into focus.

It was maybe three or four months later, when a woman whom I knew quite well came into the office with both her forearms in plaster.

'Oh my goodness! What happened to you?' I asked.

She brushed off my question but later I was told that she had been struck with a nulla[126] and had both arms broken. I was shocked beyond words. Both arms! The poor woman. She had been made helpless. She couldn't cook, wash, change her clothes or eat without help. I could sort of understand how one arm could have been broken. After all, one of my dear friends from long ago had her arm broken by her partner. But to have both arms broken. I couldn't imagine what must have happened between the two of them for this to be the result. That episode of family violence preyed on my mind … but it wasn't the worst of it … it was the third incident that affected me the most.

This story of the violence was related to me by the woman who suffered it. Her husband was a volatile man who frequently belted her. On this occasion, however, he was more than usually angry with his wife and his violence went to another level that I cannot speak about. I was horrified by her story. If it had happened in Melbourne her husband would have been put in jail.

I was an employee of the council and what went on between husbands and wives and in Yarralin families was not my business. As much as I was upset by the violence, I knew I must remain clearheaded about it, otherwise I wouldn't be able to continue to live and work in the community. So I put the incidents to the back of my mind and carried on. But I didn't forget. I hoped that one day I could do something.

Some time later as I was looking through my correspondence, I noticed that government grants were being offered to set up a women's refuge. It was a generous grant that included the cost of construction of a refuge centre. I studied the criteria carefully and ticked off the requirements. Yarralin had as good a chance as any community to get that grant. I decided to pursue it.

I knew I needed to act slowly, carefully and respectfully. I would need to undertake a survey to find out how many women suffered from family violence and whether it was a regular occurrence. Prior to conducting a survey, my first step was to share the idea with the women who worked in the office to see if they thought a women's refuge would be helpful. They knew the community far better than I and would give me guidance. The women thought the idea was worth pursuing, but by the looks on their faces I could see that they were not convinced it would go ahead. I was pleased that their lack of conviction tempered my enthusiasm as it lowered my expectations to a more objective and realistic level.

'Who should I ask first?' I requested my office advisors. As I hoped, they came up with a short list of women who could advise me and shed light on the issue. As I spoke with the women on the list, I asked them who I should talk to next. My list grew. I visited women in their houses and when I saw women who had come into the office, I asked them if we could have a quiet chat.

Early in my enquiry, I realised that it was too confronting to ask women directly about any violence they may have suffered. Instead I asked them if they knew of other women in the community who suffered from violence. In these discussions, the issue of how many times the women had been beaten came into it. We decided that regular violence was every few months or more. We honed the list so that 'one-offs' were not included, only the regulars.

I counted only the women in Yarralin, because I couldn't be sure whether it was too far for the Pigeon Hole or Lingara women to travel to use the refuge. My list grew until I had twenty-four names on it. Next I calculated how many women over fifteen years of age lived in Yarralin. By my figures, which were approximate, as the population was not static, around 25 per cent of the women in Yarralin were subjected to regular family violence.

With my data collected on the rates and regularity of family violence, I brought together a group of women who were willing to discuss the opportunity to apply for the women's refuge grant. Before I could act, I needed to seek their approval to move to the next step, which was speaking to the council. It was not easy for them to make this decision but they agreed.

Time was running out to put in the grant application. I decide to speak to the councillors individually. It was very uncomfortable for them. I didn't believe that family violence had ever before been discussed publicly. Eventually each councillor I spoke to reluctantly agreed that I should send in the application. I completed it straight away and put it in the mailbag for the next mail plane.

As was the case with grant applications, it was a matter of waiting for what seemed to be an interminable time. Then, to my delighted surprise, an approval letter arrived. As I read through the grant conditions, I noted that although I had included costings for the refuge to be furnished and fitted out with a refrigerator and washing machine, these items had not been approved. There was also no allowance for funding a refuge coordinator.

I phoned the government department to object to the funding conditions and was told that it was not government procedure to fund household furniture and appliances. Only the construction of the building was funded. Women's refuges were expected to raise their own funds to pay for the basic household goods.

'How are we expected to do that in Yarralin?' I asked heatedly.

'Well, normally, the money is raised through donations and raffles,' I was told.

I could hardly believe my ears.

'This is a remote Aboriginal community,' I said sharply. 'How many chook raffles do you think I would need to hold here to raise that sort of money?'

'I'll get back to you,' was the answer.

I was heartily relieved to receive a letter a couple of weeks later saying that the grant funding conditions had been changed to include appliances and furniture. Mind you, we weren't given any extra funding. The amount for the house had been reduced to cover the cost of furniture and appliances. It didn't matter though, there would be just enough to build the house.

Yarralin was fortunate that the police aide was a woman. Because we didn't have any money to pay her, we decided that she could live in the house rent free if she doubled as the refuge coordinator. Fortunately, she agreed. Problem solved … sort of.

The women's refuge was built and fenced and in the process of being fitted out. By this stage I had resigned from my job so I did not know whether it all worked out. I hoped that in the future it would help women when they need to escape from a violent situation. Even if it didn't, my pragmatic consolation was that, at the very least, there was another house in Yarralin in a community that was desperately short of housing.

This did not overcome my own feeling of discomfort that I had pushed the boundaries of my community development practice. The values and principles of community development are underpinned by community decision-making. That is, members of the community taking collective action to create solutions to community issues. I knew that if I hadn't raised the issue of violence against women in Yarralin, it would have been highly unlikely that the women would have approached me about it. My discomfort was further compounded by the fact that I was leaving Yarralin before the refuge was completed and not yet functional. I had no choice but to accept the uncertainty of the outcome and trust in the strong and resilient women of Yarralin to deal with my intervention.

20 Reflections

Life twists and turns in unexpected ways. Although I loved my job and living in Yarralin, my personal life was not happy. I had an unhappy relationship with my partner who also lived in Yarralin. On a happiness scale of one to ten, I hovered around five. Stiffening my shoulders and getting on with it could only work for so long before confusion and despair overwhelmed me. I knew I would have to leave. I was very fortunate that the old adage, 'when one door closes another opens', became true for me. I was selected to be the Manager of the Remote Area Management Project (RAMP), an Aboriginal training program for community councillors. The training project was based in Darwin and although I was sad to leave the community, I was consoled by the thought that I would be able to continue visiting Yarralin in my new capacity as a trainer with RAMP.

As an outsider when I accepted the council clerk job in Yarralin, I knew I would face challenges. And I did. I tried my best to be a creative and resourceful council clerk, but I was working in the unknown and had to find my way as best I could. I'm sure I could have done a better job if there had been an experienced mentor to offer guidance and support to both the council and me. It would have made my job far less stressful and frustrating. It would have also supported the council in understanding the system and how to work as best they could within it. However, no such person existed and the council and I had to wing it together.

Working in Yarralin was somewhat like being on a slow-moving roller-coaster. There were highs and deep lows as well as much in between. The spectacular success of the stock team program was one of the greatest highs. Jackie's stock team had successfully completed their first droving job and Jackie had signed a longer-term contract with VRD. He also had plans to become an accredited trainer and I hoped he would succeed. I had always thought that if Jackie had been educated and White, he could have given Robert Holmes à Court a run for his money.

With the HIPP program, Yarralin had become a very active community. A housing renovation program was underway and planning for the sewerage system had been completed. The site for the new mechanic's workshop had been filled, compacted and the concrete pad poured. A third portable home had been purchased as a motel for visiting consultants and tradesmen. The motel made life easier all round. Visitors didn't have to rush in and out of the community and the council clerk house was no longer required as accommodation.

The Batchelor College class was a triumph. It was a marvellous real-life example of the value of education being seen by the whole community. Sherrill, the Batchelor College teacher, had taken to Yarralin like a duck to water and loved her teaching. I got along well with Sherrill and it had been an enjoyable novelty for me to share a cup of tea with her in her demountable home, which, by the way, she had found very comfortable. It always gave me a boost when I had time to visit the class. Sherrill had gained a solid rapport with the students and kept things interesting by adapting her teaching material to suit the work situations the students were aiming for.

Government policies and systems can be clunky and sometimes just plain difficult to work with. It is always good people that make the difference. The community and I were fortunate there were dedicated government officers and consultants who wanted the best outcomes for the people at Yarralin. Without their support and commitment, many projects would have been infinitely more difficult to achieve.

It has been close to thirty years since I started work in Yarralin in 1995. As I look back to that time, my research and reading has given me a much deeper understanding of the history of the Aboriginal people in the Victoria River region. Murder, massacre and deathscape were words used by Deborah Bird Rose as a result of her anthropological work with the Aboriginal people of Yarralin. Although both books by Rose were on my bookshelf in Yarralin,[127] to my everlasting shame I merely skimmed through them. Her words did not penetrate my consciousness. There was too much for me to grasp as I had neither the background knowledge of Aboriginal history nor the time and energy to immerse myself in the bloody history of Yarralin Community.

I had no notion of inter-generational memory and trauma and how that impacts on the present. In any case, I was conditioned by decades of uninterested social attitudes and had grown up admiring the White history of the valiant explorers and settlers. I guess I was similar to many White people who thought the frontier violence and killings occurred in a time long past and were not important to the present. However, for the Aboriginal families and their community, history and the past weren't able to be forgotten like a light switch being turned off. The past informs the present.

As I write my stories, I have tried, and failed, to put myself in the Aboriginal position by pondering my own family history. It is one thing for me to imagine the fear and anger of my great-great-grandfather transported on a convict ship to Australia for minor theft. Or to feel the fear and hope my young great-great-grandmother may have felt in 1849 when she left the Tipperary poorhouse in Ireland to travel on the 'bride ship' *Pemberton* to Australia. However, it is quite another thing to imagine how I would have felt if at least 719 of my relatives and countrymen were slaughtered in massacres during a forty-year period, from 1884 to 1925.[128]

Although it was more than a hundred years ago, I ponder how I would feel about the White killers of my people. Would I have residual feelings of anger, resentment and hatred towards those murderers? How would I feel about those crimes against humanity that had been shrouded in silence for decades? Even today, many of the crimes are not known or acknowledged by a sizeable proportion of the Australian population. What would it feel like to live in Australia where the past murders and massacres of my people have been of little interest to generations of Australians?

My research led me to books and articles about Aboriginal people during the early days of the Northern Territory pastoral industry. It also led me to the documentation of the violent colonisation of Australia through the Colonial Frontiers Massacre interactive map.[129] It was with shock that I read some of the massacres were acts of genocide.

Was this the case in the Victoria River region? I wondered. As I worked my way through the massacre map, I counted twenty-three massacres during the years 1884 to 1925 in the Victoria River region and surrounding area.[130] These massacres killed a minimum of 719 Aboriginal people, predominantly Ngarinyman and Bilinara people from the Yarralin and Pigeon Hole locations. Because the Aboriginal people lived in small groups, the loss of life was devastating to their ability to hunt and forage for food, reproduce the next generation and carry out ceremonial obligations to Country.[131] It is worth noting that the massacre documentation records the lowest known number of those killed.[132] There may have been many more deaths than those counted for the massacre map.

Although I knew of the exploitation and appalling behaviour of pastoralists at Victoria River Downs and neighbouring Wave Hill Station, for the two years I worked at Yarralin I was not aware of the extent of the terrible violence of the colonial encounter with the First Australians. It is important to note that Victoria River Downs Station, continuously from 1879 to the present day, has been owned by extremely wealthy men and large corporations.[133] Their vast wealth makes the shocking abuse, neglect and exploitation of their Aboriginal workers all the more inexcusable.

As I write this book, I ponder what I would have done had I known of the carnage of the past? Would feelings of grief, shame, anger and outrage have overwhelmed me and inhibited my ability to work in the present? Perhaps being able to work in ignorance enabled me to remain focused on the few things I could do to help the community to achieve a slightly improved life. On the other hand, perhaps a greater understanding would have helped me to respond with more compassion and gentleness and to have made a more strategic approach with the community. I will never know.

Another historical situation little known to me was the treachery of the Commonwealth and Northern Territory governments in denying Yarralin land rights way back in 1975 when Justice Ward had said the Yarralin land claim had been 'effectively and mutually settled' between the Hooker Corporation and the Ngarinyman people.[134] Would I have behaved differently in my council-clerk role if I'd known that the title of Yarralin land was held by the Department of Consumer Affairs? What would I have done as an employee of the council had I known that the Wickham River land claim was sitting in bureaucratic never-never land waiting for three land parcels to be surveyed? Of course I will never know that either, but my answer might be that, even if I had full knowledge of the situation, I would not have been able to change a thing.

In hindsight, I realise that the history of the struggle for land rights and the roles played by both the Commonwealth and Northern Territory governments did affect me. In one way or another, the role of council clerk was just another colonial imposition foisted on Yarralin people by the system that oppressed them. I can imagine that, to the council, I was just another White person taking money from the system. I certainly didn't see myself in that way but I can readily understand it may have looked that way to the Aboriginal people.

Many changes have happened over the past thirty years. The contested 2007 Northern Territory Emergency Response[135] on Aboriginal communities, more commonly known as the Intervention, was strongly lauded by some and equally strongly criticised by others. This severe intervention was followed in 2012 by much the same policies but under a program with a more positive name, 'Stronger Futures'.[136] More recently in 2020, the updated National Agreement on Closing the Gap program has taken their place.[137] Outcomes from these interventions are variable. In some remote communities health and education indicators show improvement, in others there is a worsening.

For Yarralin, I think the biggest victory of all was not as a result of those huge commonwealth programs but the attainment of gaining land rights for Yarralin in 2016 after forty-four years of waiting. As Joe Morrison, the CEO of the Northern Land Council said at the handback ceremony, the Traditional Owners 'never gave up the fight, and today's ceremony is testament to your tenacity'.

Joe went on to say:

> Many of your ancestors died defending their rights and resisting the unwanted occupation of your lands and desecration of your waters and sacred sites. Those stories are not told in our education curricula, as I believe they should be, but they have been written down by people of good will and some of those historians and anthropologists are here today.[138]

Many years have passed since I worked at Yarralin. It was an extraordinary privilege to live in an Aboriginal community and work in a culture with a deeply embedded sense of family and place that stretches back 60,000 years. In writing this book, I am indebted to the experiences that challenged my thoughtless assumptions and deepened the notion of what it is to be Australian. I will forever be grateful for the opportunity. Thank you Yarralin.

Appendix 1

Massacres in the Victoria River Region 1884 to 1925[139]

Year	Location	Lower est. of people killed	Language group	By whom	Notes
1884	Blackgin Creek	20	Ngarinyman, Bilinara	Massacre led by Mounted Constable William Willshire	Reprisal
1890	Mistake Creek	60 men	Malngin and Nyinin	Mounted police	At Mistake Creek, police received a telegraph instructing them to release prisoners because the culprit (who allegedly killed one bullock) had been found elsewhere. Instead, they were murdered and their bodies burnt.
1890	Blackfella Creek	25	Ngarinyman, Bilinara	Pastoralists	Reprisal
1892	First Massacre Willaroo Station	30	Warlpiri	Colonisers, stockmen, drovers	A double massacre in a reprisal for looting Willaroo Station and the killing of the Willaroo manager, Syd Scott
1892	Second Massacre Willaroo Station	30	Wardaman	Mounted police, stockmen, drovers	Reprisal

247

Year	Location	Lower est. of people killed	Language group	By whom	Notes
1893	Collins Creek	53	Ngarinyman, Bilinara	Colonisers	Reprisal for the spearing of Constable Collins
1894	Victoria River	10 men, women, children	Ngarinyman, Karrangpurru, Nungali, Malngin, Wardaman, Ngaliwurru, Bilinara	Police operation reprisal led by Constable Willshire	Reprisal
1894	Wickham River	35 men	Ngarinyman, Bilinara	Colonisers	Reprisal
1894–5	Gordon Creek & VRD	60	Bilinara, Wardaman	Mounted Constable E. O'Keefe, Jack Watson and colonisers	Police sanctioned massacres
1895	Little Gregory Creek	10	Ngarinyman, Karrangpurru, Nungali, Malngin, Wardaman, Ngaliwurru, Bilinara	Colonisers	Reprisal for attack on Paddy Cahill
1895	Blackfellows Knob	15	Ngarinyman, Bilinara	Police, pastoralists	These are known as the 'killing times'
1886	Seale Gorge	30 men, women, children	Ngarinyman, Bilinara	Stockmen, drovers	After the massacre the bodies were dragged to a pyre and burnt
1886	Bradshaw Station	15	Ngarinyman, Bilinara	Pastoralists	Dispersal operation; part of a group of massacres

Year	Location	Lower est. of people killed	Language group	By whom	Notes
1896–7	Waterloo Station	100	Ngarinyman	Mounted police, pastoralists	Massacre after the spearing of 'Big Johnny Durack'. Part of a group of massacres
1905	Delamere Station	15	Wardaman	Colonisers, pastoralists	Unknown
1910	Humbert River Station	30	Ngarinyman, Karrangpurru, Nungali, Malngin, Wardaman, Ngaliwurru, Bilinara	Colonisers	Reprisal for murder of 'Brigalow Bill'
1911–14	Bull's Head Pocket	30	Ngarinyman, Bilinara	Pastoralists	The killing occurred during a corroboree
1911–14	Kidman Knob	30	Ngarinyman, Bilinara	Pastoralists	People were engaged in ceremony
1918	Auvergne Station	7	Wardaman, Bilinara, Mudburra	Station employees	Reprisal for the spearing of station employee Alexander MacDonald
1920	Coomanderoo Station	30	Manngayarri	Colonisers	Killing in reprisal for a milking cow being killed
1920	Wattie Creek	8 women	Gurindji	Colonisers/ stockmen	'A group of women refused to submit to gang rape and were shot.'
1920–2	Wave Hill Station	30	Gurindji	Stockmen	Paddy Cahill's assistance was called 'in about 1924 to deal with cattle killers. He shot over 30 bush people.'

Year	Location	Lower est. of people killed	Language group	By whom	Notes
1924	Victoria River District	20 men, women, children	Ngarinyman, Karrangpurru, Nungali, Malngin, Wardaman, Ngaliwurru, Bilinara	Pastoralists	This was the last reported massacre on Gurindji country
1925	Sturt Creek	26 men, women, children	Ngarinyman, Bilinara	Pastoralists	Reprisal

Appendix 2

Victoria River Downs Station

Ownership of Victoria River Downs Station and historical events from the initial purchase of VRD in 1879 until Yarralin gained land rights in 2016.

Year	Notes	VRD Owner
1879	First lease of VRD to Fisher & Lyons – 15,890 square miles or 41,000 square kilometres[140]	Fisher & Lyons. Fisher was one of the wealthiest men in Australia.[141]
1883	VRD stocked with 20,000 head of cattle – overlanded by Nat Buchanan[142]	As above
1889	Change of ownership: VRD taken over by auctioneering and brokerage business Goldsbrough Mort & Co. which dominated the early wool trade.[143]	Goldsbrough Mort & Co.[144]
1894	Constable Willshire was stationed at Gordon Creek (VRD) to maintain law and order over the Aboriginal population of around 4,000.[145]	As above
Late 1890s	Aborigines on VRD reported as being 'excessively troublesome'[146]	As above
1900	Change of ownership: VRD sold to Kidman Syndicate	Sydney Kidman, Isadore Emanuel and Alex Forrest
1900	Wickham Blacks' camp established on VRD providing pool of unpaid labour[147]	As above
1909	Change of ownership: Bovril registered in England in 1909 to acquire pastoral properties in the Northern Territory and Western Australia	Bovril Australian Estates
1914	Bovril northern estates were the largest in the Empire, if not the world, with an area of 37,500 square kilometres[148]	As above
1917–19	Failure of Vesteys' Darwin meatworks[149]	As above
1920s	VRD cattle sold for slaughter to Wyndham meatworks[150]	As above
1930s	The Great Depression	As above
1939–45	World War II	As above

1932–50	Bovril management recorded information about Aboriginal workers in a 'Natives' ledger. Information included the names of a worker's spouse and parents, their camp, the nature of their employment, their Indigenous name and the group of which they were a part.[151]	As above
1943	Patrol Officer Sweeney reported that 'cattle stations are generally unable or unwilling to bear the full responsibility for the dependent women and children and old people on their stations.[152]	
1952	Sweeney reported development of native welfare was slow on VRD. However, the manager had finally 'agreed to erect four pit type lavatories to serve the native camp area'.[153]	
1955	Change of ownership: One of Melbourne's most secretive and enigmatic millionaires purchased VRD[154]	W.L. Buckland
1960	Change of ownership: Buckland's sale to Hooker reputed to be the biggest land deal ever transacted in rural Australia[155]	Hooker Corporation
1966	Wave Hill walk-off: In August 1966, 200 Gurindji stockmen, domestic workers and their families initiated strike action at Wave Hill Station in the Northern Territory. The strike protested the poor conditions Aboriginal workers had experienced on the station for more than forty years.[156]	As above
1967	Referendum – Australian Constitution amended to allow the Commonwealth to make laws for Aboriginal people and include them in the census.	As above
April 1972	VRD and Humbert River walk-off. The strikers joined the Gurindji at Wattie Creek.[157]	As above
1973	VRD manager bulldozed Aboriginal living area[158]	

October 1973	VRD agreed to excision of 240 square kilometres for Yarralin. (2% VRD land)[159]	
February 1975	VRD withdrew agreement[160]	
September 1975	VRD agreed once more to claim of 240 square kilometres[161]	
September 1975	Justice Ward, Interim Land Commissioner, declared land claim was 'effectively and mutually settled'[162]	
1977	Yarralin wrote to Northern Territory Government stating 240 square kilometres was beginning of larger claim over 2,100 square kilometres north of Yarralin block[163]	
1983	Wickham River Land Claim – surveying oversight had left 3,100 ha slice of unalienated land. Land claim lodged by Northern Land Council[164]	
1984	Northern Territory Government gave one block of 149 square kilometres to Ngarinyman Yarralin Community Incorporated. The other block of 355 square kilometres was held by the Northern Territory Land Corporation – a body used to thwart Aboriginal land claims.[165]	
1984	Hooker sold VRD to Peter Sherwin for $12 million. By 1986 Sherwin had become Australia's largest cattle breeder.[166]	Peter Sherwin
1985	Yarralin land title held by a Katherine bank in lieu of unpaid debts 'from what appeared at best to be mismanagement of funds'[167]	

1989	Peter Sherwin's European staff locked gates on access roads to Pigeon Hole to thwart the Bilinara Land Rights claim.[168] Justice Nader, a Northern Territory Supreme Court judge described the treatment of Indigenous Australians by a company owned by the cattle baron, Mr Peter Sherwin, as 'extraordinary and savage'.[169]	
1989	Robert Holmes à Court purchased VRD through his Heytesbury Pastoral Company. After his death in 1990, his wife, Janet, took over.[170]	Heytesbury Pty Ltd
Mid 1990s	Ngarinyman Yarralin Community Inc. dissolved. Title seized by Northern Territory Commission for Consumer Affairs.[171]	
2009	Wickham Land Claim brought before the Aboriginal Land Commission – Northern Territory Government conceded there were Traditional Owners[172]	
2009	The Northern Territory Government and Northern Land Council agreed that the three blocks of Wickham River claim, Yarralin block (owned by Commission of Consumer Affairs), and Land Corporation block, be scheduled as Aboriginal Freehold land.	
2015	Following land surveys, the three claimed blocks were scheduled as Aboriginal land under the Aboriginal Land Rights (Northern Territory) Act 1976.[173]	
2016	Yarralin land handed back – 50,310 ha of land officially handed back as freehold land to the Traditional Owners under the Ngalkarrang-Wulngann Aboriginal Land Trust.[174]	

References

Papunya

1. Skelton, R., 2010, *King Brown Country – The betrayal of Papunya*, Allen & Unwin, p.25
2. Bartlett, B., 1998, Origins of Persisting Poor Aboriginal Health: An Historical Exploration of Poor Aboriginal Health and the Continuities of the Colonial Relationship as an Explanation of the Persistence of Poor Aboriginal Health, Submitted as requirements for MPH by Research, Department of Public Health & Community Medicine, University of Sydney, https://ses.library.usyd.edu.au/bitstream/2123/386/1/adt-NU1999.0016whole.pdf
3. Kean, J., 2021, 'Digging for Honey Ants: Revisiting the Papunya Mural Project', *Index Journal*, Issue No. 3, Monument, https://index-journal.org/issues/monument/digging-for-honey-ants-revisiting-the-papunya-mural-project
4. Kimber, R.G., 1990, 'The End of the Bad Old Days: European Settlement in Central Australia, 1871–1894', Occasional Papers No. 25, The Fifth Eric Johnston Lecture delivered at The State Library of the Northern Territory, https://citeseerx.ist.psu.edu/viewdoc/download?doi=10.1.1.991.1380&rep=rep1&type=pdf
5. Strehlow, T. 1959, Land of Altjiri, (unpublished manuscript), p.319 https://military-history.fandom.com/wiki/Coniston_massacre#cite_note-1
6. Stojanovik, M., 2021, Hermansburg, Northern Territory, https://www.odysseytraveller.com/articles/hermannsburg-northern-territory/
7. Egan, T., 2019, Hermannsburg Mission: Questions of Survival, Launch of Volume 11, Tales of Frieda Keysser & Carl Strehlow, https://alicespringsnews.com.au/2019/12/24/hermannsburg-mission-questions-of-survival/
8. Anthony, T., 2000, 'Criminal justice and transgression on northern Australian cattle stations', *Transgressions: critical Australian Indigenous histories*, Macfarlane, I. and Hannah, M. Eds. ANU E press, https://press-files.anu.edu.au/downloads/press/p21521/pdf/ch035.pdf, p.40
9. Holcombe, S., 2004, 'Socio-political perspectives on localism and regionalism in the Pintupi Luritja region of central Australia: Implications for service delivery and governance', Working Paper No. 25/2004, ISBN 0 7315 4924 4, ISSN 1442-3871, https://core.ac.uk/download/pdf/160609093.pdf

10   Holcombe, S., 2004, Working Paper No. 25/2004

11   Beudel, S., 2008, 'Desert Grasslands', *Overland* 191, Winter 2008 periodical issue, p.20–6
https://static1.squarespace.com/static/58b3f3ff86e6c04706dcc5d3/t/58ebfbc38419c26fd66bae36/1491860442622/desert_grasslands_beudel.pdf

12   Holcombe, S., 2004, 'The Politico-Historical Construction of the Pintupi Luritja and the Concept of Tribe', *Oceania*; June 2004; Vol. 74, No. 4; Research Library p.257 https://www.researchgate.net/publication/256055017_The_Politico-Historical_Construction_of_the_Pintupi_Luritja_and_the_Concept_of_Tribe

13   Holcombe, S., 2016, The Interwoven Histories of Mount Liebig and Papunya-Luritja, https://www.researchgate.net/publication/318318702_The_interwoven_histories_of_Mount_Liebig_and_Papunya-Luritja

14   Long, J., 1989, 'Leaving the Desert: Actors and sufferers in the Aboriginal exodus from the Western Desert', *Aboriginal History*, Vol.13, No. 1/2, ANU Press, pp.9–43, https://press-files.anu.edu.au/downloads/press/p72111/pdf/article027.pdf

15   ibid.

16   Holcombe, S., *The interwoven histories of Mount Liebig and Papunya-Luritja*, op. cit.

17   Northern Territory Annual Report for year 1956–57, p.39
https://aiatsis.gov.au/sites/default/files/docs/digitised_collections/remove/59315.pdf

18   Long, J., 1989, Leaving the Desert: Actors and sufferers in the Aboriginal exodus from the Western Desert, op. cit.

19   Settle Down Country: the Pintupi return home, 1982, https://www.youtube.com/watch?v=ZxboRrh_pgw

20   Long, J., 1989, Leaving the Desert: Actors and sufferers in the Aboriginal exodus from the Western Desert, op. cit.

21   https://www.abc.net.au/news/2020-03-24/maralinga-nuclear-tests-ground-zero-lesser-known-history/11882608

22   Long, J., 1989, Leaving the Desert: Actors and sufferers in the Aboriginal exodus from the Western Desert, op. cit.

23   ibid, p.11

24   Green, C., 2004, Group Soul: Who Owns the Artist Fusion?, University of Melbourne, Routledge, Third Text, Vol. 18, Issue 6, pp.595–608 https://www.researchgate.net/publication/282664414_Group_Soul_Who_owns_the_artist_fusion

25   Papunya Native Settlement (1958–1978), https://www.findandconnect.gov.au/ref/nt/biogs/YE00051b.htm#tab5

26 ibid.
27 Parker, P., 1981, Kintore Move, Tjakulpa Newsletter, October 1981, https://nla.gov.au/nla.obj-1625316825/view?partId=nla.obj-1625375479#page/n0/mode/1up
28 Tan, M., 2015, Papunya's daughters: Australia's second generation of master dot painters, https://www.theguardian.com/artanddesign/2015/sep/15/papunyas-daughters-australias-second-generation-of-master-dot-painters
29 Australian Aboriginal Kinship, https://en.wikipedia.org/wiki/Australian_Aboriginal_kinship
30 Warumpi Band, https://en.wikipedia.org/wiki/Warumpi_Band
31 Geoffrey Bardon, *Papunya Tula: Art of the Western Desert*, 1991, ISBN 0-86914-160-0 Sydney, McPhee Gribble/Penguin
32 Merlino, Vanessa, Papunya – Legacy of places past and future, https://www.dlandavidson.com.au/papunya-legacy-of-places-past-and-future
33 Kean, J. 2017, Friday Essay: how the Men's Painting Room at Papunya Transformed Australian Art, https://theconversation.com/friday-essay-how-the-mens-painting-room-at-papunya-transformed-australian-art-79909
34 Papunya Tula, https://www.wikiwand.com/en/Papunya_Tula
35 Johnson, Vivian, 2008, *Lives of the Papunya Tula Artists*, IAD Press, pp.67–70
36 ibid.
37 *Aboriginal Land Rights Act 1976*, https://en.wikipedia.org/wiki/Aboriginal_Land_Rights_Act_1976
38 Merlino, Vanessa, Papunya – Legacy of places past and future, https://www.dlandavidson.com.au/papunya-legacy-of-places-past-and-future
39 Johnson, V., Lives of the Papunya Tula Artists op. cit.
40 ibid.
41 ibid.
42 Rosewarne, C., et al, 2007, 'The Historical Context of Developing an Aboriginal Community-Controlled Health Service: A Social History of the First Ten Years of the Central Australian Aboriginal Congress, Health and History', *Aboriginal Health and History*, Vol. 9, No. 2, pp.126–8
43 Maher, P,. 1999, 'A Review of "Traditional" Aboriginal Health Beliefs', Original Article, *Australian Journal of Rural Health*, 7, pp.22936
44 Brady, M., 2011, 'Fuel, Cars and the Geography of Petrol Sniffing', *Humanities Research*, Vol. XXVII. No. 2, http://press-files.anu.edu.au/downloads/press/p152901/pdf/ch081.pdf

45   Eggertson, L., 2014, Opal fuel reduces gas-sniffing and suicides in Australia, *Canadian Medical Association Journal* (CMAJ), 13 May, 186(8): E229–E230

46   Bartlett, B., 1998, Origins of Persisting Poor Aboriginal Health, Submitted as requirements for MPH by Research, University of Sydney. https://ses.library.usyd.edu.au/bitstream/2123/386/1/adt-NU1999.0016whole.pdf

47   Waterford, J., 1978, 'Aborigines at Papunya to run own health service', *Canberra Times*, 22 February.

48   Bartlett, B., 1998, Origins of Persisting Poor Aboriginal Health, op. cit.

Coonamble references

49   Altman, John, 2016, 'Making a living differently', Inside Story, https://insidestory.org.au/making-a-living-differently/

50   Commonwealth Parliamentary Debates House of Representatives, 26 May 1977, 1921–22

51   Sanders, W., 1993, 'The rise and rise of the CDEP scheme: an Aboriginal 'workfare' program in times of persistent unemployment', No. 54, CAEPR Discussion Paper, https://openresearch-repository.anu.edu.au/bitstream/1885/145485/1/1993_DP54.pdf

52   Christison, R., 2010, Coonamble Shire Thematic History, https://coonambleshire.nsw.gov.au/Media-Downloads/coonamble-shire-thematic-history

53   Coonamble Shire Council, 2020, Local Strategic Planning Statement, https://shared-drupal-s3fs.s3-ap-southeast-2.amazonaws.com/master-test/fapub_pdf/Local+Strategic+Planning+Statements/LSPS+2020/LSPS+Regional%3B/Coonamble+Shire+Council+Local+Strategic+Planning+Statement+2020.pdf

54   Christison, R., 2010, Coonamble Shire Thematic History, op. cit.

55   Australian Museum, Wiradjuri cultural objects from Peak Hill, New South Wales, https://australian.museum/learn/cultures/atsi-collection/australian-archaeology/indigenous-objects-peak-hill-nsw/

56   Miller, S., 1999, Sharing a Wailwan Story, Powerhouse Museum, http://www.coonamble.org/murries/wailwan_education_notes.pdf

57   ibid.

58   Coonamble Shire Council, 2020, Local Strategic Planning Statement, op. cit.

59   Christison, R., 2010, Coonamble Shire Thematic History, op. cit.

60   Kopras, A., and Kryger, T., 1992, Background Paper No. 7, *Atlas of Unemployment: Unemployment Estimates*, p.26, https://www.aph.gov.au/binaries/library/pubs/bp/1992/92bp07.pdf

61 Aboriginal and Torres Strait Islander Commission, https://en.wikipedia.org/wiki/Aboriginal_and_Torres_Strait_Islander_Commission

62 Anthony, T., 2010, Learning from ATSIC, https://www.abc.net.au/news/2010-01-06/27934

63 Nedim, U. 2014, Can I go to Prison for not Paying a Fine? Downing Centre Court, Posted on 27 November 2014

64 Rutherford, W., 2019, Remembering Tin Town: Identifying and Valuing Aboriginal Reserve Sites of New South Wales, Thesis Master of Arts, University of Southern Queensland, p.19

65 Coonamble Shire Council, Culture on Country, https://coonambleshire.nsw.gov.au/visit/culture-on-country

66 Rutherford, Remembering Tin Town, op. cit. p.39

67 Rutherford, Remembering Tin Town, op. cit. pp.51–2

68 Christison, R., 2006, Thematic History of the former Coonabarabran Shire, Warrumbungle Shire Council, pp.8–13, http://www.higround.com.au/docs/THCoona.pdf

69 I owe a debt of gratitude to academic historian Heather Goodall, local Coonamble historian Joan McKenzie and William Rutherford who was born in Tin Town. Without their documentation, I would not have been able to understand the wounds of the past.

70 Goodall, H., 2006, *Invasion to Embassy – Land in Aboriginal Politics in New South Wales, 1770–1972*, Sydney University Press. pp.337–42

71 ibid.

72 ibid., p.338

73 ibid., p.337–42

74 ibid.

75 Private conversation, Nugget Whitehead, 2021

76 ibid.

Yarralin references

77 Overview of the Victoria River Catchment, Top End Waterways Project, https://denr.nt.gov.au/__data/assets/pdf_file/0003/254136/overviewvrc.pdf

78 Department of Primary Industry And Resources, Northern Territory Primary Industry and Fisheries Economic Overview 2018–19, p.13, https://industry.nt.gov.au/__data/assets/pdf_file/0004/948748/economic-overview-2018-2019.pdf

79 Australian National University Archives, Victoria River Downs, https://archivescollection.anu.edu.au/index.php/victoria-river-downs

80 Rose, D., 1991, *Hidden Histories: Black Stories from Victoria River Downs, Humbert River and Wave Hills Stations*, Aboriginal Studies Press, Canberra, p.47
81 ibid., p.18
82 ibid., p.xxi
83 Reynolds, H., 1981, pp.92–3 as cited in Lewis, D., *A Wild History*, op. cit., pp.117–18
84 Reynolds, H. Settlers and Aborigines on the Pastoral Frontier, 1974, p.161, https://espace.library.uq.edu.au/view/UQ:241782/Lectures_on_NQ_History_S1_CH11.pdf
85 Lewis, D., 2012, *A Wild History*, op. cit., p.115
86 Rose, *Hidden Histories*, op. cit., pp.37–8
87 Lewis, Darrell, The Victoria River District Doomsday Book, Darrell Lewis and National Centre for Biography, Australian National University (A.C.T.), Territory Stories, 2021, https://territorystories.nt.gov.au/p.465
88 ibid, p.35
89 Rose, D. 1992, *Dingo Makes Us Human*, op cit., p.xxi
90 Commonwealth of Australia, Initial Conference of Commonwealth and State Aboriginal Authorities, *Aboriginal Welfare*, 1937, https://aiatsis.gov.au/sites/default/files/catalogue_resources/20663.pdf
91 Rowley, C. D., *The Destruction of Aboriginal Society, Aboriginal Policy and Practice*, Vol. 1, 1970, pp.270–1, https://openresearch-repository.anu.edu.au › bitstream
92 ibid, p.211
93 ibid, p.213
94 Rose, *Hidden Histories*, op. cit., p.211
95 Rose, D., 1991, citing Rowley, 1974, Item 38/329, 60, p.142
96 Lewis, Darrell., *The Victoria River District Doomsday Book*, op. cit.
97 ibid, p.151
98 Lewis, D., 2012, Wild History, citing 'Undeveloped cattle areas. Resumptions favoured', p.82 from *Northern Standard*, 24 March 1936, p.3
99 Lewis, *Wild History*, p.82
100 Defining Moments, Wave Hill Walk-Off, https://www.nma.gov.au/defining-moments/resources/wave-hill-walk-off
101 National Museum of Australia, Collaborating for Indigenous Rights, A Petition to the Governor General, https://indigenousrights.net.au/land_rights/wave_hill_walk_off,_1966-75/a_petition_to_the_governor-general
102 Department of Prime Minister and Cabinet, Transcripts from the Prime Ministers of Australia, *Speech at the Gurundji Land Ceremony*, Daguragu, 16 August 1975, https://pmtranscripts.pmc.gov.au/release/transcript-3849

103 Rose, *Hidden Histories*, p.231
104 ibid., p.233
105 Gosford, B., *They never gave up the fight: the battle for land rights at Yarralin*, Part 2, 7 December 2015, July 2015 edition of *Land Rights News*, published by the Northern Land Council
106 Rose, D. B., *Report on the Material Conditions of Life – Yarralin and Lingara*, 14 May 1981
107 Rose, *Hidden Histories*, p.7
108 ibid., p.10
109 ibid., pp.242–3
110 ibid., p.244
111 ibid, p.244
112 McLaughlin, M. (ed) *Land Rights News*, July 2015, Northern Land Council
113 Murphy-Oates, L., Justice is delivered: Yarralin handed back to traditional owners after 40-year battle, *NITV News*, 16 June 2016, https://www.sbs.com.au/nitv/nitv-news/article/2016/06/16/we-never-gave-fight-yarralin-land-handed-back-after-40-years
114 Yarralin Hand Back, *Land Rights News*, July 2016, https://www.nlc.org.au/uploads/pdfs/LRN_July-2016_Web.pdf
115 Flanagan, R., McGuinness, B., Djama and VET: Exploring Partnerships and Practices in the Delivery of Vocational Education and Training in Rural and Remote Aboriginal Communities, Case Study 5: Introduction to Stock and Station Skills Case Study, Report number: Vol. 2, Northern Territory University: NTU Press, January 1998, https://www.academia.edu/24929354/Djama_and_VET_Exploring_Partnerships_and_Practices_in_the_Delivery_of_Vocational_Education_and_Training_in_Rural_and_Remote_Aboriginal_Communities._Case_Study_Three_The_Dhimurru_Land_Management_Aboriginal_Corporation
116 Rose, D. B., *Report on the Material Conditions of Life*, op. cit.
117 Jens Korff, J., *Barriers to Aboriginal Education*, last updated 2021, https://www.creativespirits.info/aboriginalculture/education/barriers-to-aboriginal-education
118 Guenther, J., Disbray, S., & Osborne, S., Red Dirt Education: A compilation of learnings from the Remote Education Systems project, 2016, https://www.academia.edu/28136513/Red_Dirt_Education_A_compilation_of_learnings_from_the_Remote_Education_Systems_project
119 ibid.
120 ibid.

121 James, F., 'Only a third of Indigenous children attend school on most days', *ABC News*, 22 Oct 2020, https://www.abc.net.au/news/2020-10-22/five-year-low-nt-indigenous-school-attendence/12802086

122 Yarralin water quality fact sheet, https://healthinfonet.ecu.edu.au/key-resources/21611/?title=Yarralin+water+quality+fact+sheet&contentid=21611_1

123 Legislative Assembly of the Northern Territory, Public Accounts Committee, Report on the Provision of Health Services to Aboriginal Communities in the Northern Territory, November 1996, Report Number 28, p.86, p.140, https://parliament.nt.gov.au/__data/assets/pdf_file/0005/363902/Provision-of-health-services-to-Communities.pdf

124 National Museum Australia, Arrival of the Dingo, https://www.nma.gov.au/defining-moments/resources/arrival-of-the-dingo

125 Myall is an Aboriginal word meaning wild. It was apparently applied by Europeans to Aborigines who had had no contact with whites, https://www.traveller.com.au/myall-lakes--fast-facts-5yt6

126 A hardwood club used in hunting, fighting and as a ceremonial tool by Australian Aboriginal people, https://victoriancollections.net.au/items/51bbc5692162ef16005cf3a8

127 *Hidden Histories*, 1991, op. cit, *Dingo Makes Us Human*, 1992, op. cit

128 See Appendix 2

129 https://c21ch.newcastle.edu.au/colonialmassacres/

130 https://c21ch.newcastle.edu.au/colonialmassacres/map.php

131 Definitions, Introduction to Colonial Frontier Massacres in Australia, 1788–1930, https://c21ch.newcastle.edu.au/colonialmassacres/introduction.php#methodology

132 Conservative estimates are used. For example, if records indicate 6 to 10 people were killed, the map records the lower number, 6, https://c21ch.newcastle.edu.au/colonialmassacres/introduction.php#methodology

133 See Appendix 1

134 Rose, *Hidden Histories*, op. cit., p.233

135 The Australian Human Rights Commission, Social Justice Report 2007, Chapter 3: The Northern Territory 'Emergency Response' Intervention – A human rights analysis, https://humanrights.gov.au/our-work/social-justice-report-2007-chapter-3-northern-territory-emergency-response-intervention

136 Australian Government, Closing the Gap, Stronger Futures in the Northern Territory, A ten year commitment to Aboriginal people in the Northern Territory, 2012, https://www.dss.gov.au/sites/default/files/documents/09_2012/stronger-futures-booklet-jul2012.pdf

137 The National Agreement on Closing the Gap, 2020, https://www.closingthegap.gov.au/national-agreement/national-agreement-closing-the-gap

138 *Land Rights News*, July 2016, 'Bloody Events Have Stained This Land', Speech by Joe Morrison, NLC CEO, at the Yarralin Handback Ceremony

139 Colonial Frontier Massacres in Australia, 1788–1930, The Centre for 21st Century Humanities, University of New Castle, https://c21ch.newcastle.edu.au/colonialmassacres/

140 Australian National University Archives, Victoria River Downs, https://archivescollection.anu.edu.au/index.php/victoria-river-downs

141 Flinders Ranges Research, Victoria River Downs (VRD) Big Run, https://www.southaustralianhistory.com.au/vrd.htm

142 Flinders Ranges Research, Victoria River Downs (VRD) Big Run, https://www.southaustralianhistory.com.au/vrd.htm

143 Makin, J., 1999. The Big Run, JB Books, South Australia, p.69

144 Dictionary of Sydney, NSW State Library, https://dictionaryofsydney.org/organisation/goldsbrough_mort_&_co

145 Flinders Ranges Research, Victoria River Downs (VRD) Big Run, https://www.southaustralianhistory.com.au/vrd.htm

146 Lewis, D., 2012. *A Wild History: Life and Death on the Victoria River Frontier*, Monash University Publishing, p.111.

147 Lewis, D., 2012. p.115

148 Makin, J., 1999. p.103

149 ibid. p.112

150 ibid. p.118

151 List of names of Aboriginal workers at the Victoria River Downs station, 1832 – 1950, Noel Butlin Archives Centre, Australian University Archives, https://archives.anu.edu.au/finding-aids/names-aboriginal-workers-employed-victoria-river-downs-station

152 Rose, D.B., 1991. Hidden Histories, Aboriginal Studies Press, p.211

153 Rose, D.B., 1991. P. 214

154 Makin, J., 1999. p.137

155 Makin, J., 1999. p.139

156 Wave Hill Walk-Off, National Museum Australia, https://www.nma.gov.au/defining-moments/resources/wave-hill-walk-off

157 Rose, D., p.229

158 Rose, p.231

159 Rose, p.233

160 Gosford, B., 2015. They never gave up the fight: the battle for land rights at Yarralin, Part 2, Land Rights News, July 2015 Edition, Published by Northern Land Council, https://blogs.crikey.com.au/northern/2015/12/07/they-never-gave-up-the-fight-the-battle-for-yarralin/
161 ibid.
162 ibid.
163 Rose, p.242
164 Gosford, B., 2015, op. cit.
165 Rose, p.242–3
166 *The Enigma, Lords, Looters, Larrikins and Legends,* https://4lstories.wordpress.com/
167 Rose, 1992, p.244
168 Clarke, J., 1989, Change of Hands, and Heart, over NT 'Soweto', Aboriginal Law Bulletin, http://classic.austlii.edu.au/au/journals/AboriginalLawB/1989/37.html
169 Rose, 1992. p.258
170 Flinders Ranges Research, Victoria River Downs (VRD) Big Run, https://www.southaustralianhistory.com.au/vrd.htm
171 Wickham River Land Claim Title Deed Handover, 2016. Land Rights News July 2016. https://www.nlc.org.au/uploads/pdfs/LRN_July-2016_Web.pdf
172 ibid.
173 Gosford, B., 2015. They never gave up the fight: the battle for land rights at Yarralin, Part 2, *Land Rights News*, July 2015 Edition, Published by Northern Land Council, https://blogs.crikey.com.au/northern/2015/12/07/they-never-gave-up-the-fight-the-battle-for-yarralin/
174 Gosford, B., 2015, op. cit.

Acknowledgements

I am deeply grateful to the Aboriginal people I worked with in Papunya, Coonamble and Yarralin. I knew so little when I arrived in each community and must have tested the patience of many. Thank you for accepting me into your communities. Everyone has their own perspective and no doubt they will recognise events and situations from their own point of view. I have written from my own perspective, that of an Anglo woman from the suburbs of Melbourne, who was lucky enough to find work in each of the communities.

It was a unique experience to work in the Aboriginal-controlled health service in Papunya, even more so, as it was the early days of the Kintore Homelands movement and just ten years after the beginning of the Papunya Tula art movement. The significance of both these movements resonates today. Although I was a profoundly ignorant newcomer, I remember and value the acceptance and kindness shown to me by the Lyappa health workers. My thanks to Punata Nungurrayi. It was delightful to talk with you after forty years.

It was a joy for me to work with the Aboriginal community of Coonamble. Their desire to work made the CDEP a success, as did the support of the Coonamble Shire Council, St Vincent de Paul and the townspeople generally. Special thanks go to Gail Turnbull, my counterpart, for her unstinting dedication to the CDEP and to all the CDEP participants.

When I first started work in Yarralin, I was told by Tim Baldwin, the Member for Victoria River, that Yarralin was a good community and they were good people. He was very right. It was my privilege to work in Yarralin with its strong and resilient people who knew what was best for their community. Achieving community goals requires a team effort. Thanks go to the Walangeri Ngumpinku Council, the support of the office staff and to Yarralin's committed workers in the building, plumbing, mechanics and community services teams. My thanks to Mayor Brian Pedwell of Victoria Daly Regional Council for his encouragement and support.

Without my writing group colleagues this book would not have happened. It was their interest in the stories of my experiences in the three Aboriginal communities of Papunya, Coonamble and Yarralin that kept me writing. As my stories accumulated, my fellow writers encouraged me to turn my stories into a book and *Crossing Cultures* was born.

The beauty of doing something completely new is that I had no idea how hard it would be or that it would take more than two years. I leaned on many friends to help me correct the grammar and flow of the stories. I would not have got to the finish line without my cousin Sophia Valente, her partner Michael Haywood, and Sue Bowles, who were with me from the start. Cathy Guinness from my writing group; Lynne Vasiliadis, my yoga buddy; my decades-long friend Robyn Lowe; my neighbours Betty Thompson and Jan Aitken all pointed out ways to bring events and experiences into focus and corrected mistakes. Special thanks go to my dear friend Sarah Allen, and Alex Hotchin and Nan McNab for helping me get to the finish line.

My memories were supplemented with Google searches. It is amazing what is buried in our minds. I found that a Google article or newspaper item could lead to a tiny thread of memory. When I gently pulled the thread, past memories and feelings floated to the surface. It was a fascinating and joyful rediscovery of my own past. It was also an awakening when I realised my knowledge of the past was completely inadequate. Google and the internet were invaluable in my quest to understand the context and history of the places I worked in. A big disappointment was that much of the information I yearned for was locked away in academic papers and articles in university libraries and behind paywalls and not accessible to me. What a terrible waste of all that work by researchers and academics. Bring on free access!

Although my father, Bill, passed away nearly twenty years ago, I am filled with gratitude for his help and guidance. In many ways, *Crossing Cultures* is a story of the friendship between my father and me. We shared the same wry humour and sense of the ridiculous that helped us both to keep trying our best despite the travails of our work.

Many thanks to all my encouraging friends who insisted my stories formed part of Australia's history.

My final thankyou is for the copyright holders of written material and photos who so generously allowed me to use their material.

www.ingramcontent.com/pod-product-compliance
Lightning Source LLC
Chambersburg PA
CBHW040240010526
44107CB00065B/2815